My Heart
Unveiled

A TOOL FOR HELPING DISCIPLES OF JESUS UNDERSTAND AND DISCERN THEIR HEARTS

Published by Valley Bible Church, Pleasanton CA, 3rd Edition
Copyright © 2019 by Valley Bible Church, Pleasanton CA

ISBN 9781079783735

PREFACE

My Heart Unveiled

A tool for helping disciples of Jesus understand and discern their hearts.

Current culture applauds following our hearts. And by "heart" it means our feelings. We have been taught and encouraged to pay special attention to our feelings and to trust them. A recent popular social media quotation claims, "You'll know the truth by the way it feels." Yet, feelings are fickle, and if we follow them, we will certainly be confused and misled.

It is true that we live from our hearts. Created in the image of God, we have the ability to think, feel, and choose. In Scripture the term "heart" is the center of one's inner life and represents these three functions. Our intellect, emotions, and will are designed to work together to help us as Christ-followers live a biblically balanced and satisfied life.

A Christian disciple is one who desires to live wholeheartedly for Christ and is eager and involved in making other disciples. Therefore it is essential she is aware of her heart-responses in relationships and circumstances. And as the disciple becomes more discerning, she will be better equipped to align her heart to Truth, obey Christ, and maintain heart-health.

My Heart Unveiled is a seven-part discipleship tool designed to help you, a follower of Jesus, understand and discern your heart so that you might live wholeheartedly in Christ by glorifying and enjoying Him.

In *My Heart Unveiled* you will learn what it means to entrust your heart to God—Father, Son, and Holy Spirit—and His plan to rescue mankind. Also, you will learn tools to evaluate your heart and to establish healthy heart-attitudes and disciplines.

May the Lord bless you and refine you as you work through the lessons and enjoy more fully the Satisfier of your heart.

UNVEILED

Not hidden. Revealed. Laid Bare. Disclosed.

But when one turns to the Lord, the veil is removed. Now the Lord is the Spirit, and where the Spirit of the Lord is, there is freedom. And we all, with unveiled face, beholding the glory of the Lord, are being transformed into the same image from one degree of glory to another. For this comes from the Lord who is the Spirit.

2 CORINTHIANS 3:16-18

ACKNOWLEDGEMENTS

Producing the *My Heart Unveiled* discipleship tool has been the collective effort of many wonderful individuals. In particular, we are grateful and appreciative of the following women and elders of Valley Bible Church, both Pleasanton and Livermore campuses, for their commitment to pray, brainstorm, write, edit, design, test, revise, provide testimonies, and encourage.

WRITING TEAM

Sharon Collard, Imelda Dodgen, Charlene Earle, Connie Johnson, Anna Plummer, Fritzeen Scott, and Shirley Sweetman.

TEST GROUP PARTICIPANTS

Lisa Araiza, Rita Baird, Linda Cline, Sharon Collard, Charlene Earle, Christina Foster, Sarah Grebe, Connie Johnson, Laura Johnston, Cher Hampton, Stephanie McDaniels, Sarah Meng, Caroline Roeschke, Fritzeen Scott, Elizabeth Wehmann, and Susan Wong.

LAYOUT AND DESIGN

Christina Foster

CITATIONS

Susan Wong

CONTRIBUTING PHOTOGRAPHERS

Ari Byers, Rachel Smith, and Jessica Swenson

In addition, we would like to thank the Elders of Valley Bible Church for their oversight, input, review, and support: Timothy Barley, Gary Darnell, Devon Dodgen, Jim Jahncke, Jay Scott, Gary Stafford, and Randy White.

Thank you, Father God, for allowing us the opportunity and privilege to be a part of the My Heart Unveiled project. May it be a tool to encourage and equip disciples of Jesus Christ and to further advance Your Kingdom. To God be all glory. Amen.

Sharon Collard

Former Pastor to Women
Valley Bible Church at the Crossing
Pleasanton, CA

Fritzeen Scott

Former Pastor to Women
Valley Bible Church at the Altamont
Livermore, CA

TABLE OF CONTENTS

UNDERSTANDING
GOD'S
PLAN OF
Redemption

PART 1

In Part 1 you will discover God's beautiful plan of redemption. Before the universe was made, the Godhead planned that you would be saved by grace through faith in Jesus Christ. From beginning to end, your salvation is a work of divine grace (Ephesians 1:5).

LESSON 1

God's Majesty Revealed in Creation

In Lesson 1 you will discover God's beautiful majesty revealed in creation.

As you begin your study, pray the words of David in Psalm 25:5–"Lead me in your truth and teach me, for you are the God of my salvation; for you I wait all the day long."

LEAD ME IN YOUR *truth* AND TEACH ME,

FOR

YOU ARE THE *God of my salvation;* FOR YOU I WAIT *all the day long.*

PSALM 25:5

GOD CREATED THE WORLD
—

THE TRINITY - THE FATHER, SON, AND HOLY SPIRIT CREATED THE WORLD.
Read the following Scriptures and record your observations.

GENESIS 1:1-2
In the beginning, God created the heavens and the earth. The earth was without form and void, and darkness was over the face of the deep. And the Spirit of God was hovering over the face of the waters.

The Holy Spirit was involved in creating the heavens and the earth out of nothing.

FDQ: The word "God" in these verses is the Hebrew *Elohim*. It is a plural noun yet normally represented by a singular pronoun "He." This is the first evidence of the doctrine of the Trinity—one Creator God functioning as three persons. These verses speak of our time, space, matter, and universe coming into existence. God created out of nothing! "Create" is the Hebrew word *bara*, meaning "to fashion out of nothing."

DEUTERONOMY 32:6
Do you thus repay the LORD, you foolish and senseless people? Is not he your father, who created you, who made you and established you?

Father God created, made, and established me.

ISAIAH 64:8
But now, O LORD, you are our Father; we are the clay, and you are our potter; we are all the work of your hand.

Father God made me.

MALACHI 2:10a
Have we not all one Father? Has not one God created us?

One Father who created all.

1 CORINTHIANS 8:6
[Y]et for us there is one God, the Father, from whom are all things and for whom we exist, and one Lord, Jesus Christ, through whom are all things and through whom we exist.

Through the Father and Son all things were made and exist for Him.

JOHN 1:1-5

In the beginning was the Word, and the Word was with God, and the Word was God. He was in the beginning with God. All things were made through him, and without him was not any thing made that was made. In him was life, and the life was the light of men. The light shines in the darkness, and the darkness has not overcome it.

All things were made through God's Son, Jesus. Jesus was with God from the beginning.

COLOSSIANS 1:15-17

He [Christ] is the image of the invisible God, the firstborn of all creation. For by him all things were created, in heaven and on earth, visible and invisible, whether thrones or dominions or rulers or authorities—all things were created through him and for him. And he is before all things, and in him all things hold together.

Jesus is God and He created all things in heaven and on earth. All things were created through Jesus and for Him.

HEBREWS 1:1-3

Long ago, at many times and in many ways, God spoke to our fathers by the prophets, but in these last days he has spoken to us by his Son, whom he appointed the heir of all things, through whom also he created the world. He is the radiance of the glory of God and the exact imprint of his nature, and he upholds the universe by the word of his power. After making purification for sins, he sat down at the right hand of the Majesty on high....

Jesus is God. God appointed Jesus to create and uphold the universe. The universe includes all things.

REVELATION 4:11

"Worthy are you, our Lord and God, to receive glory and honor and power, for you created all things, and by your will they existed and were created."

All glory, honor, and power are due the Lord God for He created all things; and all things exist by His will.

FDQ: Why is it important to know that each member of the Trinity was involved in creation?

Each member of the Trinity was involved in creation.

LIFE FLOURISHES IN A PERFECT ENVIRONMENT
—

READ GENESIS 1

Record how God created a perfect environment for sustaining all life on earth. Make a list of God's character and attributes as demonstrated in the creation account.

Orderly	Caring
Creates something out of nothing	Purposeful
Creative	Detailed
Intentional	Generous
Thoughtful	Power of His Word
Vast	Relational

God gave man everything he would need to survive and flourish and God and man enjoyed an intimate relationship.

What God did in the creation of the water, land, plants, and animals, He also did in the creation of man (variety, generosity, etc.).

FDQ: Looking over your list, what characteristic/attribute most impacts you? Why?

ANSWER THE FOLLOWING QUESTIONS ABOUT THE TEXT:

How did God view His creation?   "It is good."

How many times does "good" appear in Genesis 1?   7 times. (Genesis 1:4, 10, 12, 18, 21, 25, 31)

"Good" refers to the absolute best or highest quality and moral excellence.

Nothing in all creation needed to be altered or improved!

How does knowing that God perfectly created all things influence your view of Him?

_____

_____

_____

And God saw
EVERYTHING
that he had made,
and behold,
IT WAS VERY GOOD.

GENESIS 1:31a

GOD'S PLAN DEMONSTRATES GOD'S GRACE

—

WHAT WAS GOD'S PLAN FROM BEFORE TIME (CREATION) BEGAN?
Read the following Scriptures and record your response.

2 TIMOTHY 1:9
[God] who saved us and called us to a holy calling, not because of our works but because of his own purpose and grace, which he gave us in Christ Jesus before the ages began....

Before the ages began, God's plan was to save me through the saving work of Christ Jesus—by His grace, not by my works.

EPHESIANS 1:4-5
[God] chose us in him before the foundation of the world, that we should be holy and blameless before him. In love he predestined us for adoption as sons through Jesus Christ, according to the purpose of his will....

God chose me before the foundation of the world; He predestined me for adoption through the work of Jesus Christ. Grace comes to me through Jesus Christ.

Since before time began...

God had a plan to show you His grace, to pour out His forgiveness on a people who do not deserve it. Sending Jesus into the world to die and to rescue you from your sin was not an afterthought. It was God's original plan. God purposed for you to enjoy an amazing relationship with Him. Before the beginning, God knew He would create man and that man would reject Him. He knew you would need a Savior and that the only One who could save you would be His Son.

END YOUR STUDY...
Summarize what you learned from this lesson

Reflection

Read and meditate on Psalm 104 - "O Lord My God, You Are Very Great." Record your thoughts and praise Him for His majesty and His manifold works.

LESSON 2

God's Intimacy Revealed to Man

In Lesson 1 you reviewed God's perfect plan in creation. In Lesson 2 you will reflect on God's final act of creation on the sixth day, the creation of man.

Note: All references to "man" in Part 1 also refer to "woman," unless the context suggests otherwise.

READ GENESIS 1:26-31 & 2:7-24

How was man created differently from all other creation? Why is this significant?

God did not "speak into being" but rather gathered the dust from the ground and formed man. God breathed into man's nostrils the breath of life. Man became a living creature. God was intimately involved in the process of creating man and woman. Although Genesis does not expressly state that God gathered dust from the ground to create Eve, we know that He "took" the rib from Adam to create Eve, and the context implies that Eve was also created from dust. (Genesis 2:23 - "This at last is bone of my bones and flesh of my flesh; she shall be called Woman, because she was taken out of Man.")

GENESIS 2:7

[T]hen the Lord God formed the man of dust from the ground and breathed into his nostrils the breath of life, and the man became a living creature.

GENESIS 2:21-22

So the Lord God caused a deep sleep to fall upon the man, and while he slept took one of his ribs and closed up its place with flesh. And the rib that the Lord God had taken from the man he made into a woman and brought her to the man.

GOD DESIGNED & CREATED MAN

He created man "hands-on." He was personally involved when He formed Adam and Eve, gave them life, and animated them by breathing into them.

What is the significance that God chose to create man from dust?

What is the significance that God created man by putting His very breath within man?

FDQ: What do you think of when you think of dust?
Does dust have value or intrinsic worth?
Look up Psalm 104:29 — Read it aloud together.

Psalm 104:29 - "When you hide your face, they are dismayed; when you take away their breath, they die and return to their dust."
- Apart from the breath of God in us, man does not matter at all; man cannot exist apart from God's breath.
- Dust is worthless, of no value, has no life. It is God who gives man his worth. God brings life out of the ordinary and the mundane.
- The word for breath in Hebrew is *ruach*; the word imitates the very sound of breath. It is the same word for Spirit (Greek — *pneuma*, Latin — *spiritus*).
- The same word (breath) is found in Genesis 1:2 - "The earth was without form and void, and darkness was over the face of the deep. And the Spirit of God was hovering over the face of the waters."

So God created man in his own image, in the image of God he created him; male and female he created them.

GENESIS 1:27

No other creation is like man. God created (animated) man by breathing His very breath into him.

GOD'S PLAN FOR MANKIND

—

REVIEW GENESIS 1:26-28

What was God's plan for mankind? What responsibilities did God give Adam and Eve?

God created man for relationship with Him just as the Trinity is in relationship one member with another (26).
He gave them dominion/purpose over all the earth (27).
He told them to be fruitful and multiply (28).

FDQ: What does it mean to have "dominion over"?
The word "dominion" means "rule or power over." God is sovereign over all His creation. He chose to delegate His authority to mankind. Man was to rule the animals (26), to "subdue" the earth and have dominion over all animals (28). Man was to exercise his rule under the authority of God, Who delegated it to man.

GOD PROVIDED FOR MAN'S GOOD AND SATISFACTION

—

HOW DID GOD PROVIDE FOR MAN'S GOOD AND SATISFACTION?

Make a list of God's provisions from Genesis 1:26-31; 2:15-25.

God gave man the following things:
- Life (2:7)
- Purpose, authority, and responsibility over creation:
  - be fruitful and multiply (1:28)
  - subdue the earth, have dominion over it, work it (1:28)
  - work the land (2:15)
  - name the animals and be responsible for them (2:20)
- A perfect and beautiful environment (Eden – means "pleasure")
- Food (1:29-30; 2:16-17)
- A perfect helper/partner; a helper fit for him (1:27; 2:20)
- A tender and affectionate celebration
- A perfect union—relationship with God, one another, and creation
- Intimacy with God—God spoke with Adam; God knows Adam; God provided for Adam

God provided man with everything he needed to be satisfied!

GENESIS 2 IS ONLY A SHADOW OF WHAT IS TO COME!

———

Then the angel showed me the river of the water of life, bright as crystal, flowing from the throne of God and of the Lamb through the middle of the street of the city;

also, on either side of the river, the tree of life with its twelve kinds of fruit, yielding its fruit each month. The leaves of the tree were for the healing of the nations.

No longer will there be anything accursed, but the throne of God and of the Lamb will be in it, and his servants will worship him.

They will see his face, and his name will be on their foreheads.

And night will be no more. They will need no light of lamp or sun, for the Lord God will be their light, and they will reign forever and ever.

REVELATION 22:1-5

GOD CREATED MAN AND WOMAN IN HIS IMAGE

—

WHAT DOES IT MEAN TO BE "MADE IN THE IMAGE OF GOD"? HOW IS MAN LIKE GOD?
Read the following Scriptures and record your response.

GENESIS 1:27
So God created man in his own image, in the image of God he created him; male and female he created them.

GENESIS 5:1
This is the book of the generations of Adam. When God created man, he made him in the likeness of God.

God created man "like" Himself, in His image. Man resembles and represents God.

FDQ: Define "image."
"Image" means to be like someone but not identical, a representation. The image represents the real. In Hebrew the word means "likeness."

Man is unique in all creation.

It is a great privilege to be a woman. Like God, you are personal, intelligent, creative, relational, and communicative. God has given you His Word and the ability to understand it.

Through His Word you can know and enjoy Him and His world. You have a moral conscience, the ability to choose right from wrong. In addition, unlike the rest of creation, you are eternal (Ecclesiastes 3:11).

MAN'S PURPOSE IS TO GLORIFY GOD

—

God designed man for Himself to reflect His glory.

ISAIAH 43:7

[E]veryone who is called by my name, whom I created for my glory, whom I formed and made.

REVELATION 4:11

Worthy are you, our Lord and God, to receive glory and honor and power, for you created all things, and by your will they existed and were created.

The ***glory*** of God is...

"the infinite beauty and greatness of God's manifold perfections (His character, His worth, and His attributes)." [1]

To ***glorify*** God means...

to make much of Him and
"[t]o see God as glorious,
savor Him as glorious,
and to celebrate Him as glorious." [2]

In your feeling, thinking, and choosing, you are to reflect who God is and what He is like.

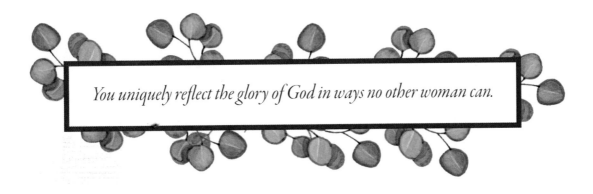

You uniquely reflect the glory of God in ways no other woman can.

O Lord, how manifold are your works!

PSALM 104:24a

The word "manifold" means "varied, multi-faceted." God's works, the creation of the world as well as the creation of each person, are manifold, multi-faceted.

1 PETER 4:10

As each has received a gift, use it to serve one another, as good stewards of God's varied [manifold] grace[.]

"

You are under God's authority,
A recipient of His blessing,
A reflection of His essence, worth, and dignity.
A dependent upon your Creator.

ANONYMOUS

END YOUR STUDY...

Summarize what you learned from this lesson

Reflection

Read Psalm 8:4-6. Meditate and reflect on God's goodness in creating you.

[W]hat is man that you are mindful of him,
and the son of man that you care for him?
Yet you have made him a little lower than the heavenly beings
and crowned him with glory and honor.
You have given him dominion over the works of your hands;
you have put all things under his feet....

PSALM 8:4-6

LESSON 3

Man's Fall Into Sin: Section A

In Lessons 1 and 2 you surveyed the beautiful creation account. When God created the world, He saved the best for last. He created man as His image-bearer, and this is mankind's privileged and unique calling.

In Lesson 3 you will examine what sin is and does and how Adam and Eve fell into Original Sin. Sin promises to be worth it, but take note—sin always lies.

SIN DEFINED

WHAT FIRST COMES TO MIND WHEN YOU THINK OF SIN?
Brainstorm your ideas.

_____

_____

_____

_____

_____

HOW WOULD YOU DEFINE SIN?
Write out your personal definition of sin.

_____

_____

_____

1 JOHN 5:17a
All wrongdoing is sin[.]

❝

The emphasis of Scripture, however, is on the godless self-centeredness of sin. Every sin is a breach of what Jesus called "the first and great commandment," not just by failing to love God with all our being but by actively refusing to acknowledge and obey him as our Creator and Lord. We have rejected the position of dependence that our createdness inevitably involves and made a bid for independence. Worse still, we have dared to proclaim our self-dependence, our autonomy, which is to claim the position occupied by God alone. Sin is not a regrettable lapse from conventional standards; its essence is hostility to God (Romans 8:7), issuing in active rebellion against him. It has been described in terms of "getting rid of the Lord God" in order to put ourselves in his place in a haughty spirit of "God-almightiness." [1]

JOHN STOTT

❝

Sin is any failure to conform to the moral law of God in act, attitude, or nature.... A life that is pleasing to God is one that has moral purity not only in its actions, but also in its desires of heart. [2]

WAYNE GRUDEM

GENESIS 3

"The Fall"

1Now the serpent was more crafty than any other beast of the field that the LORD God had made.

He said to the woman, "Did God actually say, 'You shall not eat of any tree in the garden'?" 2 And the woman said to the serpent, "We may eat of the fruit of the trees in the garden, 3 but God said, 'You shall not eat of the fruit of the tree that is in the midst of the garden, neither shall you touch it, lest you die.'" 4 But the serpent said to the woman, "You will not surely die. 5 For God knows that when you eat of it your eyes will be opened, and you will be like God, knowing good and evil." 6 So when the woman saw that the tree was good for food, and that it was a delight to the eyes, and that the tree was to be desired to make one wise, she took of its fruit and ate, and she also gave some to her husband who was with her, and he ate. 7 Then the eyes of both were opened, and they knew that they were naked. And they sewed fig leaves together and made themselves loincloths.

8 And they heard the sound of the LORD God walking in the garden in the cool of the day, and the man and his wife hid themselves from the presence of the LORD God among the trees of the garden. 9 But the LORD God called to the man and said to him, "Where are you?" 10 And he said, "I heard the sound of you in the garden, and I was afraid, because I was naked, and I hid myself." 11 He said, "Who told you that you were naked? Have you eaten of the tree of which I commanded you not to eat?" 12 The man said, "The woman whom you gave to be with me, she gave me fruit of the tree, and I ate." 13 Then the LORD God said to the woman, "What is this that you have done?" The woman said, "The serpent deceived me, and I ate."

14 The LORD God said to the serpent, "Because you have done this, cursed are you above all livestock and above all beasts of the field; on your belly you shall go, and dust you shall eat all the days of your life. 15 I will put

enmity between you and the woman, and between your offspring and her offspring; he shall bruise your head, and you shall bruise his heel."

16 To the woman he said, "I will surely multiply your pain in childbearing; in pain you shall bring forth children. Your desire shall be contrary to your husband, but he shall rule over you."

17 And to Adam he said, "Because you have listened to the voice of your wife and have eaten of the tree of which I commanded you, 'You shall not eat of it,' cursed is the ground because of you; in pain you shall eat of it all the days of your life; 18 thorns and thistles it shall bring forth for you; and you shall eat the plants of the field. 19 By the sweat of your face you shall eat bread, till you return to the ground, for out of it you were taken; for you are dust, and to dust you shall return."

20 The man called his wife's name Eve, because she was the mother of all living. 21 And the LORD God made for Adam and for his wife garments of skins and clothed them.

22 Then the LORD God said, "Behold, the man has become like one of us in knowing good and evil. Now, lest he reach out his hand and take also of the tree of life and eat, and live forever—" 23 therefore the LORD God sent him out from the garden of Eden to work the ground from which he was taken. 24 He drove out the man, and at the east of the garden of Eden he placed the cherubim and a flaming sword that turned every way to guard the way to the tree of life.

FDQ: The word "crafty" means "to be adept in the use of subtlety and cunning."

THE FALL OF MAN

SIN ENTERED THE HUMAN RACE AS RECORDED IN GENESIS 3:1-6

Chart your observations of the character, beliefs, and actions of the serpent, Adam, and Eve.

SERPENT

- The serpent was crafty/cunning/deceitful (1).
- His first attack was against God's Word (1).
- He twisted God's positive command into a negative one (1).
- He challenged and contradicted God's Word (4-5).
- He tried to get Eve to doubt God's goodness (If God has lied to me, how can He be good?) and sin's badness (If this fruit is something good for me, why does God forbid it?) (4-5).
- The serpent's lie was powerful because it was mixed with truth (5, partially fulfilled in 7).
- He enticed Eve with equality with God (This is how Satan himself fell – Isaiah 14:13-14).
- He diminished God's authority, character, generosity, and goodness.
- His goal was to separate man's relationship with God.
- "Satan sidelined the man and drew the woman into the role of spokesman in the moment of crisis. He reversed the roles that God had intended." John Piper

ADAM

- Adam took and ate the fruit (6).
- Adam abdicated his role; he did not warn or protect Eve (6).
- Adam blamed both God and Eve (12).

EVE

- Eve entered a conversation with the serpent (2).
- She misquoted God – she both added and left out (2-3).
- Eve demonstrated she was vulnerable to deception.
- She believed the serpent that God was withholding something good from her and that she could be equal with God. She believed that God's provision was not enough.
- She ate the fruit and gave it to Adam to eat (6).

"

Sin is not just the doing of bad things, but the making of good things into ultimate things. It is seeking to establish a sense of self by making something else more central to your significance, purpose, and happiness than your relationship to God. [3]

TIM KELLER

Sin is always a lowering of God and an elevating of self.

THE PATTERN OF SIN

___

CIRCLE THE VERBS FOUND IN GENESIS 3:6.

GENESIS 3:6
So when the woman saw that the tree was good for food, and that it was a delight to the eyes, and that the tree was to be desired to make one wise, she took of its fruit and ate, and she also gave some to her husband who was with her, and he ate.

WHAT IS THE PATTERN OF TEMPTATION AND SIN?

I see it   I want it   I take it   I share it

Do not love the world or the things in the world. If anyone loves the world, the love of the Father is not in him. For all that is in the world—the desires of the flesh and the desires of the eyes and pride of life—is not from the Father but is from the world.

I JOHN 2:15-16

HOW HAVE YOU SEEN THIS PATTERN IN YOUR OWN LIFE?

_____

_____

_____

_____

_____

FDQ: Do you see this pattern in your own life? Give an example.

How do we "share" our sin?

There are always consequences to others from our sin. Sin will always negatively impact others through our attitudes and actions.

NO ONE FALLS PREY TO SIN "ALL OF A SUDDEN." WHAT DOES THIS MEAN?

Satan incrementally and intentionally deceives, leading a person to exchange truth for a lie.

_____

_____

_____

WE MUST RECOGNIZE THE WAY SATAN WORKS IN ORDER TO DETECT HIS LIES AND HIS SEEDS OF DOUBT. READ 2 CORINTHIANS 11:3, 14. WHAT IS PAUL'S FEAR?

2 CORINTHIANS 11: 3, 14

But I am afraid that as the serpent deceived Eve by his cunning, your thoughts will be led astray from a sincere and pure devotion to Christ.... And no wonder, for even Satan disguises himself as an angel of light.

_____

_____

_____

_____

SATAN LURES EVE
—

HOW DID SATAN LURE EVE? (REVIEW GENESIS 3)

○ He drew Eve into a discussion with him.

○ He planted the seed of doubt regarding God's Word and God's character (His goodness and intentions toward them).

○ He exposed Eve's incomplete understanding of God's command.

○ He directly contradicted God.

○ He diverted Eve's attention from the consequence of disobedience to the lie that she deserved more than what God gave her.

WHAT HAPPENED AS A RESULT OF ADAM AND EVE EATING THE FRUIT? WHAT DID THEY EXPERIENCE? HOW DID THEY RESPOND?

Experienced shame (7)
Knew they had sinned
Had an awareness of good and evil
Attempted to cover their shame with a flimsy fig leaf (7)
Hid from God (8, 10)
Feared God (10)
Blamed each other and God (12,13)

Sometimes you will clearly and immediately experience the consequences of sin, but other times sin is more subversive and the consequences may be less obvious and pronounced. But be aware: sin is always dangerous and destructive.

Reflect on a time when you did not immediately experience the consequences of sin but later were impacted by it.

END YOUR STUDY...
Summarize what you learned from this lesson

Reflection

Ask the Holy Spirit to reveal to you areas of temptation in your life. Have any of these temptations become sin? If so, confess these to God and repent and thank Him for His forgiveness.

—— **LESSON 4** ——

Man's Fall Into Sin: Section B

In Lesson 3 you uncovered Satan's strategy that resulted in Adam and Eve choosing to rebel against God–to sin. They chose to believe Satan over God, thus inserting their own authority above God's.

In Lesson 4 you will note how the effects of Adam and Eve's Original Sin spread to all mankind.

What God commands

you are to

Believe, Trust,
& Obey.

GOD'S RESPONSE TO SIN

——

ONCE AGAIN, READ THROUGH THE ACCOUNT OF THE FALL OF MAN RECORDED IN GENESIS 3.

How does God respond to Adam and Eve's sin? (9-13) What does this demonstrate about God's character?

God pursued Adam and Eve; He desired them to be restored. In their sin, Adam and Eve distanced themselves from God's presence, but God continued to pursue them. He sought them, asked them questions, and began the process of restoration. He addressed them each personally.

Jesus' first coming and His death and resurrection are evidence of God's ultimate pursuit of us to reconcile us into fellowship with Himself.

God asked Adam a question. He extended mercy and gives Adam an opportunity to confess, repent, and be restored. God is a merciful, forgiving, and gracious initiator.

When Adam and Eve sinned, they felt shame (condemnation). God literally called out to Adam and Eve in order to bring them out of hiding and into restoration.

In the same way, when you sin, the Holy Spirit convicts you and makes you aware of your sin so that you can confess and be restored.

WHAT IS GOD'S PLAN?

ROMANS 8:19-21
For the creation waits with eager longing for the revealing of the sons of God. For the creation was subjected to futility, not willingly, but because of him who subjected it, in hope that the creation itself will be set free from its bondage to corruption and obtain the freedom of the glory of the children of God.

God has a plan to restore all things, including man.

What does it look like when you are rebelling against God?

I run from God's presence. I refuse to listen to His Word. I withdraw. I am fearful. I am anxious. I blame others. I refuse to take ownership for my sin. I justify my sin.

I try to provide for myself what I think He is withholding from me.

When I rebel against God, I choose to hide and distance myself from Him. This puts me at risk in all areas and relationships.

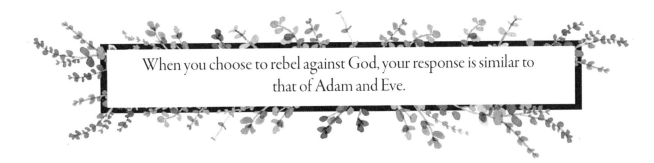

When you choose to rebel against God, your response is similar to that of Adam and Eve.

GOD CURSES THE SERPENT

—

What is God's curse on the serpent? (14-15)

ROMANS 16:20a

The God of peace will soon crush Satan under your feet.

The serpent is cursed above all livestock and beasts of the field. He is no longer upright but is sentenced to crawl on the ground. He will eat dust all the days of his life. There is enmity between he and the Woman, between his offspring and her offspring. Eve's offspring will "bruise [his] head."

Through Jesus, I share in the victory over Satan. (Romans 16:20a)

The real battle is between Satan and the offspring of the Woman. The offspring who will bruise ("crush" NIV) the head of the serpent is Christ Himself; Who comes from the Woman (Genesis 3:15). This is the first gospel message. It is termed the *protoevangelium*.

Women will bear the consequence of Eve's sin. (16)

- She will bring forth children in pain (16a) – The literal translation is "causing to be great, I shall cause to be great your sorrow"–an intense statement, repeated for emphasis.

  FDQ: Consider the long-term implications: a woman may suffer in menstrual cycle, conception, pregnancy, and child-rearing. Children are a source of joy but may also be a source of pain, sorrow, disappointment, and heartache. The consequence of Eve's sin extends to all women regardless of whether she ever marries or bears children. It affects the longings of her heart and her unfulfilled desires.

- A parallel passage to Genesis 3:16b is found fifteen verses later in Genesis 4:7. Genesis 3:16b – "Your desire shall be contrary to your husband, and he shall rule over you." Genesis 4:7 – "Sin is crouching at your door. Its desire is contrary to you, but you must rule over it." The same word for desire is used in both passages (tᵉšûqà), nom. desire, request, longing, appetite (H9592). "As in Genesis 4:7, there is a struggle in Genesis 3:16 between the one who has the desire (wife) and the one who must/should rule or master (husband). Cain did not win his battle with sin, and the victory of the husband is not necessarily assured by God in Genesis 3:16b. The 'curse' here describes the beginning of the battle of the sexes. After the fall, the husband no longer rules easily; he must fight for his headship. The woman's desire is to control her husband (to usurp divinely appointed headship), and he must master her, if he can. Sin has corrupted both the willing submission of the wife and the loving headship of the husband. And so, the rule of love founded in paradise is replaced by struggle, tyranny, domination, and manipulation."[1]

- There will be a fracturing from the equality and complementarity that man and woman enjoyed, to a mutual desire to dominate. "I am placing my desires and my will before yours."

Men will bear the consequences of Adam's sin. (17-19)

- Man's primary role is to work the ground and bring forth abundance. Before the fall, the ground produced only what was good, and man received joy from his work. After the fall, man will labor in painful toil just to subsist. Work will be hard during this life.

- Man's final end–death. The result of Adam's sin extended to the entire human race.

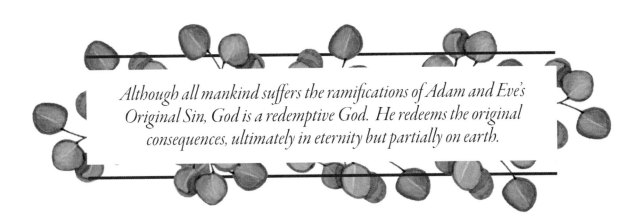

Although all mankind suffers the ramifications of Adam and Eve's Original Sin, God is a redemptive God. He redeems the original consequences, ultimately in eternity but partially on earth.

THE FOLLOWING SCRIPTURES SHOW EXAMPLES OF GOD'S REDEMPTIVE ACTS REGARDING CHILDREN, MARRIAGE, AND LABOR.

PSALM 127:3
Behold, children are a heritage from the Lord, the fruit of the womb a reward.

EPHESIANS 5:22-25
Wives, submit to your own husbands, as to the Lord. For the husband is the head of the wife even as Christ is the head of the church, his body, and is himself its Savior. Now as the church submits to Christ, so also wives should submit in everything to their husbands. Husbands, love your wives, as Christ loved the church and gave himself up for her....

PSALM 128:2
You shall eat the fruit of the labor of your hands; you shall be blessed, and it shall be well with you.

ADAM'S SIN BECAME YOUR SIN

——

HOW DO THE FOLLOWING VERSES SHOW THAT ADAM'S SIN EXTENDED TO THE ENTIRE HUMAN RACE?

Read each verse and record your response.

ROMANS 5:12

Therefore, just as sin came into the world through one man, and death through sin, and so death spread to all men because all sinned....

Because of Adam, sin entered the world.
Death came to all mankind.

ROMANS 5:18-19

[O]ne trespass led to condemnation for all men...[and] by the one man's disobedience the many were made sinners....

All men were condemned. (18)
All men were made sinners. (19)

"

The problem with the human race is not most deeply that everybody does various kinds of sins - those sins are real, they are huge and they are enough to condemn us. Paul is very concerned about them. But the deepest problem is that behind all our depravity and all our guilt and all our sinning, there is a deep mysterious connection with Adam whose sin became our sin and whose judgment became our judgment. [2]

JOHN PIPER

WITH SIN CAME DEATH

—

Physical Death
The separation of the soul from the body.

Spiritual Death
The separation of the soul from God.

What are the implications of spiritual death?

In present life:
Spiritual death is the loss of God's favor and the loss of knowing God.
A person is separated from relationship with God.
She does not desire God or the things of God.
She is unable to understand God's Word.
Scripture is clear that everyone begins life "dead in trespasses and sins" (Ephesians 2:1-5). The result is living life focused on her sinful desires.

After physical death:
She is eternally separated from God (Matthew 25:41) and in constant torment (Luke 16:19-31).

Why is it significant that God clothed Adam and Eve in garments made from an animal skin? (Genesis 3:21)

In order for Adam and Eve to be clothed, a sacrifice had to be made. An animal had to die. God clothed them—He covered their shame and restored their dignity.

> "[W]ithout the shedding of blood there is no forgiveness of sins."

HEBREWS 9:22b

FDQ: Discuss the following: Only God can make a garment that can cover your shame. You are clothed with a garment of righteousness that was purchased with the blood of another, Jesus Christ.

Why must blood be shed for the forgiveness of sin?
(See Leviticus 17:11)

A MESSAGE OF HOPE
—

GENESIS 3 OFFERS A MESSAGE OF HOPE.

The gospel is proclaimed in Genesis 3—Jesus is declared a victor over Satan. "He shall bruise his heel" (Genesis 3:15).

What depiction of the gospel message, God's mercy and grace, do you see?

God continued to pursue a relationship with Adam and Eve and mercifully chose to sacrifice an animal's life to cover their shame. This is a pointer to Christ's ultimate sacrifice to cover/atone for our sins so that we are righteous before the Father.

"For the wages of sin is death, but the free gift of God is eternal life in Christ Jesus our Lord."

ROMANS 6:23

END YOUR STUDY...

Summarize what you learned from this lesson

Reflection

Meditate on the fact that although you were born into sin and separated from God, the blood sacrifice of Christ has brought you into relationship with Him.

LESSON 5

Jesus is the Remedy

In Lessons 3 and 4 you examined the devastating fall of man into sin, but in Lesson 5 you will rejoice in the Good News—Jesus is the Remedy!

JESUS REMEDIES
the sin problem.

HE FORMED US
and
HE FOUND US.

ANONYMOUS

"You know that he appeared in order to take away sins, and in him there is no sin."

1 JOHN 3:5

Created in God's image, man enjoyed perfect harmony with God in a perfect environment. Everything man needed to thrive was provided to him. Yet man chose to disobey God by challenging God's authority and goodness. As a consequence, man's relationship with God was broken, leading to spiritual death.

In Romans 5:12 Paul states, "Therefore, just as sin came into the world through one man, and death through sin, and so death spread to all men because all sinned[.]"

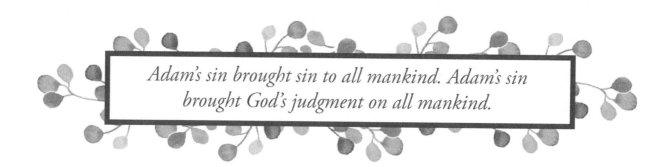

Adam's sin brought sin to all mankind. Adam's sin brought God's judgment on all mankind.

THE CONDITION OF MAN

—

READ WHAT THE FOLLOWING SCRIPTURES STATE REGARDING THE CONDITION OF MAN.

PSALM 14:1-3

The fool says in his heart, "There is no God." They are corrupt, they do abominable deeds, there is none who does good. The Lord looks down from heaven on the children of man, to see if there are any who understand, who seek after God. They have all turned aside; together they have become corrupt; there is none who does good, not even one.

PSALM 51:5

Surely I was sinful at birth, sinful from the time my mother conceived me. (NIV)

ISAIAH 53:6

All we like sheep have gone astray; we have turned—every one—to his own way; and the Lord has laid on him the iniquity of us all.

ROMANS 3:23

[F]or all have sinned and fall short of the glory of God,

EPHESIANS 2:1-3

And you were dead in the trespasses and sins in which you once walked, following the course of this world, following the prince of the power of the air, the spirit that is now at work in the sons of disobedience—among whom we all once lived in the passions of our flesh, carrying out the desires of the body and the mind, and were by nature children of wrath, like the rest of mankind.

JESUS, THE REMEDY

———

But God in His utter graciousness provides His Son as the means by which we are reconciled to God and spared from His wrath.

"

For the essence of sin is man substituting himself for God [Genesis 3:1-7], while the essence of salvation is God substituting himself for man [2 Corinthians 5:21]. Man asserts himself against God and puts himself where only God deserves to be; God sacrifices himself for man and puts himself where only man deserves to be. [1]

JOHN STOTT

WRITE OUT OR TRACE 2 CORINTHIANS 5:21 BELOW.

FOR OUR SAKE HE MADE HIM TO BE

SIN

WHO KNEW NO SIN, SO THAT IN HIM

we might become

THE RIGHTEOUSNESS OF GOD.

2 CORINTHIANS 5:21

Only God can PROVIDE A GARMENT that will COVER YOUR SHAME.

The Robe of Righteousness

We are all born naked, physically and spiritually, because of Adam and Eve's sin and resulting curse. Though physically you learn to clothe yourself, you can never clothe yourself spiritually. Only God through Christ can spiritually clothe you.

When Adam and Eve sinned, their eyes were opened and they realized they stood bare before God. They were ashamed and tried to sew together fig leaves to hide their nakedness. But God responded by clothing them with garments of skin from an animal he had slain (Genesis 3:21). God in His kindness restored their dignity.

Like Adam and Eve, all your sin is laid bare before God ("Nothing is covered up that will not be revealed, or hidden that will not be known. Therefore whatever you have said in the dark shall be heard in the light, and what you have whispered in private rooms shall be proclaimed on the housetops." Luke 12:2-3); and none of your "righteous deeds" is sufficient to cover your spiritual nakedness. You cannot save yourself. Though you may try to spiritually clothe yourself by good works, "[w]e have all become like one who is unclean, and all our righteous deeds are like a polluted garment" (Isaiah 64:6a).

Only God can provide a garment that will cover your shame. But instead of the skin of an animal as He did for Adam and Eve, He now clothes you with the ultimate garment—a garment of righteousness that was purchased with the blood of his Son, Jesus Christ. ("Without the shedding of blood there is no forgiveness of sins." Hebrews 9:22; "For our sake he made him to be sin who knew no sin, so that in him we might become the righteousness of God." 2 Corinthians 5:21)

The blood of Jesus covers your sins, and you are forgiven and made righteous. "Blessed are those whose lawless deeds are forgiven, and whose sins are covered" (Romans 4:7).

"I will greatly rejoice in the Lord; my soul shall exult in my God, for he has clothed me with the garments of salvation; he has covered me with the robe of righteousness, as a bridegroom decks himself like a priest with a beautiful headdress, and as a bride adorns herself with her jewels" (Isaiah 61:10).

The parable of the prodigal son is a beautiful picture of how God longs to clothe you in His righteousness. When the father sees his prodigal son from a distance, he runs to him receiving him home. The father instructs his servants to adorn his repentant son with his best robe. ("But the father said to his servants, 'Bring quickly the best robe, and put it on him....'" Luke 15:22)

Jesus told another parable of a wedding feast. When the master finds a man at the wedding banquet without his wedding garment, he throws him out (Matthew 22:1-14). In the same way, you cannot enter the Kingdom of God without the Robe of Righteousness bought by Christ's blood.

Revelation also includes the imagery of a white robe. Chapter 6 tells of the martyred saints each being given a white robe to wear until the end. ("Then they were each given a white robe and told to rest a little longer, until the number of their fellow servants and their brothers should be complete, who were to be killed as they themselves had been." Revelation 6:11) And Chapter 19 reveals that the Church as His Bride will be granted "fine linen, clean and white" (KJV) to wear for The Wedding. ("Let us rejoice and exult and give him the glory, for the marriage of the Lamb has come, and his Bride has made herself ready; it was granted her to clothe herself with fine linen, bright and pure—for the fine linen is the righteous deeds of the saints." Revelation 19:7-8)

This is your only ticket to heaven — the blood of Christ shed on the cross. Without faith in the atoning work of His blood, you are uncovered and laid bare before Him. You cannot clothe yourself; you cannot cover yourself; you cannot save yourself.

———

"Thanks be to God for his inexpressible gift!"
2 CORINTHIANS 9:15

"When we've been there ten thousand years,
Bright shining as the sun,
We've no less days to sing God's praise
Than when we first begun."

AMAZING GRACE, JOHN NEWTON, 1779

God reconciled man to Himself by making Jesus, Who knew no sin, to be sin on our behalf, so that we could be right with God. The context of 2 Corinthians 5:21 centers on reconciliation to God (18-20). The Greek word for reconciliation in these verses is *katallages*– "the exchange of hostility for a friendly relationship." Hostility existed between holy God and sinful man which Jesus dealt with on the cross (2 Corinthians 5:14-15; Ephesians 2:13-16).

So there was an extraordinary exchange. Christ died as your substitute. God treated the Son as the object of His judgment and wrath, and Jesus voluntarily received God's judgment and wrath so that you might be reconciled to God (John 10:17-18).

John Stott states, "He became sin with our sin so that we may become righteous with his righteousness.... What was transferred to Christ was not moral qualities but legal consequences; he voluntarily accepted liability for our sins." [2]

God's punishment administered on Jesus was **thorough** and **complete**. Thus God was **fully** satisfied and has no need to further punish those who put their trust in Christ. In this sense the Father "made" Jesus to be sin (Romans 3:25; Hebrews 2:17; 1 John 2:2; 1 John 4:10).

The implications are far-reaching. For all eternity Christ-followers will marvel at God's kindness and grace to save us through the sacrifice of His Son (Ephesians 2:7).

FDQ: Read the following verses aloud together.
Galatians 3:13 - Christ redeemed us from the curse of the law by becoming a curse for us—for it is written, "Cursed is everyone who is hanged on a tree."
Hebrews 9:28 - [S]o Christ, having been offered once to bear the sins of many, will appear a second time, not to deal with sin but to save those who are eagerly waiting for him.
1 Peter 2:24 - He himself bore our sins in his body on the tree, that we might die to sin and live to righteousness. By his wounds you have been healed.

WHAT DO YOU LEARN ABOUT BEING "MADE RIGHT WITH GOD"?

Read the following passage and record your response.

ROMANS 3:21-26

But now the righteousness of God has been manifested apart from the law, although the Law and the Prophets bear witness to it—the righteousness of God through faith in Jesus Christ for all who believe. For there is no distinction: for all have sinned and fall short of the glory of God, and are justified by his grace as a gift, through the redemption that is in Christ Jesus, whom God put forward as a propitiation by his blood, to be received by faith. This was to show God's righteousness, because in his divine forbearance he had passed over former sins. It was to show his righteousness at the present time, so that he might be just and the justifier of the one who has faith in Jesus.

The righteousness is from God (21).
It is given through faith in Jesus Christ to all who believe (22).
It is available to all (22).
I have a need to be made right (23).
Christ's gracious gift justified me; I did not earn it (24).
Christ redeemed me; a price was paid (25).
God sacrificed His Son as the payment for all sin—past, present, future (25).
God sacrificed His Son at the perfect time (26).
God is just and the One who justifies those who have faith in Jesus (26).

Propitiation:

The turning away of wrath by an offering; an atoning sacrifice (Romans 3:25; Hebrews 2:17; 1John 2:2; 1 John 4:10).

THE CROSS IS SUFFICIENT

——

Though you may always remember with a sense of sorrow and regret the hurt and harm your sin has caused others and yourself, embracing Christ's completed work on the cross on your behalf will guard you against believing the lie that you must take a further step to forgive yourself.

To "forgive oneself" is not a biblical truth. The idea implies that Christ's work was incomplete and insufficient and something more is necessary to be truly forgiven.

If you really could forgive yourself, you would have no need for the Savior. It is imperative to understand that the shedding of Christ's blood paid for your sins once for all–past, present, and future. His forgiveness is complete; there is nothing you can add. Christ came to redeem and restore you, and as you walk in this truth, you will experience greater understanding of and gratitude for God's grace and the freedom Christ purchased for you.

What does it look like to embrace forgiveness?

_____

_____

_____

_____

When you embrace forgiveness, you are choosing to actually trust, believe in, and lay hold of the finished work of Christ on the cross. You may have regret for your sin after you confess; however, God wants you to walk in freedom from the guilt and shame of your sin. What Christ accomplished on the cross allows you to do that.

If you battle believing you are forgiven, talk to Jesus and consider/pray the following Scriptures: Psalm 103:8-13; Psalm 51:12; Galatians 5:1; Hebrews 10:22.

HAVE YOU IN THE PAST OR ARE YOU CURRENTLY STRUGGLING WITH FEELINGS OF GUILT OR SHAME?

Consider the following teaching, and ask the Holy Spirit to confirm these truths in your heart.

Conviction versus Condemnation

Conviction is grief or sorrow over specific sins that should bring you to repent of your sins and to embrace forgiveness. It is godly sorrow described in 2 Corinthians 7:9-10. Because of His love for you, the Holy Spirit convicts you to save you from your sin and its harmful effects (John 16:8; Psalm 32:3-5). It is God's gracious gift to you that you feel His displeasure so that you can repent and experience God's ongoing forgiveness (sanctification: 1 John 1:9; Colossians 1:13-14). Jesus' death and resurrection secured your standing before God once for all (justification: Hebrews 10:10). He has presented you to the Father as holy, blameless, and above reproach (Colossians 1:22). Because sin grieves God, mars your fellowship with Him, and destroys the quality of life God intends for you to enjoy, in His kindness He is faithful and persistent to convict you of your specific sin and lead you to repentance.

Christ died and became your condemnation. "There is therefore now no condemnation for those who are in Christ Jesus" (Romans 8:1; condemnation – _katakrima_ – the punishment following a guilty sentence). Yet at times you may experience condemning feelings or thoughts, which may come from judgment (perceived or real) from your own heart (1 John 3:19-20), from others, or from your accuser, the devil (Revelation 12:10). Condemnation is general and sweeping in nature and often leads to guilt or shame followed by feelings of discouragement, defeat, and even despair ("I will never change."). Condemning feelings must be countered with biblical truth (See Micah 7:7-9. See also, Part 2 Lesson 4 and Part 4 Lesson 5).

For a helpful article on why to "forgive oneself" is not a biblical truth, see "Say No to the Gospel of Self-Forgiveness" by John Beeson (April 17, 2019) at thegospelcoalition.org.

THE GIFT OF SALVATION

———

Scripture depicts salvation in three ways:

JUSTIFICATION	SANCTIFICATION	GLORIFICATION
I have been made righteous.	*I am being conformed to the image of Christ.*	*I will be perfect in future glory as He is perfect.*
•Romans 5:18-19•	•2 Corinthians 3:18•	•1 John 3:2•

JUSTIFICATION

———

That Which is Past

Justification:

Being made right with God. The gospel deals with the *penalty* of sin.

ROMANS 5:18-19

Therefore, as one trespass led to condemnation for all men, so one act of righteousness leads to justification and life for all men. For as by the one man's disobedience the many were made sinners, so by the one man's obedience the many will be made righteous.

PSALM 103:10-12

He does not deal with us according to our sins, nor repay us according to our iniquities. For as high as the heavens are above the earth, so great is his steadfast love toward those who fear him; as far as the east is from the west, so far does he remove our transgressions from us.

Through the shedding of His blood, Christ bore the penalty of your sin. He became your substitute and took upon Himself the full force of God's wrath that you deserved. God declared you "not guilty" and set you free from the penalty of death. As a result, when God sees you He sees Christ. You stand before God perfect and unblemished because you stand in the righteousness of Christ.

You are declared righteous at the moment you receive Christ as your Lord and Savior.

WHAT ARE SOME OF THE WONDERFUL THINGS THAT HAPPENED TO YOU THE MOMENT YOU TRUSTED CHRIST AND ACCEPTED HIS PAYMENT FOR YOUR SINS?

Consider the following verses and record your response.

COLOSSIANS 2:13-14

And you, who were dead in your trespasses and the uncircumcision of your flesh, God made alive together with him, having forgiven us all our trespasses, by canceling the record of debt that stood against us with its legal demands. This he set aside, nailing it to the cross.

All my sins were forgiven and God made me alive in Him.

COLOSSIANS 1:13

He has delivered us from the domain of darkness and transferred us to the kingdom of his beloved Son...

God transferred me from Satan's domain into the kingdom of his Son.

COLOSSIANS 1:21-22

And you, who once were alienated and hostile in mind, doing evil deeds, he has now reconciled in his body of flesh by his death, in order to present you holy and blameless and above reproach before him...

I am now holy and blameless and above reproach before God.

JOHN 1:12

But to all who did receive him, who believed in his name, he gave the right to become children of God.

I became a child of God.

JOHN 5:24

Truly, truly, I say to you, whoever hears my word and believes him who sent me has eternal life. He does not come into judgment, but has passed from death to life.

I received eternal life.

ROMANS 6:6

We know that our old self was crucified with him in order that the body of sin might be brought to nothing, so that we would no longer be enslaved to sin.

I am no longer enslaved to sin (not bound to sin).

1 JOHN 4:9-10

In this the love of God was made manifest among us, that God sent his only Son into the world, so that we might live through him. In this is love, not that we have loved God but that he loved us and sent his Son to be the propitiation for our sins.

I am now to live through Christ.

1 PETER 3:18

For Christ also suffered once for sins, the righteous for the unrighteous, that he might bring us to God, being put to death in the flesh but made alive in the spirit....

I have access to God's presence.

FDQ: How might you use the above verses when you are struggling in sin or struggling to believe Christ has paid the penalty of your sin?

The main gift in the gospel is God Himself.

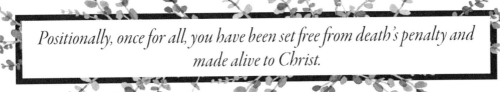

Positionally, once for all, you have been set free from death's penalty and made alive to Christ.

SANCTIFICATION

That Which is Present

Sanctification:

The ongoing process of becoming more like Christ each day. The gospel deals with the *power* of sin.

God is graciously renewing your heart and your character to be more and more like His. You have been sealed with the Holy Spirit (Ephesians 1:13) and have God's power within you (Ephesians 1:19). As a result you can choose righteousness, and sin is gradually overcome. Day-by-day, you are being set apart for God's purpose and set free from sin's power.

Sanctification is the work of God within you, but it also requires your part.

PHILIPPIANS 2:12-13
Therefore, my beloved, as you have always obeyed, so now, not only as in my presence but much more in my absence, work out your own salvation with fear and trembling, for it is God who works in you, both to will and to work for his good pleasure.

WHAT DO YOU LEARN ABOUT THE PROCESS OF SANCTIFICATION?
Read the following verses and record your response.

ROMANS 6:11-14
So you also must consider yourselves dead to sin and alive to God in Christ Jesus. Let not sin therefore reign in your mortal body, to make you obey its passions. Do not present your members to sin as instruments for unrighteousness, but present yourselves to God as those who have been brought from death to life, and your members to God as instruments for righteousness. For sin will have no dominion over you, since you are not under law but under grace.

I am dead to sin and alive to God in Christ Jesus (11).
I must not give in to sin and obey it (12).
I can and must choose righteousness (13).
I am under grace so sin has no authority or control over me (14).

The first command in Romans 6 is found in verse 11. It is to "consider," which means "to reckon, consider what is true continuously." It is a non-emotional truth—to consider as fact and to put your reflective thinking upon it.

GLORIFICATION

—

That Which is Future

Glorification:

When Christ returns, you will be *perfected*. This completion is called glorification.

In heaven, the work started on earth will be finished, and you will be free from the presence, struggle, and effects of sin. At Christ's coming, the glory of God–His honor, praise, majesty, and holiness–will be realized in every Christ-follower. You will have complete access to God's presence.

Your future is bright and it is guaranteed!

WHAT DO YOU LEARN ABOUT YOUR FUTURE GLORIFICATION?

Read the following verses and **record** your response.

PHILIPPIANS 3:20-21

But our citizenship is in heaven, and from it we await a Savior, the Lord Jesus Christ, who will transform our lowly body to be like his glorious body, by the power that enables him even to subject all things to himself.

My citizenship is in heaven. I am given a new, glorious body.

1 PETER 1:3-5

Blessed be the God and Father of our Lord Jesus Christ! According to his great mercy, he has caused us to be born again to a living hope through the resurrection of Jesus Christ from the dead, to an inheritance that is imperishable, undefiled, and unfading, kept in heaven for you, who by God's power are being guarded through faith for a salvation ready to be revealed in the last time.

My inheritance cannot perish. I am being guarded by God's power through my faith for this inheritance.

REVELATION 21:4

He will wipe away every tear from their eyes, and death shall be no more, neither shall there be mourning, nor crying, nor pain anymore, for the former things have passed away.

There will be no more tears, nor death, nor mourning, nor crying, nor pain. The former things have passed away!

FREEDOM FROM SIN IS YOUR FUTURE CERTAINTY

In the coming kingdom you will enjoy "a way of life utterly sinless, integrity untarnished, work and responsibility without fatigue, deep emotions without tears, worship without restraint or disharmony or shame, and best of all the presence of God in an unqualified and unrestricted and personal way." [3]

"

What is most valuable to you at this point of time?
Nothing can be of greater value than the cross of Christ. Without a cross-centered life, you will find yourself in perpetual defeat–not rising above your circumstances, not fulfilling your destiny.

TIM BARLEY

END YOUR STUDY...
Summarize what you learned from this lesson

Reflection

Take a moment to thank God for His gift of salvation, and spend some time writing out your two-minute testimony. One way to do this is to include answers to the following questions:

- What was your life like before Christ?
- How did He draw you to Himself?
- How has your life changed?

See Appendix A (Two-Minute Testimony Guidelines)

FDQ: Over the next several weeks, have the ladies take turns sharing their testimonies.

If a woman feels she does not have a testimony of her salvation (when she was saved), direct her to these questions: How has God demonstrated His character in your life? What life experiences have grown you? What fruit do you see in your life?

PART 1 WORKS CITED

Lesson 1: God's Majesty Revealed in Creation

No works cited.

Lesson 2: God's Intimacy Revealed to Man

1 • Piper, John. "What Is God's Glory?" Desiring God, 22 July 2014, www.desiringgod.org/interviews/what-is-god-s-glory. Accessed 16 Nov. 2016.
2 • Piper, John. "God's Glory Illustrated for Kids." Desiring God, 26 August 2016, www.desiringgod.org/interviews/god-s-glory-illustrated-for-kids. Accessed 16 Nov. 2016.
3 • Piper, John. "Glorifying God...Period." Desiring God, 15 July 2013, www.desiringgod.org/messages/glorifying-god-period. Accessed 16 Nov. 2016.

Lesson 3: Man's Fall into Sin - Section A

1 • Stott, John. The Cross of Christ. InterVarsity Press, 2006, pg. 92.
2 • Grudem, Wayne. Systematic Theology. Inter-Varsity Press and Zondervan Publishing, 1994, pg. 490.
3 • Keller, Timothy. The Reason for God. Dutton, 2008, pg. 162.

Lesson 4: Man's Fall into Sin - Section B

1 • Foh, Susan T. Women & The Word of God — A Biblical Response to Feminism, Presbyterian and Reformed Publishing Co., 1980, p. 69.
2 • Piper, John. "Adam, Christ, and Justification: Part 1." Desiring God, 18 June 2000, www.desiringgod.org/messages/adam-christ-and-justification-part-1. Accessed 16 Nov. 2016.

Lesson 5: Jesus is the Remedy

1 • Stott, John. The Cross of Christ. InterVarsity Press, 1986, pg. 160.
2 • Stott, John. The Cross of Christ. InterVarsity Press, 1986, pg. 148.
3 • Carson, D.A. Jesus' Sermon on the Mount. Baker Books, 1987, pg. 81.

UNDERSTANDING
My Heart

PART 2

As you recognized in Part 1, Eve's desire to be equal to God trumped her delight in Him. She was deceived into believing that God was not enough to satisfy her heart. As a result, she turned from worshiping God to trusting self.

Deceived Eve:
• Believed God's provision was not enough.
• Believed God was holding something back.
• Believed something beyond God would more fully satisfy her.

In Part 2 you will learn what the Scripture means when it refers to the heart of man.

── LESSON 1 ──

God Alone Will Satisfy My Heart

To begin, Lesson 1 will contrast a misdirected heart with one that finds its satisfaction in God.

All is vanity

AND A STRIVING

after wind.

ECCLESIASTES 1:14b

A MISDIRECTED HEART

———

Like Adam and Eve, all people in their natural state wrestle with a misdirected heart. A misdirected heart is one that believes something or someone other than God will ultimately satisfy man's core need for Him.

God created mankind with the innate desire to be happy—to be known intimately and loved deeply. The world promises happiness in a myriad of ways, many of which seek to minimize God or to replace Him altogether. But all that the world offers can never completely satisfy you in the way that knowing God will. Being known and loved by God and knowing and loving Him in return is ultimate satisfaction. (See Psalm 107:9; Isaiah 55:2-3; John 6:35)

ALL THAT THE WORLD OFFERS CAN NEVER TRULY SATISFY

———

King Solomon recorded in Ecclesiastes how he tried to find pleasure and satisfaction in the things of this world but discovered that "all is vanity and a striving after the wind."

ECCLESIASTES 2:1-11, 17

I said in my heart, "Come now, I will test you with pleasure; enjoy yourself." But behold, this also was vanity.... I searched with my heart how to cheer my body with wine.... I made great works. I built houses and planted vineyards for myself. I made myself gardens and parks.... I made myself pools.... I bought male and female slaves.... I had also great possessions of herds and flocks.... I also gathered for myself silver and gold.... I got singers...and many concubines.... So I became great and surpassed all who were before me in Jerusalem.... And whatever my eyes desired I did not keep from them. I kept my heart from no pleasure.... Then I considered all that my hands had done and the toil I had expended in doing it, and behold, all was vanity and a striving after wind, and there was nothing to be gained under the sun.... So I hated life, because what is done under the sun was grievous to me, for all is vanity and a striving after wind.

Solomon concluded by exhorting the reader to remember and fear God and obey Him.

ECCLESIASTES 12:1, 13

Remember also your Creator in the days of your youth, before the evil days come and the years draw near of which you will say, "I have no pleasure in them".... Fear God and keep his commandments, for this is the whole duty of man.

What are some things people believe will satisfy them?

_____

_____

_____

_____

What are some things you are tempted to go to apart from God for comfort and satisfaction?

_____

_____

_____

_____

Identify an experience from your life that illustrates how you have tried to find satisfaction on your own.

_____

_____

_____

_____

GOD IS THE "ALL-SATISFYING OBJECT"

———

"

As C.S. Lewis says, God in the Psalms is the 'all-satisfying Object.' His people adore Him unashamedly for the 'exceeding joy' they find in Him (Psalm 43:4). He is the source of complete and unending pleasure. [1]

JOHN PIPER

In your natural state you cannot see that God is the ultimate end of your heart's desire, but when you become born again (John 3:3), you gain the capacity to see Him as He is: all-satisfying.

PSALM 63:3a
[Y]our steadfast love is better than life....

JOHN 6:35
Jesus said to them, "I am the bread of life; whoever comes to me shall not hunger, and whoever believes in me shall never thirst."

JOHN 17:3
"And this is eternal life, that they know you, the only true God, and Jesus Christ whom you have sent."

YOUR STEADFAST *love* IS BETTER THAN *life.*

PSALM 63:3a

THE FOLLOWING PSALMS DESCRIBE GOD AS ALL-SATISFYING.

Hand-write each of the following verses.

PSALM 34:8

O taste and see that the LORD is good! Blessed is the man that takes refuge in him.

PSALM 37:4

Delight yourself in the LORD, and he will give you the desires of your heart.

PSALM 42:1-2

As a deer pants for flowing streams, so pants my soul for you, O God. My soul thirsts for God, for the living God. When shall I come and appear before God?

PSALM 63:1

O God, you are my God; earnestly I seek you; my soul thirsts for you; my flesh faint for you, as in a dry and weary land where there is no water.

PSALM 73:25

Whom have I in heaven but you? And there is nothing on earth that I desire besides you.

PSALM 107:9

For he satisfies the longing soul, and the hungry soul he fills with good things.

PSALM 119:103

How sweet are your words to my taste, sweeter than honey to my mouth.

NOW THAT YOU HAVE WRITTEN OUT THESE VERSES, GO BACK AND PERSONALIZE THEM.

Re-write one or more of the verses in the space below. Use first person and make it your prayer.

PSALM 37:4 EXAMPLE

Oh Lord God, when I come expectantly to You as the Object of my delight, You align my desires to Your desires. Help me be quick to come to You and believe and experience You as the source of my joy. I praise You that You delight to give me more of You and to deepen our relationship. Increase my desire for You, Lord.

ENJOYING GOD, PEOPLE, AND CREATION
——

GOD DESIGNED YOU TO EXPERIENCE DELIGHT IN HIMSELF, IN PEOPLE, AND IN CREATION. OUR OVERALL DISPOSITION ABOUT ALL OF LIFE SHOULD BE THAT IT IS A GIFT TO BE ENJOYED. THESE ARE THE MEANS BY WHICH YOU MAY EXPERIENCE HIM AS ALL-SATISFYING.

Read the following verses and record what you learn about each area.

1. FOREMOST, IN YOUR RELATIONSHIP WITH HIM.

PSALM 16:11

You make known to me the path of life; in your presence there is fullness of joy; at your right hand are pleasures forevermore.

This is the way I am to live life. I was created to be intimate with the living God. So I am to seek Him, for in His presence is the fullest joy and ultimate satisfaction.

PSALM 84:1-2

How lovely is your dwelling place, O LORD of hosts! My soul longs, yes, faints for the courts of the LORD; my heart and flesh sing for joy to the living God.

There is nothing grander than being in God's presence. I was made for God.

2. IN YOUR RELATIONSHIP WITH OTHERS.

GENESIS 2:18

Then the LORD God said, "It is not good that the man should be alone; I will make him a helper fit for him."

God gives me companions.

PSALM 133:1

Behold, how good and pleasant it is when brothers dwell in unity!

How does finding your satisfaction in God affect your relationship with others? On the other hand, if you are not finding your satisfaction in God, what does that look like?

If I am not finding my satisfaction in God, I am using others as resources to meet my needs.
There should be a steadiness and confidence in my relationship with others rather than being critical, comparing, demanding, and/or idolizing.
I can easily become a victim because others are not meeting my needs.

3. IN YOUR INVOLVEMENT WITH AND USE OF THE MATERIAL UNIVERSE.

ECCLESIASTES 9:7-9

Go, eat your bread with joy, and drink your wine with a merry heart, for God has already approved what you do. Let your garments be always white. Let not oil be lacking on your head. Enjoy life with the wife whom you love, all the days of your vain life that he has given you under the sun, because that is your portion in life and in your toil at which you toil under the sun.

I TIMOTHY 4:4-5

For everything created by God is good, and nothing is to be rejected if it is received with thanksgiving, for it is made holy by the word of God and prayer.

What are some indicators that your interaction with the material world is not honoring to God?

FDQ: You may want to read together these two verses:
1 Corinthians 10:31
Colossians 3:17

FDQ: God means for us to feel delight in these three areas. However, if a woman is not experiencing delight for whatever reason, she should be encouraged to go to the Word to exult in God and cultivate delight in Him.

As your love for and understanding of God increases, your love for others and your enjoyment of all that He has given you in the world will also increase.

JESUS AND THE SAMARITAN WOMAN
—

Look at one more passage that beautifully describes the intimacy and satisfaction you can enjoy with Jesus.

CAREFULLY READ JOHN 4:7-26.

Read the passage and answer the following questions.

What do you observe? What need did Jesus satisfy for the woman?

Jesus asks a Samaritan woman at the well for a drink of water and explains, "Whoever drinks of the water that I will give him will never be thirsty again. The water I will give him will become in him a spring of water welling up to eternal life." "True worshipers will worship in spirit and in truth."

Jesus knows the woman. Without highlighting her sins or her status, He comes to her, initiates a conversation with her, and accepts her as she is. Jesus offers her what she has not been able to find (longing for someone to satisfy her needs). The woman is excited to go into town and share what Jesus has done for her. She is fully known by Jesus and is not ashamed; she is free from condemnation.

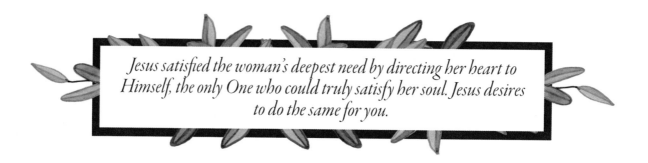

Jesus satisfied the woman's deepest need by directing her heart to Himself, the only One who could truly satisfy her soul. Jesus desires to do the same for you.

END YOUR STUDY...
Summarize what you learned from this lesson

Reflection

- Do you believe God will satisfy your longings?
- Do you believe God created you to enjoy an intimate, satisfying relationship with Him?
- How does this affect the way you view God, other people, and creation?

—— LESSON 2 ——

God's Nature Reflected in My Heart

In Lesson 1 you noted that true satisfaction is found in God alone.

In Lesson 2 you will explore how your heart functions. In the Bible the heart represents all that you are: the whole inner person. It is at the core of your being and from it comes what you think, what you feel, and what you choose.

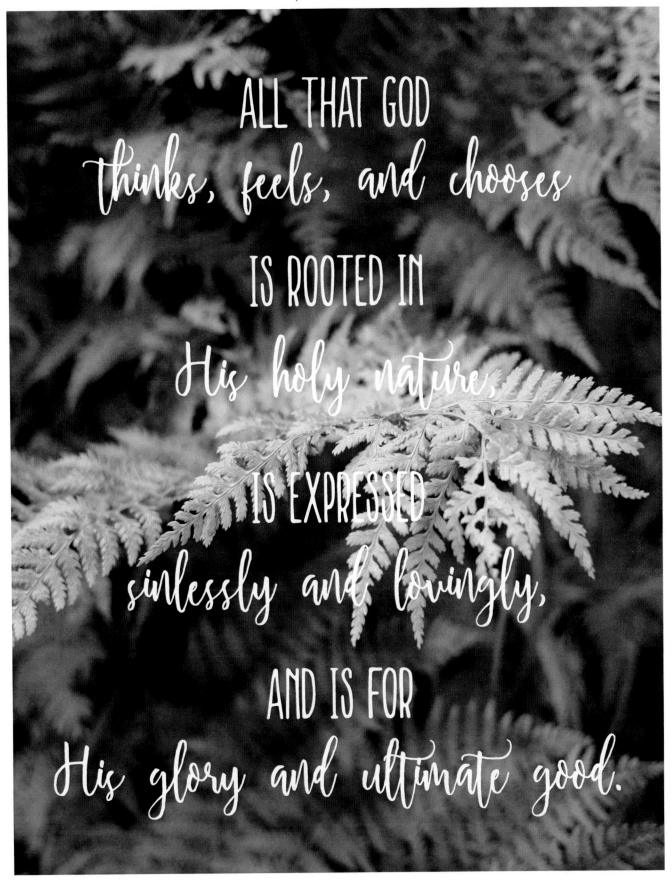

ALL THAT GOD
thinks, feels, and chooses

IS ROOTED IN

His holy nature,

IS EXPRESSED

sinlessly and lovingly,

AND IS FOR

His glory and ultimate good.

My Whole Heart

Intellect
thinking

Will
choosing

Holy Spirit

Emotions
feelings

GOD'S IMAGE-BEARER

Man's ability to think, feel, and choose reflects God's nature;
God created man as His image-bearer.

God is personal and has...

INTELLECT

ISAIAH 40:13-14

Who has measured the Spirit of the LORD, or what man shows him his counsel? Whom did he consult, and who made him understand? Who taught him the path of justice, and taught him knowledge, and showed him the way of understanding?

SEE ALSO ISAIAH 55:8-9

EMOTIONS

EXODUS 34:6

The Lord passed before him and proclaimed, "The LORD, the LORD, a God merciful and gracious, slow to anger, and abounding in steadfast love and faithfulness...."

SEE ALSO DEUTERONOMY 5:9 AND PSALM 7:11.

WILL

ISAIAH 14:24

The LORD of hosts has sworn: "As I have planned, so shall it be, and as I have purposed, so shall it stand...."

SEE ALSO ACTS 14:16-17

How do you respond to the reality that God is personal and has intellect, emotions, and a will? Is it easy for you to grasp or difficult?

_____

_____

_____

What blocks your ability to relate to God?

_____

_____

_____

FUNCTIONS OF THE HEART

—

You live from your heart. To understand your capacity to trust and obey God, it is important to understand how the heart functions. It is common in American culture to view the heart and mind as two separate parts, wherein the heart houses the emotions and the mind houses the thinking. The Bible does not divide man as such but presents the heart as the well-spring from which flows man's thinking, feeling, and choosing. Most likely you do not differentiate between the three functions of the heart as you go throughout your day. However, you are always thinking, feeling, and choosing whether you are conscious of it or not. You may observe that you are a thinker more than a feeler or vice versa. Your tendency to be more aware of one function or the other may be based on your God-given personality and past experiences.

In the Old Testament the word "heart" (*leb*) occurs over 600 times. In the New Testament the equivalent term (*kardia*) occurs about 200 times.

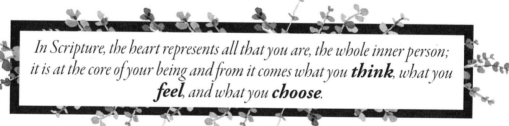

*In Scripture, the heart represents all that you are, the whole inner person; it is at the core of your being and from it comes what you **think**, what you **feel**, and what you **choose**.*

FDQ: Some ladies may find this definition confusing. Be sure that they understand that the heart includes all three functions—thinking, feeling, and choosing.

The Intellect

The term *heart* refers to your thinking, understanding, and reasoning: the focus of your attention, what you believe, and your conscience. What you are thinking is a reflection of what you are believing. Your ability to think rightly will determine what you feel and choose.

HOW DO THE FOLLOWING VERSES DEMONSTRATE THE HEART'S ABILITY TO THINK?

Review each verse and underline key phrases.

MATTHEW 13:14b-15

"'You will indeed hear but never understand, and you will indeed see but never perceive.'" For this people's heart has grown dull, and with their ears they can barely hear, and their eyes they have closed, lest they should see with their eyes and hear with their ears and understand with their heart and turn, and I would heal them."

HEBREWS 4:12

For the word of God is living and active, sharper than any two-edged sword, piercing to the division of soul and of spirit, of joints and of marrow, and discerning the thoughts and intentions of the heart.

HEBREWS 8:10

"For this is the covenant that I will make with the house of Israel after those days, declares the Lord: I will put my laws into their minds, and write them on their hearts, and I will be their God, and they shall be my people."

What does it mean to think rightly?

Thinking that aligns with God's Word.

Your intellect gives you the ability to make judgments and to be discerning.

The Emotions

The term " heart " also refers to your emotions.

Some people believe emotions are bad and should not be expressed. If this is the case, emotions may be suppressed or minimized. Other people believe emotions are paramount, and they allow their emotions to define them. If this is the case, they will live out of and be ruled by their emotions.

In truth, emotions appropriately expressed are a means to experience life more fully. They are a response to your beliefs, longings, desires, motives, and circumstances. They serve as a gauge to your inner and outer world, though they should not direct or control you. Nevertheless, God always cares about what you are feeling.

God's emotions are perfect responses to every situation and are always perfectly expressed. But your emotions are marred by the fall so that you cannot always trust them to accurately discern truth.

HOW DO THE FOLLOWING VERSES DEMONSTRATE THE HEART'S ABILITY TO FEEL?

Review each verse and **underline** key phrases.

PHILIPPIANS 4:6

Do not be anxious about anything, but in everything by prayer and supplication with thanksgiving let your requests be made known to God.

anxiety

ROMANS 12:15

Rejoice with those who rejoice, weep with those who weep.

happiness, sadness

ECCLESIASTES 7:9

Be not quick in your spirit to become angry, for anger lodges in the heart of fools.

anger

PSALM 16:11

You make known to me the path of life; in your presence there is fullness of joy; at your right hand are pleasures forevermore.

joy, gladness

PSALM 42:5a

Why are you cast down, O my soul, and why are you in turmoil within me?

turmoil, sadness

How do you view emotions?

_____

_____

_____

What has shaped your emotions or perhaps your inability to feel your emotions?

_____

_____

_____

_____

_____

_____

The Will

The term "heart" also refers to your will. The will determines what actions you take. God gives you the ability to choose. Your right choosing flows from your right thinking. When you choose to follow God's truth, your emotions may not immediately fall in line. You may even feel like you are being hypocritical because you are making a decision against your feelings. But as you choose to trust God and obey Him, your feelings will eventually align with your godly choice. Remember these two things: 1) You are called to follow biblical truth, not your feelings; and 2) You always have the ability to choose to obey.

HOW DO THE FOLLOWING VERSES DEMONSTRATE THE HEART'S ABILITY TO CHOOSE?

Review each verse and underline key phrases.

JOSHUA 24:15a

"[C]hoose this day whom you will serve...."

PSALM 25:12

Who is the man who fears the LORD? Him will he instruct in the way that he should choose.

God instructs the person who fears Him in the way he should choose.

PSALM 119:30

I have chosen the way of faithfulness; I set your rules before me.

I can choose the way of faithfulness.

EZRA 7:10

For Ezra had set his heart to study the Law of the LORD, and to do it and to teach his statutes and rules in Israel.

Ezra chose to study the Word of God and obey it.

HEBREWS 11:24-25

By faith Moses, when he was grown up, refused to be called the son of Pharaoh's daughter, choosing rather to be mistreated with the people of God than to enjoy the fleeting pleasures of sin.

Moses made a choice to be mistreated rather than enjoy the fleeting pleasures of sin.

Although you may not always choose the circumstances in which you find yourself, you always have a choice to surrender to God in every circumstance and receive His grace to help you in your time of need (Hebrews 4:16).

Share a time when you thought you did not have a choice.

_____

_____

_____

_____

_____

_____

Describe a time when you did not feel like obeying but you chose to do the right thing.

_____

_____

_____

_____

_____

_____

_____

_____

_____

_____

An example: "God is calling me to tell truth in love in a very difficult situation. I am choosing obedience and have made an appointment to meet with this person. I am still anxious and fearful, but I am determined to do what God is laying on my heart to do, so I am keeping my appointment, trusting God is able to protect my heart as I walk in obedience, even if my emotions are not keeping in step with my God-honoring actions."

FDQ: We should validate every emotion but we need to be careful not to encourage people to live out of their emotions. It is important to be aware of times when feelings are dictating behavior rather than biblical thinking guiding behavior.

END YOUR STUDY...

Summarize what you learned from this lesson

Reflection

Refer to the Whole Heart Diagram as you pray through Psalm 86:11.

Teach me your way, LORD, that I may rely on your faithfulness; give me an
undivided heart, that I may fear your name. (NIV)

PSALM 86:11

--- **LESSON 3** ---

God Gave Me A New Heart

In Lesson 2 you explored the three heart functions.

In this lesson you will examine how God spiritually revived your heart. Now you have the ability to fight sin because sin no longer rules your heart. Be encouraged! Your regenerated heart can trust and obey God, resulting in you wholeheartedly loving God and being satisfied in Him.

A HEART TRANSPLANT

As a Christ-follower, you have been given a new heart.

EZEKIEL 36:26

And I will give you a new heart, and a new spirit I will put within you. And I will remove the heart of stone from your flesh and give you a heart of flesh. (See also Ezekiel 11:19; Jeremiah 24:7)

AT SALVATION GOD GAVE YOU A NEW HEART. WHAT DOES IT MEAN THAT YOU ARE REGENERATED AND RENEWED BY THE HOLY SPIRIT?

Read the following passage and record your response.

TITUS 3:3-7

For we ourselves were once foolish, disobedient, led astray, slaves to various passions and pleasures, passing our days in malice and envy, hated by others and hating one another. But when the goodness and loving kindness of God our Savior appeared, he saved us, not because of works done by us in righteousness, but according to his own mercy, by the washing of regeneration and renewal of the Holy Spirit, whom he poured out on us richly through Jesus Christ our Savior, so that being justified by his grace we might become heirs according to the hope of eternal life.

God saved me, not because of my good works, but according to His own mercy, by the washing of *regeneration* (rebirth; made spiritually alive) and *renewal* (continuing to make new) of the Holy Spirit.

LOOK UP THE DICTIONARY DEFINITIONS OF "REGENERATION" AND "RENEWAL."

Regeneration
Rebirth; made spiritually alive

Renewal
Continuing to make new

In a real sense, the Holy Spirit makes alive your spiritually dead heart so that it can be receptive to God and His beauty. God drew you to His heart and performed in you a heart transplant.

Pause and thank God for giving you a new heart.

FDQ: What is one way that God has changed you? Explain.

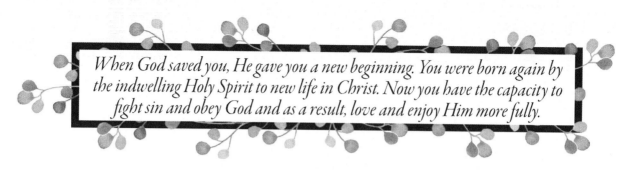

When God saved you, He gave you a new beginning. You were born again by the indwelling Holy Spirit to new life in Christ. Now you have the capacity to fight sin and obey God and as a result, love and enjoy Him more fully.

SIN NO LONGER RULES YOUR HEART

ROMANS 6:3-14

Do you not know that all of us who have been baptized into Christ Jesus were baptized into his death? We were buried therefore with him by baptism into death, in order that, just as Christ was raised from the dead by the glory of the Father, we too might walk in newness of life.

For if we have been united with him in a death like his, we shall certainly be united with him in a resurrection like his. We know that our old self was crucified with him in order that the body of sin might be brought to nothing, so that we would no longer be enslaved to sin. For one who has died has been set free from sin. Now if we have died with Christ, we believe that we will also live with him. We know that Christ, being raised from the dead, will never die again; death no longer has dominion over him. For the death he died he died to sin, once for all, but the life he lives he lives to God. So you also must consider yourselves dead to sin and alive to God in Christ Jesus.

Let not sin therefore reign in your mortal body, to make you obey its passions. Do not present your members to sin as instruments for unrighteousness, but present yourselves to God as those who have been brought from death to life, and your members to God as instruments for righteousness. For sin will have no dominion over you, since you are not under law but under grace.

CONSIDER THE FOLLOWING POINTS FROM THE TEXT:

Romans 6:3-10 explains what God has done to stop sin's rule in you.

The Spirit immersed you into Jesus and thus into His death and resurrection; this immersion makes possible a new kind of life. This is what is symbolized in water baptism—that you were buried with Him into His death and risen with Him in your new identity and life. You have been brought from death into life!

ROMANS 6:3-4

Do you not know that all of us who have been baptized into Christ Jesus were baptized into his death? We were buried therefore with him by baptism into death, in order that, just as Christ was raised from the dead by the glory of the Father, we too might walk in newness of life.

1 JOHN 3:14a

We know that we have passed out of death into life....

This immersion, or grafting into Jesus, gives you the benefits of both His death and resurrection; thus, you stand freed from sin's rule.

ROMANS 6:5-7

For if we have been united [grafted] with him in a death like his, we shall certainly be united with him in a resurrection like his. We know that our old self was crucified with him in order that the body of sin might be brought to nothing, so that we would no longer be enslaved to sin. For one who has died has been set free from sin.

Your union with Christ is permanent and once-for-all.

ROMANS 6:8-10

Now if we have died with Christ, we believe that we will also live with him. We know that Christ, being raised from the dead, will never die again; death no longer has dominion over him. For the death he died he died to sin, once for all, but the life he lives he lives to God.

HOW ARE YOU TO RESPOND TO THE ABOVE TRUTHS?

1. Accept as a fact that you died to the sin nature and are now living to God because of your union with Christ.

ROMANS 6:11

So you also must consider [accept as fact like a non-emotional philosopher] yourselves dead to sin and alive to God in Christ Jesus.

2. As a result of this fact, do not allow sin to reign over you by being obedient to its desires.

ROMANS 6:12

Let not sin therefore reign in your mortal body, to make you obey its passions.

How do you work out this verse? How do you not allow sin to reign in yourself?

- See the temptation for what it is: a promise of happiness in exchange for offending God.
- Denounce it and run to Him who is the Source of true and lasting happiness.

3. Your response to Paul's final command reveals whether or not you are yielding to the Master.

ROMANS 6:13

Do not present your members to sin as instruments for unrighteousness, but present yourselves to God as those who have been brought from death to life, and your members to God as instruments for righteousness.

1 JOHN 3:9

No one born of God makes a practice of sinning, for God's seed abides in him, and he cannot keep on sinning because he has been born of God.

ROMANS 6:17-19

But thanks be to God, that you who were once slaves of sin have become obedient from the heart to the standard of teaching to which you were committed, and, having been set free from sin, have become slaves of righteousness. I am speaking in human terms, because of your natural limitations. For just as you once presented your members as slaves to impurity and to lawlessness leading to more lawlessness, so now present your members as slaves to righteousness leading to sanctification.

4. Paul concludes this section with these encouraging truths: Sin no longer will lord over you. Therefore, you are free to obey God. So, sin no more!

ROMANS 6:14-15

For sin will have no dominion over you, since you are not under law but under grace. What then? Are we to sin because we are not under law but under grace? By no means!

ROMANS 6:7

For one who has died has been set free from sin.

A NEW BEGINNING BUT A CONTINUING FIGHT

—

Though you have a new heart, you must daily (and moment-by-moment) choose to walk in the newness of Life (Romans 6:4). In order to do this, it is important to understand the process of temptation.

What are some common misconceptions about temptation?

The things that tempt me are only things that are bad. Temptation is a sin. Temptations only come from outside forces (e.g., Satan, the world).

WHAT IS THE DEVIOUS PROCESS OF TEMPTATION?

Followers of Jesus must develop the discipline to recognize that temptation is a process that CAN lead to sinning, but it does not have to.

JAMES 1:12-15

Blessed is the man who remains steadfast under trial, for when he has stood the test he will receive the crown of life, which God has promised to those who love him. Let no one say when he is tempted, "I am being tempted by God," for God cannot be tempted with evil, and he himself tempts no one. But each person is tempted when he is lured and enticed by his own desire. Then desire when it has conceived gives birth to sin, and sin when it is fully grown brings forth death.

Eve was tempted in the same way James describes: Temptation first came to her as a thought from the tempter, "God could be withholding something good from me." She was lured when she "entertained" the thought and continued talking to Satan. She was enticed by the thought and desired the fruit. Her desire became so strong that she took and ate it.

You benefit in your relationship with God when you successfully navigate through temptations/trials/tests (12).

God NEVER solicits you to do evil; His motives are entirely pure (13).

Temptation follows a predictable pattern (14-15).

- It begins when you start desiring something more than you desire pleasing and honoring God. This is an internal (heart) struggle. This desire can last a short or long period of time.
- Following this initial or intermittent longing, if you succumb to the allurement or enticement, you will "own" it. At this point the temptation becomes sin, whether it is an attitude of the heart or an outward action.

FDQ: These words (lured and enticed) were applied to the hunter or fisherman who lures his prey from its retreat and entices it by bait into his trap, hook or net. James Hardy Ropes. A Critical and Exegetical Commentary on the Epistle of St James. The International Critical Commentary. Edinburgh: T. & T. Clark, 1916. James Adamson. The Epistle of James. The New International Commentary on the New Testament. Grand Rapids: Eerdmans, 1977.

- This temptation-turned-sin results in a "death" in your quality of life rather than God's desire for you to have abundant life.

FDQ: Regarding Jesus overcoming his temptations, see Matthew 4:1-11; Luke 4:1-13. Though Satan tempted Jesus to sin, Jesus did not sin. Yet we know that Jesus truly was tempted while He "learned obedience." Hebrews 4:15-- For we do not have a high priest who is unable to sympathize with our weaknesses, but one who in every respect has been tempted as we are, yet without sin. Hebrews 5:8-- Although he was a son, he learned obedience through what he suffered.

"'He learned obedience' means that Jesus moved from untested obedience into suffering, and then through suffering into tested and proven obedience." John Piper, "Ask Pastor John," Episode 892 (June 30, 2016).

Give an example of a temptation you have experienced that has followed James's pattern.

Name one or more desires that regularly lure and entice you. Why is it important to know what they are?

STOP SINNING!

WHAT IS SO WRONG WITH SIN?

Sin leads to "death" in all its senses.

GENESIS 2:16-17

And the Lord God commanded the man, saying, "You may surely eat of every tree of the garden, but of the tree of the knowledge of good and evil you shall not eat, for in the day that you eat of it you shall surely die."

ROMANS 8:6

For to set the mind on the flesh is death, but to set the mind on the Spirit is life and peace.

BE AWARE THAT THE SIN NATURE DESIRES TO INFLUENCE YOU.

See a few examples below.

1. The sin nature seeks to create within you the desire to practice evil.

GALATIANS 5:16-21

But I say, walk by the Spirit, and you will not gratify the desires of the flesh. For the desires of the flesh are against the Spirit, and the desires of the Spirit are against the flesh, for these are opposed to each other, to keep you from doing the things you want to do. But if you are led by the Spirit, you are not under the law. Now the works of the flesh are evident: sexual immorality, impurity, sensuality, idolatry, sorcery, enmity, strife, jealousy, fits of anger, rivalries, dissensions, divisions, envy, drunkenness, orgies, and things like these. I warn you, as I warned you before, that those who do such things will not inherit the kingdom of God.

List the works of "the flesh" (sin nature). What is the benefit of knowing these things? To increase your understanding, you may want to take the time to look up the definition of each word. With what do you particularly struggle? Remember, all sin divides your heart.

2. The sin nature seeks to get you to "withdraw" from God and His people.

HEBREWS 3:12-13

Take care, brothers, lest there be in any of you an evil, unbelieving heart, leading you to fall away from the living God. But exhort one another every day, as long as it is called "today," that none of you may be hardened by the deceitfulness of sin.

Have you experienced a time when you have withdrawn (or been tempted to withdraw) from community? Can you identify why? Describe the situation—what you were thinking, feeling, choosing.

Who regularly encourages you to live authentically as a Christ-follower? Who do you regularly encourage?

3. The sin nature can deceive you about reality and it desires things contrary to the Spirit; this leads to an insensitivity regarding Jesus and His truth.

MARK 4:19

[B]ut the cares of the world and the deceitfulness of riches and the desires for other things enter in and choke the word, and it proves unfruitful.

What are the three things Mark lists that make God's Word of no benefit in your life? Give an example of how this can happen in your own life.

EPHESIANS 4:20-24

But that is not the way you learned Christ!— assuming that you have heard about him and were taught in him, as the truth is in Jesus, to put off your old self, which belongs to your former manner of life and is corrupt through deceitful desires, and to be renewed in the spirit of your minds, and to put on the new self, created after the likeness of God in true righteousness and holiness.

4. The sin nature seeks to garner your allegiance.

ROMANS 6:12

Let not sin therefore reign in your mortal body, to make you obey its passions.

ROMANS 13:14

But put on the Lord Jesus Christ, and make no provision for the flesh, to gratify its desires.

5. The sin nature always leads to further corruption in the quality of your life.

SEE EPHESIANS 4:22-24.

Be encouraged that though you are in a fight and your sin nature is always with you, you are no longer bound to sin. You need to learn to continue putting off your old self and putting on Christ. Like the Apostle Paul, commit to fight the good fight against sin.

"

What God creates in the new birth is not a sinless Christian. What he creates is an embattled, not-yet perfect, Spirit-empowered, persevering, Christ-treasuring, sin-hating, new being—a new creation in Christ. And don't miss those words "embattled" and "sin-hating." The new creation in Christ is a fighter. Paul said at the end of his life, "I have fought the good fight" (2 Timothy 4:7). And he tells Timothy, "Fight the good fight" (1 Timothy 6:12).... The outcome is guaranteed, but the battle is real.[1]

JOHN PIPER

GOD CARES FOR YOUR HEART

—

Remember, God in His kindness cares for your heart and helps you in your ongoing battle with sin.

HOW DOES GOD CARE FOR YOUR HEART?

Consider the following truths:

He creates in you a clean heart (Psalm 51:10).
He searches your heart (1 Chronicles 28:9; Revelation 2:23).
He tests your heart (1 Chronicles 29:17; Psalm 26:2; Psalm 139:23-24).
He revives your contrite heart (Isaiah 57:15, 18).
He places His Word in your heart (Psalm 16:7; Psalm 119:11).
He instructs your heart (Psalm 16:7).

How have you experienced God's care for your heart?

END YOUR STUDY...

Summarize what you learned from this lesson

Reflection

Marvel at the fact that God has given you a new heart. Reflect on the truths presented in this lesson.

"Who can discern his errors? Declare me innocent from hidden faults. Keep back
your servant also from presumptuous sins; let them not have dominion over me!
Then I shall be blameless and innocent of great transgression. Let the words of my
mouth and the meditation of my heart be acceptable in your sight, O Lord, my rock
and my redeemer."

PSALM 19:12-14

Pray and ask God to keep you from sin and to forgive you for sinning. Thanks be to God that He has granted
you forgiveness and the power to keep you from sinning. He has made you right with Him (justification) and
He is continuing to make you like Him as you walk with Him (sanctification).

LESSON 4

Renewing My Mind To Grow My Heart

Created in God's image, you have been given the ability to think, feel, and choose. When these three heart functions align with God's Word, you have the capacity to live wholeheartedly and experience your relationship with Him, others, and the material world as delightful gifts to enjoy.

At the moment of your salvation, you were made new. As a result, sin no longer reigns in your heart! Yet, in Lesson 3 you faced the reality that though sin does not rule your heart, you will remain in a continual fight against it for the rest of your life. To better understand the battle and to be prepared to fight sin, you looked at the process of temptation and sin's devious nature.

In Lesson 4 you will examine the key weapon in your fight against sin: the renewing of your mind. By the power of the Holy Spirit, you will be transformed as you effectively practice this discipline.

GROWING IN MATURITY

—

"

When we were born again as spiritual beings in right standing with God, we were still tilted toward the world's way of thinking.... [W]e find it hard to break away. Indeed, when Paul wrote the Christians at Corinth, he called them men of flesh. Though born of the Spirit and equipped with all provisions in Christ, these individuals had yet to develop into the complete, mature believers God intended them to be.[1]

ROBERT S. McGEE

CONTRAST ONE WHO IS SPIRITUALLY IMMATURE WITH ONE WHO IS MATURE.

Read the following verses and record your response.

HEBREWS 5:11-14
About this we have much to say, and it is hard to explain, since you have become dull of hearing. For though by this time you ought to be teachers, you need someone to teach you again the basic principles of the oracles of God. You need milk, not solid food, for everyone who lives on milk is unskilled in the word of righteousness, since he is a child. But solid food is for the mature, for those who have their powers of discernment trained by constant practice to distinguish good from evil.

JAMES 1:22-25
But be doers of the word, and not hearers only, deceiving yourselves. For if anyone is a hearer of the word and not a doer, he is like a man who looks intently at his natural face in a mirror. For he looks at himself and goes away and at once forgets what he was like. But the one who looks into the perfect law, the law of liberty, and perseveres, being no hearer who forgets but a doer who acts, he will be blessed in his doing.

The spiritually mature person is discerning and able to distinguish good from evil. She knows the Word and perseveres to obey it.

Do you recognize any specific areas of spiritual immaturity in your life?

EVIDENCE OF A MATURE MIND

——

WHAT IS THE EVIDENCE OF A MATURE MIND?

Read the following verses and record your response.

PSALM 9:1-2

I will give thanks to the Lord with my whole heart; I will recount all of your wonderful deeds. I will be glad and exult in you; I will sing praise to your name, O Most High.

remembering what He has done and giving thanks

ISAIAH 26:3

You keep him in perfect peace whose mind is stayed on you, because he trusts in you.

experiencing peace

1 CORINTHIANS 2:12-13

Now we have received not the spirit of the world, but the Spirit who is from God, that we might understand the things freely given us by God. And we impart this in words not taught by human wisdom but taught by the Spirit, interpreting spiritual truths to those who are spiritual.

understanding the Word; The Holy Spirit imparts to my spirit an understanding of His Word.

GALATIANS 5:22-23a

But the fruit of the Spirit is love, joy, peace, patience, kindness, goodness, faithfulness, gentleness, self-control....

demonstrating the fruit of the Spirit

1 PETER 2:1-3

So put away all malice and all deceit and hypocrisy and envy and all slander. Like newborn infants, long for the pure spiritual milk, that by it you may grow up into salvation—if indeed you have tasted that the Lord is good.

longing for the Word and growing in godly character

What stands out to you from these verses?

BE DISCERNING

As you are sanctified and continue to mature in your walk with the Lord, you will become more discerning, able to distinguish truth from falsehood.

"

But what is this discernment? The word used in Psalm 119:66 means "taste." It is the ability to make discriminating judgments, to distinguish between, and to recognize the moral implications of, different situations and courses of action. It includes the ability to "weigh up" and assess the moral and spiritual status of individuals, groups, and even movements....

Jesus' discernment penetrated to the deepest reaches of the heart. But the Christian is called to develop similar discernment. For the only worthwhile discernment we possess is that which we receive in union with Christ, by the Spirit, through God's Word.

So discernment is learning to think God's thoughts after Him, practically and spiritually; it means having a sense of how things look in God's eyes and seeing them in some measure "uncovered and laid bare" (Heb. 4:13).[2]

SINCLAIR FERGUSON

FDQ: What does it mean to "weigh-up" and assess your moral and spiritual status? God's Word is the standard by which we evaluate our thoughts, motives, and actions. Do you consider yourself a discerning person?

WRITE OUT A PRAYER FOR DISCERNMENT
Read the following verses and record your prayer.

PHILIPPIANS 1:9-10
And it is my prayer that your love may abound more and more, with knowledge and all discernment, so that you may approve what is excellent, and so be pure and blameless for the day of Christ....

"

The effect of love, knowledge, and discernment in you will be the moral, active approval of what is excellent with the result and intent that we will be pure and blameless. This is the sanctifying process.[3]

JOHN PIPER

WHAT DOES IT MEAN TO BE PURE AND BLAMELESS AT THE DAY OF CHRIST?

It does not mean sinless (Philippians 3:12), but...

- if you are aware of any sin, you confess it and make war on it by the Spirit (Romans 8:13),
- and you actively pursue holiness (Hebrews 12:14) and seek to please the Lord in everything (2 Corinthians 5:9),
- as you trust Christ to be your sinless perfection (Romans 5:19). [4]

THE HOLY SPIRIT EMPOWERS THE TRANSFORMATION PROCESS

——

The way you entered life in Christ is identical to the way you are to live life in Him each day. When you responded in faith to the gospel, you became a follower of Christ. In the same way, you are to "live by the Spirit, [and] keep in step with the Spirit" (Galatians 5:25). To "keep in step" means that by the power of the Holy Spirit, moment-by-moment, you are to walk by faith in the same direction and at the same pace as Him. As you respond daily in faith and in obedience to the promises and commands of God, the Spirit will Himself help you and transform you into the likeness of Christ.

Paul in Romans 8:4 states that the follower of Christ walks by the Spirit, not the flesh. The verb "walk" refers to the way a person conducts her life; it indicates a habit of living. Living according to the Spirit requires you to set your mind on Jesus.

IN ROMANS 8:5-7 HOW MANY TIMES DOES PAUL USE A FORM OF "SET THE MIND"? WHAT TWO OPTIONS DOES PAUL SPECIFY AS THE OBJECT OF A PERSON'S THINKING? WHAT IS THE OUTCOME OF EACH? WHAT IS THE MENTALITY OF THE FLESH?

Read the following verses and **record** your response.

ROMANS 8:5-7

For those who live according to the flesh set their minds on the things of the flesh, but those who live according to the Spirit set their minds on the things of the Spirit. For to set the mind on the flesh is death, but to set the mind on the Spirit is life and peace. For the mind that is set on the flesh is hostile to God, for it does not submit to God's law; indeed, it cannot.

To "set the mind" (*proneō*) refers to what your whole heart—your thinking, feeling, and choosing—is absorbed by: what preoccupies your thinking; what influences your affections; how you spend your time and energies. This is the process by which the Holy Spirit transforms you (sanctification).

To set your mind on the Spirit is to walk "in step with the Spirit" (Galatians 5:25) and is life-giving.

In addition, Romans 8:5-6 directs the follower of Christ to be spiritually mindful during all her waking hours.
- We live in an environment of pervasive and aggressive evil, so you must not be passive or believe this age is neutral.

Galatians 1:4 – [Jesus] who gave himself for our sins to deliver us from the present evil age, according to the will of our God and Father....
- This age is exerting force to entice you to adopt its values and lifestyle. It is aggressively trying to pervert the quality of your life. This is why Paul commands the reader not to be conformed to this world. (See Romans 12:1-2 below.)

Ephesians 5:15-16 – Look carefully then how you walk, not as unwise but as wise, making the best use of the time, because the days are evil.
- To protect yourself from daily evil, be wise and mindful how you use your time.

Resisting evil is empowered by the Holy Spirit and begins with your thought life. What you set your mind on will influence and shape your beliefs and actions. It is that important!

TO SET THE MIND ON THE SPIRIT
is life & peace.

ROMANS 8:6b

RENEW YOUR MIND

——

WHAT DO YOU LEARN ABOUT RENEWING YOUR MIND FROM THE FOLLOWING VERSES?

Read the following verses and record your response.

EPHESIANS 4:17-24

Now this I say and testify in the Lord, that you must no longer walk as the Gentiles do, in the futility of their minds. They are darkened in their understanding, alienated from the life of God because of the ignorance that is in them, due to their hardness of heart. They have become callous and have given themselves up to sensuality, greedy to practice every kind of impurity. But that is not the way you learned Christ!—assuming that you have heard about him and were taught in him, as the truth is in Jesus, to put off your old self, which belongs to your former manner of life and is corrupt through deceitful desires, and to be renewed in the spirit of your minds, and to put on the new self, created after the likeness of God in true righteousness and holiness.

I am to "put off" the old self by being "renewed in the spirit of my mind"; and I am to put on the new self, and walk in the righteousness and holiness of my new identity.

ROMANS 12:1-2

I appeal to you therefore, brothers, by the mercies of God, to present your bodies as a living sacrifice, holy and acceptable to God, which is your spiritual worship. Do not be conformed to this world, but be transformed by the renewal of your mind, that by testing you may discern what is the will of God, what is good and acceptable and perfect.

In order not to conform to the things of this world, I must renew my mind by examining if what I believe is true, and discerning what is good, acceptable, and perfect. This is an ongoing process.

COLOSSIANS 3:1-2, 10

If then you have been raised with Christ, seek the things that are above, where Christ is, seated at the right hand of God. Set your minds on things that are above, not on things that are on earth... and have put on the new self, which is being renewed in knowledge after the image of its creator.

I am to seek and set my mind on eternal things rather than earthly things. I am to "put on" (clothe myself with the things of Christ) the new self, which is being renewed to be more and more Christ-like.

1 PETER 1:13-15

Therefore, preparing your minds for action, and being sober-minded, set your hope fully on the grace that will be brought to you at the revelation of Jesus Christ. As obedient children, do not be conformed to the passions of your former ignorance, but as he who called you is holy, you also be holy in all your conduct....

I am to be intentional and serious about setting my mind/my thinking on the hope of the gospel in order to guard against being entrapped by old patterns of sinful conduct. I am called to live a holy life.

Peter is urging his readers to be alert! To prepare your mind for action is to gird up your mind and has the idea of an athlete who would tuck his tunic into his belt so that he could run unencumbered.

What is encumbering your thoughts, preventing you from thinking on what is true?

STEPS TO RENEWING YOUR MIND[4]

———

This is a practical tool to help you renew your mind.

CONSIDER your thoughts and ask the Holy Spirit to help you identify those that are not aligned to God's truth.

2 CORINTHIANS 10:5

We destroy arguments and every lofty opinion raised against the knowledge of God, and take every thought captive to obey Christ....

CONFESS (agree with God) that some thoughts are not honoring to Him, acknowledging them as sin. In addition, if you recognize you have embraced a lie, confess it as such.

1 JOHN 1:9

If we confess our sins, he is faithful and just to forgive us our sins and to cleanse us from all unrighteousness.

CALL UPON the Holy Spirit's power to help you set your mind on Jesus and His Word.

2 PETER 1:3 (NIV)

His divine power has given us everything we need for life and godliness through our knowledge of him who called us by his own glory and goodness.

CHOOSE to replace your sinful thought with a God-honoring thought. Select a Scripture with which to renew your mind and think on it often throughout the day.

PHILIPPIANS 4:8-9

Finally, brothers, whatever is true, whatever is honorable, whatever is just, whatever is pure, whatever is lovely, whatever is commendable, if there is any excellence, if there is anything worthy of praise, think about these things. What you have learned and received and heard and seen in me—practice these things, and the God of peace will be with you.

REPEAT these steps when sinful thoughts or attitudes recur.

Resist the Devil

In order to renew your mind, you must be familiar with your adversary, the devil, and resist his ploys.

1 PETER 5:8-9a
"Be sober-minded; be watchful. Your adversary the devil prowls about like a roaring lion, seeking someone to devour. Resist him, firm in your faith...."

- The Nature of Satan – Satan is a liar and deceiver (John 8:44-45; 2 Corinthians 11:3) who only and always seeks to destroy you (2 Corinthians 11:14). He will do all he can to make you believe that: 1) God is holding out on you; 2) Jesus is impotent; and 3) You are not righteous in your standing before God. Satan is purely evil and unredeemable. He is relentlessly hostile to God and people.

- The Strategies of Satan – Satan seduces people into dismissing him as a real threat. His goal is to neutralize sin and normalize evil so that you become convinced that you are just doing what everyone else is doing. (See 2 Corinthians 2:11)

- The Limitations of Satan – Satan has authentic power in the world (1 John 5:19; Ephesians 6:10-18). But Satan's power is limited and always under the sovereign control of God (Job 1:12) and is temporary (Romans 16:20).

God has set boundaries and Satan cannot operate outside of them. But within these boundaries he can produce a lot of damage! He is not omnipotent, omniscient nor omnipresent, but he does not need to be because he has a legion of demonic minions at his disposal who are scattered all over the earth, eager to do his bidding.

Though Satan cannot read your mind, you reveal your heart to him through your words and your actions on a regular basis.

So, you must resist and fight Satan with God's resources, standing firm in your faith, renewing your mind, and trusting in God's promises, provision, and presence through the indwelling Holy Spirit (Ephesians 6:10-18; James 4:7-8).

The devil wants you to think you are the only one facing a particular temptation, trial, test or struggle. He wants you to despair and give in to his ploys. Be assured that you are not alone (1 Peter 5:9b). You "do not have a high priest who is unable to sympathize with [y]our weaknesses, but one who in every respect has been tempted as [you] are, yet without sin" (Hebrews 4:15). Jesus understands your struggles and He knows you need His help. The great news is He is always gracious and eager to help you.

Satan has no hold on you because Jesus has covered over your sins. Satan has no case against you because the Judge has acquitted you by the death of His Son (Hebrews 2:14-15 – "Since therefore the children share in flesh and blood, he himself likewise partook of the same things, that through death he might destroy the one who has the power of death, that is, the devil, and deliver all those who through fear of death were subject to lifelong slavery.") So, "[r]esist him, firm in your faith" (1 Peter 5:9).

It is important to note that renewing your mind will be an ongoing process—even for the same thought. Just as Jesus encouraged Peter to forgive his brother "seventy-seven times" (Matthew 18:22), so you must continue to do the work of renewing your mind so that you may increasingly "set your mind on things above" (Colossians 3:2).

END YOUR STUDY...
Summarize what you learned from this lesson

Reflection

- Do you practice renewing your mind?
- Do you catch your thoughts when they are not pleasing to the Lord?
- How does your life demonstrate the qualities of a renewed mind?

Father, please continue to show me my heart, that I may see my desperate need for Your grace, know more fully You as the Object of my satisfaction, and obey You without reservation. Help me to renew my mind each day with Your Word so that I might rightly think, choose, and feel. In Jesus' name, Amen.

LESSON 5

God Desires My Whole Heart

In Lesson 4 you noted that you must renew your mind to mature in your relationship with God. God unites your heart to His will as you renew your mind. When your heart is not aligned to God, you are living with a divided heart.

In this lesson you will have an opportunity to discern your heart through using the My Heart Unveiled Chart in order to live wholeheartedly for God.

WHOLEHEARTED LIVING

WHAT DO THE FOLLOWING SCRIPTURES TELL YOU ABOUT LIVING WHOLEHEARTEDLY FOR GOD?

Read the following verses and record your response.

PSALM 86:11-12

Teach me your way, O Lord, that I may walk in your truth; unite my heart to fear your name. I give thanks to you, O Lord my God, with my whole heart, and I will glorify your name forever.

I am to ask God to teach me His ways and unite my heart to His heart. He will do this and I am to thank Him with my whole heart.

PSALM 119:2

Blessed are those who keep his testimonies, who seek him with their whole heart....

I am blessed when I seek God and keep His instructions.

PSALM 119:10

With my whole heart I seek you; let me not wander from your commandments!

I am to seek God and depend on Him to keep me from wandering.

PSALM 119:34

Give me understanding, that I may keep your law and observe it with my whole heart.

I am to ask God for understanding of His Word and obey it.

To know your heart, you must be able to recognize what you are thinking, choosing, and feeling, which will identify what you believe. What you think and feel reflects what you believe to be true, although much of the time you may not realize it. In addition, what you claim to believe may differ from how you actually live.

In Lesson 5 you will learn a practical heart evaluation tool. The goal is to help you discern your heart. As you use this tool please be prayerful, asking God to reveal your heart to you as David did in Psalm 139:23-24.

> *Search me, O God, and know my heart! Try me and know my thoughts! And see if there be any grievous way in me, and lead me in the way everlasting!*

When you ask God to search your heart, you are coming to Him with a posture of humility and submission.

TAKE EVERY THOUGHT CAPTIVE to obey Christ.

2 CORINTHIANS 10:5b

PREPARATION TO DISCERN YOUR HEART

WHAT DO THE FOLLOWING SCRIPTURES TEACH YOU ABOUT A RIGHT HEART POSTURE TOWARD GOD?

Read the following verses and record your response.

I PETER 5:6-7

Humble yourselves, therefore, under the mighty hand of God so that at the proper time he may exalt you, casting all your anxieties on him, because he cares for you.

I must humble myself before God and cast all my anxiety on Him.

JAMES 4:7-8

Submit yourselves therefore to God. Resist the devil, and he will flee from you. Draw near to God, and he will draw near to you. Cleanse your hands, you sinners, and purify your hearts, you double-minded.

I must submit to God and actively resist the devil. When I draw near to God I see how He is caring for me and providing for me.

A prideful heart will refuse to draw near to God or to submit to Him. You will try to manage your own fears and anxieties and you will not trust in God.

PROVERBS 28:13

Whoever conceals his transgressions will not prosper, but he who confesses and forsakes them will obtain mercy.

I must confess my sins to the Lord and turn from them. God will always respond mercifully to me.

2 CORINTHIANS 10:5

We destroy arguments and every lofty opinion raised against the knowledge of God, and take every thought captive to obey Christ....

I must catch my wrong thinking and replace it with truth.

In order to destroy arguments and opinions raised against the knowledge of God, you must first know what the Word of God says. Second, you must prayerfully examine your heart (thoughts, choices, feelings) to determine if it is aligned to the knowledge of God or if some thoughts need to be "caught" and changed so they will align with the knowledge and will of God.

MY HEART UNVEILED

———

Review the My Heart Unveiled Chart (at the end of this lesson). The heart evaluation exercise will help you discern the underlying motives of your heart. It is a tool you can use when you have an unsettled heart. An unsettled heart does not necessarily mean you have sinned. It is important to talk with God and ask Him to reveal your heart to you.

The chart may be used individually or with a peer. You will practice using it both ways.

You will notice the chart is divided into eight sections. Your heart is always thinking, feeling, and choosing, though you may not be aware of any of these functions. Your responses indicate your underlying core belief and desire. Remember, you may not be aware of the internal working of your heart until you ask the Holy Spirit to reveal these things to you and begin the process of examining your heart.

The process normally begins by reflecting on a situation or circumstance; however, there may be times when you experience a flood of emotions but cannot connect them to any situation. In that case begin by examining your emotions. Remember, each step in the process is done prayerfully, asking the Spirit of God to reveal your heart to you. As you go through each step, write down your responses. You may want to keep a separate journal for your heart evaluation work.

Generally you will complete Situation, Feeling, and Thinking sections on your own. They are things only you know. You may want or need help from a peer in processing through Perceived Need/Desire, Choosing, Underlying Belief/Fears, God's Truth, and Action Steps sections. As you process through these five sections it is not necessary to go in the order they are shown; however, it is important to go through each of them.

MY HEART UNVEILED EXERCISE

———

Now it is time to practice using the chart. Begin by praying. Ask the Holy Spirit to quiet your heart and to direct you to choose a current situation or one from the past. Use the following instructions. Complete the My Heart Unveiled chart to the best of your ability. Do not feel like you must complete this process in one sitting. Put it down and come back to it, always asking the Holy Spirit to guide you into truth.

FDQ: At your next meeting, you will need to assign pairs to go through the My Heart Unveiled chart with one another. When one person is sharing her chart, the partner should be an active listener and only ask questions to further her partner's processing.

MY HEART UNVEILED INSTRUCTIONS

SITUATION

Describe in as much detail as possible the situation. Who? What? When? Is this a one-time or ongoing situation?

FEELINGS

What are you feeling regarding the above situation? At times you may suppress your feelings, particularly if they produce fear, guilt or pain. In this process allow yourself to experience your emotions. It is not uncommon to experience conflicting emotions, such as fear and excitement or joy and grief. You may feel guilty for feeling a certain way. Do not dismiss it. Your emotions may not make sense as you identify them, but they are windows into your heart. Record all that you are feeling about the situation. If you typically analyze more than you recognize your feelings, this may be a hard exercise but a very important one.

THINKING

What thoughts come to mind regarding the above situation? If it is easier for you to recognize your feelings than your thoughts, it may take you some time to put words to what you are thinking. Keep in mind that at this point your thoughts and feelings may not be in agreement. You may also have conflicting thoughts. Record everything you are thinking.

CHOOSING

What are you choosing now? It may be an outward action or just an internal attitude. How is what you are choosing benefiting you/not benefiting you? How is what you are choosing impacting others? Did you discover you feel the need to control a person or situation? Have you taken action to do that? Do you have a plan or agenda regarding the situation?

PERCEIVED NEED/DESIRE

Initially you may not be aware of your perceived need or desire; however, try to answer these questions for yourself. What is underneath your feelings or thinking? Are you thinking or feeling like you need something to be okay, safe, happy, etc.? Are you thinking or feeling like you need to control a circumstance or person in order to meet this need/desire? Do you have an expectation that is not being met?

CONTROL-RESPONSES

In Part 5 Lessons 2 and 3 you will receive instruction and another opportunity to work through the chart, including this section. The fight or flight responses identify common control strategies and fears.

UNDERLYING BELIEF/FEARS

An underlying belief usually manifests itself as an underlying fear. As you begin to recognize your perceived need or desire and how you are choosing to meet that need/desire, these questions may help determine what you really believe about the situation. Are you believing truth or a lie? Are you trusting God to take care of you in this situation? Are there things you feel you must do because you cannot be sure of God's will? Are you afraid God might ask you to do something you may not want to do? Do you trust God's timetable? Is this outside of God's control? Is this something too insignificant to ask God about?

GOD'S TRUTH

Regarding what you discovered you actually believe, what does God's Word say? How does your belief align with God's Word? How does it not? Search the Scriptures if you are not sure what God's Word says. (Ask a mentor or trusted friend to help you.)

ACTION STEPS

If you recognized a sinful attitude or behavior, confess it and thank God for His forgiveness. What attitude or behavior did you identify needs changing? What Scriptures can you use to renew your mind? Write these out so that you can review them often. Is there anyone you need to forgive or from whom you need to seek forgiveness? Do you need to seek accountability in an area?

My Heart Unveiled

My situation

My response

FEELING	THINKING	CHOOSING

Why am I responding this way?

PERCEIVED NEED/DESIRE	CONTROL-RESPONSES	UNDERLYING BELIEF/FEARS

Steps to walk in obedience

GOD'S TRUTH	ACTION STEPS

(Refer to My Heart Unveiled Instructions on p. 118)

My Heart Unveiled - Example

My situation

I catch myself saying hurtful words to my young adult child whenever he disappoints me.

My response

FEELING	THINKING	CHOOSING
Disrespected	I blew it	Ignore him
Hurt	I did it again	Tell my husband
Disappointed	He always disobeys	Find a way to reconcile
Sense of loss	He does not respect me	
Guilt		

Why am I responding this way?

PERCEIVED NEED/DESIRE	CONTROL-RESPONSES	UNDERLYING BELIEF/FEARS
Validated as an authority	Anger	Need to ensure I have influence
Obedience	Manipulating by making him	or else he will be deep in his
Respect, honor	feel guilty	worldly ways
Love		

Steps to walk in obedience

GOD'S TRUTH	ACTION STEPS
We are all fallen (Romans 3:23)	Confess my fears and pride to God
God is after our children	Own my sinfulnes and ask for an apology
He does not want anyone to perish (2 Peter 3:9)	Pray for a change of heart through the renewing of
I can entrust my fears to Him (Psalm 33:4)	my mind and yielding to His Spirit
	Forgive and love our son

(Refer to My Heart Unveiled Instructions on p. 118)

120

ADDITIONAL NOTES:

- When you have come to the end of this process, thank God for revealing your heart to you. Thank Him for showing you the steps of obedience. Thank Him for giving you His Spirit that empowers you to do what He calls you to do.

- Do not be discouraged if you have struggled to complete these sections. You will have an opportunity to work through the process with your facilitator.

END YOUR STUDY...
Summarize what you learned from this lesson

Reflection

Meditate on the following two passages. Thank God that He gives you everything you need to discern your heart and live wholeheartedly for Him.

And God is able to make all grace abound to you, so that having all sufficiency in all things at all times, you may abound in every good work.

2 CORINTHIANS 9:8

His divine power has granted to us all things that pertain to life and godliness, through the knowledge of him who called us to his own glory and excellence, by which he has granted to us his precious and very great promises, so that through them you may become partakers of the divine nature, having escaped from the corruption that is in the world because of sinful desire.

2 PETER 1:3-4

My Heart Unveiled

My situation

My response

FEELING	THINKING	CHOOSING

Why am I responding this way?

PERCEIVED NEED/DESIRE	CONTROL-RESPONSES	UNDERLYING BELIEF/FEARS

Steps to walk in obedience

GOD'S TRUTH	ACTION STEPS

(Refer to My Heart Unveiled Instructions on p. 118)

My Heart Unveiled

My situation

_____

_____

_____

My response

FEELING	THINKING	CHOOSING

Why am I responding this way?

PERCEIVED NEED/DESIRE	CONTROL-RESPONSES	UNDERLYING BELIEF/FEARS

Steps to walk in obedience

GOD'S TRUTH	ACTION STEPS

(Refer to My Heart Unveiled Instructions on p. 118)

PART 2 WORKS CITED

Lesson 1: God Alone Will Satisfy My Heart

1 • Piper, John. "The All-Satisfying Object." Desiring God, 1 Oct 2016, http://www.desiringgod.org/articles/the-all-satisfying-object. Accessed 19 Dec. 2016.

Lesson 2: God's Nature Reflected in My Heart

No works cited.

Lesson 3: God Gave Me A New Heart

1 • Piper, John. "If I'm Dead to Sin, Why Must I Kill It Every Day?" Desiring God, 22 Aug. 2016, http://www.desiringgod.org/interviews/if-i-m-dead-to-sin-why-must-i-kill-it-every-day. Accessed 19 Dec. 2016.

Lesson 4: Renewing My Mind To Grow My Heart

1 • McGee, Robert S. The Search For Significance. Thomas Nelson Inc., 1998, 2003, pg. 69.
2 • Ferguson, Sinclair. "What is Discernment?" Ligonier Ministries, 6 Oct. 2014, http://www.ligonier.org/blog/discernment-thinking-gods-thoughts/. Accessed 19 Dec. 2016.
3 • Piper, John. "I Don't Feel Blameless, Am I?" Look at the Book, Desiring God, 29 August 2017, www.desiringgod.org. Accessed Nov. 2017.
4 • Ibid
5 • Adapted and used with permission from Called to Obedience Ministries.

Lesson 5: God Desires My Whole Heart

No works cited.

Knowing GOD

PART 3

In Part 3 you will immerse in God's nature. Just as you must get to know a person before you begin to trust her, so you must seek to know God (John 1:12-13)—His character, plan, and promises—before you can grow in wholeheartedly trusting Him.

── LESSON 1 ──

God is My Perfect Father

In Lesson 1 you will revel in the fact that God is your perfect Abba Father.

See what kind of love the Father has given to us, that we should be called children of God; and so we are.

1 JOHN 3:1a

YOU ARE A CHILD OF GOD

——

If you have committed your life to be a follower of Christ...
you are God's child and He is your Father. In fact, the Father subjected His only Son to a criminal's punishment and death in order to bring you into His family.

JOHN 1:12-13
But to all who did receive him, who believed in his name, he gave the right to become children of God, who were born, not of blood nor of the will of the flesh nor of the will of man, but of God.

EPHESIANS 1:5, 7
[H]e predestined us for adoption as sons through Jesus Christ, according to the purpose of his will.... In him we have redemption through his blood, the forgiveness of our trespasses, according to the riches of his grace....

"

The notion that we are children of God, His own sons and daughters...is the mainspring of Christian living.... Our sonship to God is the apex of creation and the goal of redemption.[1]

SINCLAIR FERGUSON

YOU HAVE BEEN *adopted* AS HIS CHILD.

YOU ARE AN HEIR WITH CHRIST

——

WHAT RIGHTS OF SONSHIP DID YOU RECEIVE?

Read the following passage and record your response.

GALATIANS 4:4-7

But when the fullness of time had come, God sent forth his Son, born of woman, born under the law, to redeem those who were under the law, so that we might receive adoption as sons. And because you are sons, God has sent the Spirit of his Son into our hearts, crying, "Abba! Father!" So you are no longer a slave, but a son, and if a son, then an heir through God.

Slave – Son – Heir. This is a beautiful progression. First I was set free from slavery. Then I was declared "son" and adopted into God's family. Then, as son, I was made an heir.
Through Jesus Christ I became God's child legally.
Jesus removed all penalty of debt.
I received a new status and full rights of sonship.
I received the Holy Spirit, and I became God's child experientially.

See also Romans 8:17 – [A]nd if children, then heirs—heirs of God and fellow heirs with Christ, provided we suffer with him in order that we may also be glorified with him.

You are an heir with Christ. When God looks upon you, He sees Christ in you, which means you can walk with Christ confidently, securely, and boldly. Your inherited status can never change; it is "an inheritance that is imperishable, undefiled, and unfading, kept in heaven for you" (1 Peter 1:4).

As an heir you have received a glorious inheritance, the sum total of all God has promised you through salvation (Ephesians 1:3-14), culminating in heaven. (Part 7 Lesson 5 will address this topic more fully.)

ABBA, FATHER!

———

"Abba" is an Aramaic affectionate address of a small child to his father. As a Christ-follower, you have the same access to God the Father that God the Son had (Romans 8:15). Jesus addressed God the Father as "Daddy" or "Papa" when He prayed, "Abba, Father" as recorded in Mark 14:36– "And he said, 'Abba, Father, all things are possible for you. Remove this cup from me. Yet not what I will, but what you will.'"

The term "Abba" carries with it a sense of intimacy and closeness. You have been adopted into God's family. You are His precious daughter and He is your Daddy.

FDQ: Do you experience God as Daddy or is this difficult for you? Explain.

WHAT IS YOUR STATUS AS A CHILD OF GOD?

Carefully read the following passage and record your response.

ROMANS 8:14-17

For all who are led by the Spirit of God are sons of God. For you did not receive the spirit of slavery to fall back into fear, but you have received the Spirit of adoption as sons, by whom we cry, "Abba! Father!" The Spirit himself bears witness with our spirit that we are children of God, and if children, then heirs—heirs of God and fellow heirs with Christ, provided we suffer with him in order that we may also be glorified with him.

I have been fully accepted into God's family.
I am not an outsider; I am an adopted daughter.
I have no need to fear.
I can cry out to God and depend on Him.
I am a co-heir with Christ.
I am saved not only as God's witness or worker, but also to be part of His family.
I will experience the rewards of redemption, including the opportunity to suffer with Christ.

"

Literally, through Christ we receive "the sonship." This is a legal term. In the Greco-Roman world, a childless, wealthy man could take one of his servants and adopt him. At the moment of adoption, he ceased to be a slave and received all the financial and legal privileges within the estate and outside in the world as the son and heir. Though by birth he was a slave without a relationship with the father, he now receives the legal status of son. It is a new life of privilege. It is a remarkable metaphor for what Jesus has given us.[2]

TIMOTHY KELLER

How does it make you feel to be God's precious child? In what area(s) of life are you having a difficult time walking confidently and securely as His child? What truths can you recall to renew your mind?

_____

_____

_____

_____

"

The astounding bottom line of sonship is that God now treats us as if we have done everything Jesus has done. We are treated as if we are "only sons," like Jesus. [3]

TIMOTHY KELLER

How does/did your earthly father influence your view of God?

_____

_____

_____

_____

How would you describe a good dad? What character traits make a good dad?

_____

_____

_____

_____

Does your view of God as Father encompass these things?

_____

_____

_____

THE FATHER'S BENEFITS BESTOWED ON YOU

WHAT ARE SOME OF THE BENEFITS THE FATHER HAS BESTOWED ON YOU?

Read the following Scriptures and record your response.

JOHN 14:6-7

Jesus said to him, "I am the way, and the truth, and the life. No one comes to the Father except through me. If you had known me, you would have known my Father also. From now on you do know him and have seen him."

I have access to God through Christ and I can know Him.

ROMANS 5:1-2

Therefore, since we have been justified by faith, we have peace with God through our Lord Jesus Christ. Through him we have also obtained access by faith into this grace in which we stand, and we rejoice in hope of the glory of God.

Benefits of being justified by faith are the following: I have received peace with God, access into His grace, and joy in hope of future glory.

EPHESIANS 1:3-7

Blessed be the God and Father of our Lord Jesus Christ, who has blessed us in Christ with every spiritual blessing in the heavenly places, even as he chose us in him before the foundation of the world, that we should be holy and blameless before him. In love he predestined us for adoption as sons through Jesus Christ, according to the purpose of his will, to the praise of his glorious grace, with which he has blessed us in the Beloved. In him we have redemption through his blood, the forgiveness of our trespasses, according to the riches of his grace....

God has bestowed on me every spiritual blessing. He chose me to be holy and blameless before Him. He made me His child (son) through adoption. He has blessed me with His glorious grace. He redeemed and forgave me.

God has provided you access to Himself through Christ (justification by faith) and as a result the Father makes Himself known to you. The word "access" (*prosagóge*) means to bring near, to introduce. In the same way one must receive an introduction to enter the chamber of a monarch, so God through the offering of His Son has granted you access to the Father—access that is impossible on your own status and in your own strength–and not only access but also a future glorious inheritance.

FDQ: Recently, how have you experienced God's care for you?

GOD IS COMMITTED TO YOU

─

If you are still experiencing a disconnect when thinking of God as your loving and active Father, start renewing your mind daily with the following truths.

God is committed to you in the following ways:

To Love You
as His child

•1 John 3:1•

To Be Near
to you

•Lamentations 3:55-57•

To Discipline You
because He loves you

•Hebrews 12:5-11•

To Know You
intimately

•Psalm 139:1-15•

To Hear
your prayers

•Jeremiah 33:3; Matthew 6:8-9•

To Provide For You
in everything you need

•1 Timothy 6:17; Psalm 37:25; 2 Peter 1:3-4•

To Help You
at all times

•Psalm 121:2-4•

To Protect You
in all circumstances

•Psalm 23•

To Care For You
in a tender way

•Isaiah 40:11•

To Fulfill His Purposes
for you

•Psalm 57:1-3; Isaiah 46:8-11; Ephesians 2:10•

To Rejoice
over you

•Zephaniah 3:17•

To Teach You
and lead you

•Psalm 25:4-5•

IN HIM WE HAVE
REDEMPTION
through his blood,

THE FORGIVENESS OF OUR TRESPASSES,

ACCORDING TO THE

riches of his grace.

EPHESIANS 1:7

END YOUR STUDY...
Summarize what you learned from this lesson

"MY PERFECT FATHER"

———

A personal testimony

Strong, yet deep down I was not okay. It was at this time that I was introduced to Jesus through the ministry of Young Life. I learned my need for Jesus, and He tenderly brought me into relationship with Him as my Savior and Lord.

In my young adult years, I was active in church and campus ministry, and after college I married my high school sweetheart. Sadly, however, I remained a safe distance from people and from God. Though I believed in God as Creator and Jesus as Savior, I did not have the capacity to embrace God as my Father. No way. Too Risky. Because I had not received love from my earthly father, I struggled to believe and receive the heavenly Father's unconditional love for me. I was stuck trying to earn His love and others' love. This impacted all my relationships—with my friends, with my children, but most significantly with my husband. I was unable to share my heart and I resisted intimacy. I was scared and critical of myself and often critical and disappointed with others.

But God met me in this place. He saw me. In fact, He has always seen me. When He formed me in my mother's womb, He saw me. When I hid for safety under my bed or behind a leadership or acting role, He saw me. When I responded to "How are you?" with "I am fine," because I always had to be "fine," He saw me. When I had difficulty relating emotionally, He saw me. He knew my broken heart and He has changed me and is continuing to do so!

I am so grateful that God has blessed me with a patient and loving husband as well as some wonderful and mature friends who, over several years, have helped me understand the value of emotions, as well as identify my wrong thinking, beliefs, and fears. They have helped me see that God's love is a love that initiates; it is never a response and therefore cannot be earned nor limited nor removed. His love can be trusted. And slowly, over many years as my love for and understanding of God's Word has grown, so has my love for and trust in Him. God has grown my faith through His Word. And now I can look back over my life and see His hand in it—how He has drawn me to Himself.

Several Scriptures have helped me understand God's love for me. 1 John 4:8 teaches, "Anyone who does not love does not know God, because God is love." God loves me because it is His nature to love. He has taught me how to love. Also, Romans 5:8 states, "but God shows his love for us in that while we were still sinners, Christ died for us." I can do nothing to save myself. God loves me so much He sent His Son to die for me that I might be saved and enjoy Him and others and the life He has planned for me.

He is my perfect Father. He sees me; He loves me; and I desire to love Him wholeheartedly.

How Great the Father's Love For Us

The Father's great love for us is powerfully displayed in the sacrifice of His Son. As we look through the lens of the story of Abraham and Isaac, the Father and Son's sacrifice becomes all the more precious and meaningful.

In obedience to God and because he loved God supremely and believed that God would raise Isaac from the dead, Abraham was willing to sacrifice on the altar his most precious possession on earth, his son. But his faith and knowledge did not make it easy for Abraham to obey God. What he was about to do to Isaac with his own hands must have been excruciating for him during their three days' journey to Mount Moriah.

But what God the Father had planned to do to His only Son for our sake "before the foundation of the world" (see Ephesians 1:4-10) must also have been excruciating for the Father.

"Abraham had three days in which to think upon, and consider the death of his son; three days in which to look into that beloved face, and to anticipate the hour in which it would wear the icy pallor of death. But the Eternal Father foreknew and foreordained the sacrifice of His only-begotten Son, not three days, nor three years, nor 3,000 years, but before the earth was, Jesus was to His Father, 'the Lamb slain from the foundation of the world.' Long before His birth at Bethlehem it was foretold..." - Charles Spurgeon.

And unlike Abraham, who was stopped just in time from slaying his son, God the Father did not "spare His own son but gave Him up for us all..." (Romans 8:32a). In fact, it was in the hands of the Father that Christ suffered.

"Yet it was the will of the LORD to crush him; he has put him to grief" Isaiah 53:10a.

"Surely he has borne our griefs and carried our sorrows; yet we esteemed him stricken, smitten by God, and afflicted. But he was pierced for our transgressions; he was crushed for our iniquities; upon him was the chastisement that brought us peace, and with his wounds we are healed" Isaiah 53:4-5.

"For our sake he made him to be sin who knew no sin, so that in him we might become the righteousness of God" 2 Corinthians 5:21.

"

How deep the Father's love for us, How vast beyond all measure, That He should give His only Son To make a wretch His treasure. How great the pain of searing loss - The Father turns His face away, As wounds which mar the Chosen One, Bring many sons to glory.

STUART TOWNEND

[Adapted from Charles Spurgeon's sermon found on www.spurgeongems.org/vols13-15/chs869.pdf.]

Reflection

Meditate on the wonderful reality that the Father has given you access to Himself through Christ, and as such you can enjoy Him as your Abba Father.

LESSON 2

My Prodigal God

In Lesson 1 you pondered the beautiful truth that God is your Abba Father and you are His adopted child. This is marvelous beyond description! In Lesson 2 you will see what kind of extravagant love your Father has for you. A poignant example of the Father's love is found in the Parable of the Prodigal Son.

MY PRODIGAL GOD

DEFINE "PRODIGAL"

Look up and write out the definition of "prodigal."

Wastefully or recklessly extravagant; giving or yielding profusely; lavish; lavishly abundant.

FDQ: "It means to spend until you have nothing left" (Timothy Keller, *The Prodigal God*, Publisher: Penguin Books; Reprint edition, 2011, Introduction, xvii).

God your Father is a prodigal God because He lavishes His love on you (Ephesians 1:7-8), His prodigal child. All of us are prodigals by nature. Left to ourselves, we would expend all our efforts and love on things that do not ultimately satisfy.

FDQ: A parable is a story that illustrates a truth.

THE PARABLE OF THE PRODIGAL SON

READ LUKE 15:11-32.

And he said, "There was a man who had two sons. And the younger of them said to his father, 'Father, give me the share of property that is coming to me.' And he divided his property between them. Not many days later, the younger son gathered all he had and took a journey into a far country, and there he squandered his property in reckless living. And when he had spent everything, a severe famine arose in that country, and he began to be in need. So he went and hired himself out to one of the citizens of that country, who sent him into his fields to feed pigs. And he was longing to be fed with the pods that the pigs ate, and no one gave him anything.

"But when he came to himself, he said, 'How many of my father's hired servants have more than enough bread, but I perish here with hunger! I will arise and go to my father, and I will say to him, "Father, I have sinned against heaven and before you. I am no longer worthy to be called your son. Treat me as one of your hired servants."' And he arose and came to his father. But while he was still a long way off, his father saw him and felt compassion, and ran and embraced him and kissed him. And the son said to him, 'Father, I have sinned against heaven and before you. I am no longer worthy to be called your son.'

But the father said to his servants, 'Bring quickly the best robe, and put it on him, and put a ring on his hand, and shoes on his feet. And bring the fattened calf and kill it, and let us eat and celebrate. For this my son was dead, and is alive again; he was lost, and is found.' And they began to celebrate.

"Now his older son was in the field, and as he came and drew near to the house, he heard music and dancing. And he called one of the servants and asked what these things meant. And he said to him, 'Your brother has come, and your father has killed the fattened calf, because he has received him back safe and sound.' But he was angry and refused to go in. His father came out and entreated him, but he answered his father, 'Look, these many years I have served you, and I never disobeyed your command, yet you never gave me a young goat, that I might celebrate with my friends. But when this son of yours came, who has devoured your property with prostitutes, you killed the fattened calf for him!' And he said to him, 'Son, you are always with me, and all that is mine is yours. It was fitting to celebrate and be glad, for this your brother was dead, and is alive; he was lost, and is found.'"

The Younger Son

What did the younger son demand?

"Give me the share of property that is coming to me." (12)

Usually the inheritance was given after a father's death. The younger son was asking for an exception.

FDQ: "The younger son asks for his inheritance now, which was a sign of deep disrespect. To ask this while the father still lived was the same as to wish him dead." (Timothy Keller, *The Prodigal God*, 18).

What was the father's initial reaction to his son's request? How does this illustrate God's love?

Though the father knew his son would most likely squander his inheritance, he divided his property and gave him his share. He allowed his son to choose his path and He respected his son's will, which did include rebellion. (12)

Father God pursues me but He is not pushy. He allows my will, even if it includes rebellion.

How did the son manage his inheritance? What was the result?

He wasted his inheritance with "prodigal" (wastefully extravagant) living. No one supported him in his prodigal life. He was left to care for himself and he became destitute and desperate. (14-16)

When the lost son returned home to his father, what did he say and what does it model for you?

"Father, I have sinned against heaven and before you. I am no longer worthy to be called your son." (21)

He came to his senses. He confessed to his father, acknowledged his rebellion, and took ownership of his choices.

I am to yield, recognize my need for the Father, and be quick to confess my sin.

The younger son's petition, "Give me my share" (Luke 15:12), was a rebellious demand that led to disastrous consequences. The son was left poor and destitute. His later confession, "Father, I have sinned against heaven and before you. I am no longer worthy to be called your son" (Luke 15:21), demonstrates a repentant and humble heart.

FDQ: Why is it significant that the son acted on his resolve to return home?

His father could not have received him if he had not returned home. It demonstrated the son's humility.

The Prodigal Father

Re-read the second paragraph of the parable and describe the father's joyful reception of his lost son.

The father was waiting for his son's return. He had a love that waited with hopeful expectation.

He saw his son from afar. He was looking for him and ran to greet him.

He showed compassion on his son.

He was eager and elated to receive him back. He embraced him and kissed him.

He gave his son lavish gifts. The father gave him a robe, ring, sandals, and a fattened calf. None of these things were necessities; they were all meant to honor the son and demonstrate the father's unconditional love.

FDQ: According to Timothy Keller, the father ran toward the son with his robes gathered in his arms. This demonstrated how his exuberance over his son returning out-shadowed the decorum of the day—showing his bare legs, showing his undergarments. A distinguished man never ran.

The Father waited with hopeful expectation for his son to return. He eagerly received him back with unconditional love.

How does the father's response illustrate God's prodigal love?

God's love is steadfast. He is compassionate, lavish, extravagant, and abounding.

When I return to Him, He is quick to receive me and He always forgives me, and He wipes away my sin.

God sees me through Jesus.

God sees you for who you are. He knows your heart, and He will never refuse you when you humbly turn to Him.

"

God has compassion on the woes and miseries of men…. When sinners come to God, He gives them a loving reception, and a hearty welcome…. Oh, the immeasurable love of God to sinners who come and cast themselves upon His mercy! [1]

C.H. SPURGEON

What might you feel, think or do when you lack assurance of the Father's unconditional love for you? Record your possible responses.

Some possible responses may include:

Feel–Guilt, shame, fearful, despondent, defeated, unhappy, lost, unsafe, insecure, hopeless.

Think–When things go wrong in my life, or my prayers go unanswered, I wonder if God is displeased with me and if I am supposed to do something to gain His love.

Do–When others criticize me, I fall apart and become defensive.

I need and seek the approval of others.

My prayer life is dry. It is not relational and intimate

I try to find happiness elsewhere.

I am rule-oriented (legalistic).

From this lesson and the previous one, what truths can you recall to renew your mind?

_____

_____

_____

"

God's love and forgiveness can pardon and restore any and every kind of sin or wrongdoing. It doesn't matter who you are or what you've done.... There is no evil that the father's love cannot pardon and cover, there is no sin that is a match for his grace.... Nothing, not even abject contrition, merits the favor of God. The Father's love and acceptance are absolutely free.[2]

TIMOTHY KELLER

Though you did not merit God's favor or pardon, He made a way for you to be reconciled to Him.

ROMANS 5:8

[B]ut God shows his love for us in that while we were still sinners, Christ died for us.

Though by nature you were God's enemy, He made you His own. He pursued you and drew you to Himself and made you His beloved child.

ROMANS 5:10

For if while we were enemies we were reconciled to God by the death of his Son, much more, now that we are reconciled, shall we be saved by his life.

1 JOHN 4:9-10

God showed how much he loved us by sending his one and only Son into the world so that we might have eternal life through him. This is real love.... he loved us and sent his Son as a sacrifice to take away our sins. (NLT)

1 JOHN 3:1a

See what kind of love the Father has given to us, that we should be called children of God; and so we are.

The Older Son

In the parable, the younger son is not the only one who needs a heart adjustment! The older son's heart is bitter and resentful as demonstrated in Luke 15:25-32.

What was the older son's response?

The older son was angry and resentful and refused to go in.

He made exaggerations—"I never disobeyed," "You never gave." These kinds of exaggerations are common for those who harbor bitterness.

On the outside, the older son was very obedient. He did everything he was supposed to do; yet his heart was far from his father's heart. He was begrudging.

The older son obeyed to get things from his father.

He was acting like a Pharisee. He was unforgiving and judgmental. ("Your son....")

His focus was on himself and how much he was wronged. He acted as a victim.

What was the father's response toward him?

The father unconditionally loved the older son as well. He came out and pursued him and tried to persuade him to come into the celebration.

"

Elder brothers expect their goodness to pay off, and if it doesn't, there is confusion and rage....
Elder brothers base their self-images on being hardworking, or moral, or members of an elite clan,
or extremely smart and savvy.... In fact, competitive comparison is the main way elder brothers
achieve a sense of their own significance.[3]

TIMOTHY KELLER

What does the older son's response demonstrate?

He was self-righteous and was condescending and critical of his younger brother and his father.

He believed that he deserved recognition so he was resentful of his father's attention toward his younger brother.

He does not truly love or respect his father.

He does not understand the father's love for him.

"

If you have not grasped the gospel fully and deeply, you will return to being condescending, condemning, anxious, insecure, joyless, and angry all the time.[4]

TIMOTHY KELLER

While the younger son recognized his need, returned to his father, and repented of his foolishness, the older son remained self-righteous and stubborn. He refused his father's entreaties.

What do their responses demonstrate about their respective spiritual conditions?

_____

_____

_____

_____

_____

In what ways do you identify as a prodigal son and/or as an older brother? What does this reveal regarding your heart? Explain.

_____

_____

_____

END YOUR STUDY...

Summarize what you learned from this lesson

Reflection

Think about the ways you have hurt the Father as a prodigal son or older brother. Confess and repent to the Lord and receive His forgiveness. How does this picture of the prodigal Father encourage you?

LESSON 3

Understanding God's Sovereignty

In Lessons 1 and 2 you learned how God, your perfect Father, is committed to you as His precious child.

In Lesson 3 you will explore what it means that your Father is in control over every detail of your life. He holds you in His hands, so you can trust Him with your whole heart.

"SOVEREIGNTY" DEFINED

———

God's sovereignty means that He is in absolute control over every detail in your life as well as every detail of human history—He is sovereign over microscopic details and macroscopic details—for His glory and for your good. Nothing happens apart from His purpose and His will. Sovereignty means that God not only knows what will happen but that He plans what will happen.

Because God controls all things, He can and does work all things together for a believer's good (Romans 8:28). "All things"—both good and bad. Solomon in Ecclesiastes states, "He has made everything beautiful in its time. Also, he has put eternity into man's heart, yet so that he cannot find out what God has done from the beginning to the end" (Ecclesiastes 3:11). God always works things out according to His purposes. But the working out of His purposes may not be on your timeline or in your lifetime. You will not see what God has done from the beginning to the end.

"

Nothing can hinder him or compel him or stop him.
He is able to do as he pleases always, everywhere, forever.[1]

A.W. TOZER

God will only and always allow what is meant for His ultimate glory and your greatest good.

WHAT DOES SCRIPTURE REVEAL ABOUT GOD'S SOVEREIGN WILL?

Read the following verses and **record** your response.

PSALM 115:3

Our God is in the heavens; he does all that he pleases.

God can do anything He desires to do.

PROVERBS 16:9

The heart of man plans his way, but the LORD establishes his steps.

Though I may plan and dream, it is God who brings about His plan.

PROVERBS 21:1

The king's heart is a stream of water in the hand of the LORD; he turns it wherever he will.

Even rulers and government authorities are subject to God's ultimate and specific authority.

DANIEL 4:35

[A]ll the inhabitants of the earth are accounted as nothing, and he does according to his will among the host of heaven and among the inhabitants of the earth; and none can stay his hand or say to him, "What have you done?"

God can do anything He desires in heaven or on earth.

ISAIAH 46:8-11

"Remember this and stand firm, recall it to mind, you transgressors, remember the former things of old; for I am God, and there is no other; I am God, and there is none like me, declaring the end from the beginning and from ancient times things not yet done, saying, 'My counsel shall stand, and I will accomplish all my purpose,'… I have spoken, and I will bring it to pass; I have purposed, and I will do it."

ACTS 17:26

"From one man he made every nation of men, that they should inhabit the whole earth; and he determined the times set for them and the exact places where they should live…." (NIV84)

ADDITIONAL REFERENCES · 2 CHRONICLES 20:6; JAMES 4:13-15.

"

The truth we must believe is that God is sovereign. He carries out His own good purposes without ever being thwarted, and He so directs and controls all events and all actions of His creatures that they never act outside of His sovereign will. We must believe this and cling to this in the face of adversity and tragedy, if we are to glorify God by trusting Him. We honor God by choosing to trust Him when we don't understand what He is doing or why He has allowed some adverse circumstances to occur. As we seek God's glory, we may be sure that He has purposed our good and that He will not be frustrated in fulfilling that purpose.[2]

JERRY BRIDGES

What is your heart's response to God's sovereignty? Do you trust that God is in control and that His ways are best? If so, you will experience comfort and peace. Or do you find yourself frustrated and fearful, trying to control people and things? This is evidence that you are having a difficult time believing that God is in control. Confess your response to the Lord.

In Part 5 you will more thoroughly work through the topic of your perceived need to control.

FDQ: How would it affect you if God were not sovereign over all?

THE EXAMPLE OF ESTHER

Consider God's sovereignty in light of the story of Esther.

READ THROUGH OR LISTEN TO THE BOOK OF ESTHER.

The Circumstances

Esther was an orphan who was brought up by her uncle Mordecai. She lived during the Jewish exile in Persia, when the Persian King Xerxes was on the throne. When the King became disenchanted with his queen wife, he went to look for another queen among the inhabitants of his kingdom.

Esther was brought to the king's court to be counted among the maidens, and King Xerxes chose Esther to be his queen. When Haman, one of the King's counselors plotted to have the Jews annihilated, Mordecai persuaded Esther to go to the King, uttering the now-famous quote, that Esther may have been elevated to queen "for such a time as this" (Esther 4:14).

After ordering all Jews to a three-day fast and prayer, Esther went to the King and swayed him to stop Haman's devious plan. And thus the Jews were miraculously spared from extermination.

God Demonstrates His Sovereignty

1. Because Esther was an orphan, "Mordecai took her as his own daughter" (Esther 2:7).

2. Being a Jew, Esther's rise to queen status in Persia was a miracle that God wrought for His purposes.

3. Esther's queen position was key in thwarting Haman's evil plan. She was indeed born and placed in Xerxes's kingdom "for such a time as this" (Esther 4:14).

Esther's Response

Esther acted in violation of Persian protocol. She did not have permission to appear before the king, thus she could have been executed. However, she trusted Mordecai's advice and put her life in God's sovereign hands, saying, "if I perish, I perish" (Esther 4:1).

Esther recognized God's sovereignty.

How does the story of Esther help you take comfort in God's sovereignty?

_____

_____

_____

"

Life is not a straight line leading from one blessing to the next and then finally to heaven. Life is a winding and troubled road. Switchback after switchback. And the point of biblical stories like Joseph and Job and Esther and Ruth is to help us feel in our bones (not just know in our heads) that God is for us in all these strange turns. God is not just showing up after the trouble and cleaning it up. He is plotting the course and managing the troubles with far-reaching purposes for our good and for the glory of Jesus Christ. [3]

JOHN PIPER

How do you see God's hand at work in your life? Do you choose to believe that God is sovereign over your life?

_____

_____

_____

_____

_____

_____

DIFFICULT YET IMPORTANT QUESTIONS

——

THE TOPIC OF GOD'S SOVEREIGNTY BRINGS US TO DIFFICULT YET IMPORTANT QUESTIONS.

If God is sovereign, is He also the author of evil? Why does He allow evil and suffering in the world and in our lives? (Part 7 Lesson 4 will discuss this topic in more detail.)

God is not the author of evil. God does not sin and He performs no evil (James 1:13). There is, however, apparent tension in the Bible between God's sovereignty and man's free will. Scriptures teach that God is absolutely in control over every detail and yet man has the freedom to choose between good and evil. God permits people to act contrary to and in defiance of His moral code as revealed in Scripture. Though you are responsible for your choice to do good or to sin, you cannot act apart from His sovereign will. And the fact that people's sinful intents and actions serve the sovereign purpose of God does not make God the author of their sin nor make them any less culpable for their actions.

SEE JOB 1:21b-22; JOHN 9:1-3; JOHN 11:1-6

How does your free will interact with God's sovereignty?

The Bible teaches both the sovereignty of God and the free moral choices of men with equal emphasis, but it never attempts to explain or minimize this great mystery. Much of what God does will remain a mystery to man.

DEUTERONOMY 29:29

"The secret things belong to the Lord our God, but the things that are revealed belong to us and to our children forever, that we may do all the words of this law...."

ACTS 4:27-28

"[F]or truly in this city there were gathered together against your holy servant Jesus, whom you anointed, both Herod and Pontius Pilate, along with the Gentiles and the peoples of Israel, to do whatever your hand and your plan had predestined to take place."

GOD IS SOVEREIGN OVER NATURAL DISASTERS AND OTHER TRAGEDIES

——

Moreover, God, in His sovereignty and goodness, allows natural disasters and other tragedies to occur that are not necessarily a result of human sin. Why? We know that Satan is the prince of this world and is bent on our destruction, and he is able to bring tragedies and natural disasters into our lives (see Job 1-2). Nevertheless, God limits Satan in what he is allowed to do (see Job 1:6-12; Luke 22:31-32—"Simon, Simon, behold, Satan demanded to have you, that he might sift you like wheat...."). Again, why God allows Satan to have destructive powers over our lives is also a great mystery. But we know that we still live in a fallen world, and our hope is in His ultimate salvation and in the coming age when all things will be renewed and made right.

ROMANS 8:19-22

For the creation waits with eager longing for the revealing of the sons of God. For the creation was subjected to futility, not willingly, but because of him who subjected it, in hope that the creation itself will be set free from its bondage to corruption and obtain the freedom of the glory of the children of God. For we know that the whole creation has been groaning together in the pains of childbirth until now.

As a result of sin, we live in a fallen world, which is in bondage and in futility. Bad things will happen to you, some through natural disasters and others as a result of evil acts done by others or yourself. As a follower of Christ, one day you will be freed from these sufferings.

"

All human suffering, especially the suffering of the Son of God, is meant to portray to dull souls the unimaginable moral ugliness of sin and the unimaginable offensiveness of sin to God.[4]

JOHN PIPER

IN THE FOLLOWING PSALM, UNDERLINE OTHER PURPOSES FOR SUFFERING.

PSALM 83:13-18

O my God, make them like whirling dust, like chaff before the wind. As fire consumes the forest, as the flame sets the mountains ablaze, so may you pursue them with your tempest and terrify them with your hurricane! Fill their faces with shame, that they may seek your name, O Lord. Let them be put to shame and dismayed forever; let them perish in disgrace, that they may know that you alone, whose name is the Lord, are the Most High over all the earth.

FDQ: In addition to releasing a person or circumstance to God, He may also be calling you to take another specific action (see Part 2 Lessons 4-5). We will discuss this further in Part 5.

What person or circumstance is difficult for you to release and entrust to God and His sovereign will? This may be a big thing in your life or the mundane things that come up day-to-day.

_____

_____

_____

_____

_____

_____

_____

_____

What are you thinking, feeling, and choosing regarding this person or circumstance? You may want to use the My Heart Unveiled chart to work through this struggle.

_____

_____

_____

_____

_____

_____

_____

YOUR FUTURE HOPE

—

In God's sovereign plan, there will be an end to sin and suffering. He will make all things new.

REVELATION 21:1-4

Then I saw a new heaven and a new earth, for the first heaven and the first earth had passed away, and the sea was no more. And I saw the holy city, new Jerusalem, coming down out of heaven from God, prepared as a bride adorned for her husband. And I heard a loud voice from the throne saying, "Behold, the dwelling place of God is with man. He will dwell with them, and they will be his people, and God himself will be with them as their God. He will wipe away every tear from their eyes, and death shall be no more, neither shall there be mourning, nor crying, nor pain anymore, for the former things have passed away."

When Christ returns and makes all things new, which God will bring about in His own time (1 Timothy 6:14-15), you will be free at last! This is your hope. Until then you must live your life with your hands open, releasing your grip on people and circumstances, knowing that God is sovereign and good.

END YOUR STUDY...

Summarize what you learned from this lesson

Reflection

Meditate on the following Psalm and ask the Lord to align your heart to the Psalmist's heart as expressed.

O Lord, my heart is not lifted up;
my eyes are not raised too high;
I do not occupy myself with things
too great and too marvelous for me.

But I have calmed and quieted my soul,
like a weaned child with its mother;
like a weaned child is my soul within me.

O Israel, hope in the Lord
from this time forth and forevermore.

PSALM 131

Father God, I praise You and thank You, for You do as You please and all You please is good. Creator and Sustainer of the universe, You are sovereign over all. Nothing escapes Your attention or Your care, from the greatest to the most insignificant. Help me trust You with the things I do not understand. Calm and quiet my soul, O Lord. In Jesus' name I pray, Amen.

LESSON 4

Understanding God's Holiness

(And His Justice, Wrath, & Mercy)

In Lessons 1 and 2 you learned about God's love as demonstrated in God as our loving Father. In Lesson 3 you learned that God is sovereign over every detail of your life.

In Lesson 4 you will explore God's holiness and how His holiness is displayed in His justice, wrath, and mercy. It is from the perspective of God's holiness that you are able to grasp His justice, wrath, and mercy more fully.

HOLINESS OF GOD

—

"Holy, holy, holy, is the Lord God Almighty, who was and is and is to come!"

REVELATION 4:8

WHAT DOES IT MEAN GOD IS HOLY?

The Hebrew word for "holy" is *qadowsh* and means "apartness, set apartness, separateness, sacredness."

Read the following Scriptures and **describe** an aspect of God's holiness.

ISAIAH 57:15a

For thus says the One who is high and lifted up, who inhabits eternity, whose name is Holy....

God is above and outside of creation.

1 JOHN 1:5

This is the message we have heard from him and proclaim to you, that God is light, and in him is no darkness at all.

God is perfect.

EXODUS 15:11

"Who is like you, O Lord, among the gods? Who is like you, majestic in holiness, awesome in glorious deeds, doing wonders?"

Nothing and no one can compare to God.

REVELATION 15:4

"Who will not fear, O Lord, and glorify your name? For you alone are holy. All nations will come and worship you, for your righteous acts have been revealed."

God is the only holy one.

FOR THE

Lord your God

IS A

merciful God.

DEUTERONOMY 4:31a

LOOK UP THE FOLLOWING SCRIPTURES IN CONTEXT; DESCRIBE THE RESPONSE OF EACH INDIVIDUAL TO GOD'S HOLINESS.

ISAIAH 6:3b-7

"Holy, holy, holy is the Lord of hosts;
the whole earth is full of his glory!"

And the foundations of the thresholds shook at the voice of him who called, and the house was filled with smoke. And I said: "Woe is me! For I am lost; for I am a man of unclean lips, and I dwell in the midst of a people of unclean lips; for my eyes have seen the King, the Lord of hosts!"

Then one of the seraphim flew to me, having in his hand a burning coal that he had taken with tongs from the altar. And he touched my mouth and said: "Behold, this has touched your lips; your guilt is taken away, and your sin atoned for."

Isaiah recognized he was unclean. He recognized his sin.

PSALM 29:2

Ascribe to the Lord the glory due his name; worship the Lord in the splendor of holiness.

Recognizing the holiness of God caused David to worship.

1 SAMUEL 2:2

"There is none holy like the Lord; for there is none besides you; there is no rock like our God."

Hannah affirmed God's holiness and was confident in trusting God. God is totally different from all created things and beings.

"

God's holiness is his quality of being set apart, of being completely unlike anything or anyone else. His holiness pervades all he is and all he does. There is a sense in which his holiness modifies his other attributes, so that his love is a holy love and his justice is a holy justice.[1]

TIM CHALLIES

What is your personal response to the holiness of God?

_____

_____

_____

_____

_____

GOD'S HOLINESS REQUIRES JUSTICE—WRATH AGAINST SIN

―――

"

God is holy and therefore He cannot overlook sin. If He did He would be denying part of who He is. The anger or wrath of God flows from His holiness. "It is not a capricious, arbitrary, bad-tempered and conceited anger which pagans attribute to their gods. It is not the sinful, resentful, malicious, infantile anger which we find among humans. It is a function of that holiness which is expressed in the demands of God's moral law." God's holy character cannot be compromised, so His response to sin is both necessary and right.[2]

J. I. PACKER

"

God's anger and wrath must always be seen in relation to his maintaining and defending his attributes of love and holiness, as well as his righteousness and justice. The emotion or passion that moves God to this maintaining and defending is expressed by the terms "displeasure," "indignation," "anger," and "wrath." A consequence of his wrath is vengeance, punishment, and death.[3]

GERARD VAN GRONINGEN

God's perfection and holiness requires that He not overlook or ignore sin. Since all of humanity is sinful (Psalm 14:3; Romans 3:23), God is just and right to respond wrathfully toward mankind. God is perfect in all His ways, including His wrath. (Deuteronomy 32:4—"The Rock, his work is perfect, for all his ways are justice. A God of faithfulness and without iniquity, just and upright is he.")

God's holy wrath is revealed throughout the Old and New Testament, as demonstrated in the following Scriptures:

JEREMIAH 30:23

Behold the storm of the Lord! Wrath has gone forth, a whirling tempest; it will burst upon the head of the wicked.

NAHUM 1:2

The Lord is a jealous and avenging God; the Lord is avenging and wrathful; the Lord takes vengeance on his adversaries and keeps wrath for his enemies.

ROMANS 1:18

For the wrath of God is revealed from heaven against all ungodliness and unrighteousness of men, who by their unrighteousness suppress the truth.

JOHN 3:36b

[W]hoever does not obey the Son shall not see life, but the wrath of God remains on him.

REVELATION 19:15

From his mouth comes a sharp sword with which to strike down the nations, and he will rule them with a rod of iron. He will tread the winepress of the fury of the wrath of God the Almighty.

FDQ: Have you thought much about God's wrath? Why is it good for a person to think about God's wrath?

HOW DO SINFUL PEOPLE STAND UNDER GOD'S WRATH? THEY STAND BECAUSE OF HIS MERCY!

———

Although God is right and good to respond wrathfully to sin, He chooses to respond in mercy. What is the mercy of God? According to Noah Webster's 1828 Dictionary, "mercy" is "that benevolence, mildness or tenderness of heart which disposes a person to overlook injuries, or to treat an offender better than he deserves; the disposition that tempers justice... to forbear punishment... or inflict less than law or justice will warrant." God does not punish you as your sins deserve. The Hebrew word for mercy is *hesed*, and it means "steadfast loyalty; God's covenant lovingkindness."

Romans 3:25b says that "in [God's] divine forbearance he had passed over former sins" until Christ came in "the fullness of time" (Galatians 4:4). In other words, before Christ's sacrifice on the cross, God patiently displayed His mercy by not immediately punishing sin. When Jesus came and died on the cross to take the punishment that you deserved for your sins, He took God's wrath upon Himself.

"

What is mercy? Mercy is God acting patient[ly]. It is God extending patience to those who deserve to be punished. Mercy is not something God owes to us—by definition mercy cannot be owed—but is something God extends in kindness and grace to those who do not deserve it. God does not owe you or anyone else his mercy.[4]

TIM CHALLIES

God's wrath is powerful and dreadful (Hebrews 10:31), but God is also merciful, slow to anger, and abounding in steadfast love and faithfulness (Exodus 34:6).

GOD'S MERCY IS REVEALED THROUGHOUT THE OLD TESTAMENT.

Read the following Scriptures that show His mercy toward a rebellious people.

DEUTERONOMY 4:31

"For the LORD your God is a merciful God. He will not leave you or destroy you or forget the covenant with your fathers that he swore to them."

PSALM 78:37-38

[T]heir hearts were not loyal to him, they were not faithful to his covenant. Yet he was merciful; he forgave their iniquities and did not destroy them. Time after time he restrained his anger and did not stir up his full wrath. (NIV)

2 CHRONICLES 30:9

"For if you return to the LORD your brothers and your children will find compassion with their captors and return to this land. For the LORD your God is gracious and merciful and will not turn away his face from you, if you return to him."

NEHEMIAH 9:18-19

"Even when they had made for themselves a golden calf and said, 'This is your God who brought you up out of Egypt,' and had committed great blasphemies, you in your great mercies did not forsake them in the wilderness. The pillar of cloud to lead them in the way did not depart from them by day, nor the pillar of fire by night to light for them the way by which they should go."

JEREMIAH 3:12b-13a

"Return, faithless Israel, declares the LORD. I will not look on you in anger, for I am merciful, declares the LORD; I will not be angry forever. Only acknowledge your guilt, that you rebelled against the LORD your God...."

JOEL 2:12-13

"Yet even now," declares the LORD, "return to me with all your heart, with fasting, with weeping, and with mourning; and rend your hearts and not your garments." Return to the LORD your God, for he is gracious and merciful, slow to anger, and abounding in steadfast love; and he relents over disaster.

GOD'S MERCY IS REVEALED THROUGHOUT THE NEW TESTAMENT.

1 PETER 1:3

Blessed be the God and Father of our Lord Jesus Christ! According to his great mercy, he has caused us to be born again to a living hope through the resurrection of Jesus Christ from the dead....

1 PETER 2:10

Once you were not a people, but now you are God's people; once you had not received mercy, but now you have received mercy.

God's mercy provided a way for you to avoid His wrath. Because Jesus took God's wrath upon Himself (Isaiah 53:4-5; 1 John 2:2), you are now a recipient of His mercy, never to experience His wrath. You cannot stand before God on your own merit, but as a follower of Christ, you stand in the presence of your Holy Father because of the righteous covering of Christ (2 Corinthians 5:21, Colossians 3:3). Those who never come to a saving faith in Jesus, however, will one day experience God's wrath because their sins have not been paid for by Christ's death (Matthew 25:46; Colossians 3:6; Revelation 19:15). God's holiness demands payment for sins.

READ THE FOLLOWING VERSES.

ROMANS 5:9

Since, therefore, we have now been justified by his blood, much more shall we be saved by him from the wrath of God.

1 THESSALONIANS 5:9-10

For God has not destined us for wrath, but to obtain salvation through our Lord Jesus Christ, who died for us so that whether we are awake or asleep we might live with him.

This is the wonderful truth of God's mercy in relation to His holiness, justice, and wrath: God sent His Son to be "just and the justifier of the one who has faith in Jesus" (Romans 3:26). He both demanded the payment for sin and provided the offering.

Think about the truth that you no longer have the wrath of God upon you. Holy, merciful Father God invites you into His presence through the sacrifice of your Savior, Jesus Christ. Describe your thoughts and feelings below.

So she called the name
of the LORD who spoke to her

"*You are a God of seeing,*"

for she said,

"*Truly here I have seen
him who looks after me.*"

GENESIS 16:13

THE STORY OF HAGAR

Hagar is an example of God's mercy to an undeserving woman. She was not part of the chosen people of Israel but an Egyptian maidservant to Sarai. She had no rights and no say, and yet God chose to respond kindly toward her. Similarly, some of you (who are not of the Jewish race) were "wild olive shoots" who have been grafted into the "nourishing root of the olive tree" (Romans 11:17). Just as God had mercy on Hagar, He had mercy on you and saved you even though you may not have been a part of the chosen people of Israel.

READ GENESIS 16.

God had made a covenant promise to Abram to give him many descendants who would become a mighty nation (Genesis 15). Years passed and Sarai had yet to bear a son, so Abram and Sarai took things into their own hands. Hagar was a victim of Abram and Sarai's impatience and foolishness when Sarai gave Hagar to Abram as his wife. Tension between them increased and Sarai responded harshly to Hagar's contempt. Mistreated, Hagar fled to the wilderness where she was left to care for herself and her unborn child. But the Lord was there. An angel of the Lord found Hagar, spoke to her, and delivered a promise. She would bear a son and he would be named Ishmael "because the Lord has listened to your affliction" (Genesis 16:11).

Hagar called out to God, "You are a God of seeing," for she said, "Truly here I have seen Him who looks after me" (Genesis 16:13).

Hagar had nothing to offer God, yet she experienced His mercy.

In what ways did Hagar experience God's mercy?

- Saw Hagar
- Addressed Hagar by name
- Sought Hagar out by asking her questions
- Listened to Hagar's affliction
- Looked after Hagar
- Made Himself known to Hagar

In the wilderness, Hagar experienced God intimately and personally. Yet, it was not just in this moment that God saw Hagar; He always had her in His sight because He is the God who sees—all the time and everything.

FDQ: You may want to compare and contrast Hagar's encounter with God with that of the woman caught in adultery.

DIFFICULT CIRCUMSTANCES IN YOUR LIFE
—

REFLECT ON A DIFFICULT CIRCUMSTANCE IN YOUR PRESENT OR FROM YOUR PAST.

Describe the situation.

_____

_____

_____

_____

_____

Have you been able to recognize God's mercy in the circumstance?

_____

_____

_____

_____

_____

How can remembering God's mercy help you in your daily life?

_____

_____

_____

_____

_____

What is one verse from this lesson that will help you remember God's mercy in a difficult circumstance?

_____

_____

GOD'S MERCY TOWARD AN UNDESERVING WOMAN

———

John 8:1-11 tells of Christ's encounter with a woman who was about to be stoned for her sin. It is another beautiful picture of God's mercy.

READ JOHN 8:1-11.

What sin was the woman caught in?

adultery

What was the accusers' charge and their final response against her?

The scribes and Pharisees condemned the woman. They wanted to stone her. (They did not really care about the woman; they wanted to test Jesus.)

After hearing Jesus' response, there was nothing they could do but slip away.

How did Christ respond to the situation?

Christ addressed the real issue, their hypocritical hearts.

Anyone who has not sinned can cast the first stone.

"Woman, where are they?" Jesus wanted the woman to see she no longer had accusers.

He offered forgiveness, not condemnation.

"Neither do I condemn you; go, and from now on sin no more." (John 8:11)

"Neither do I condemn you; go, and from now on sin no more."

JOHN 8:11

Though the passage does not directly state the woman's response, she must have been relieved and amazed by Jesus' authority over her accusers and His gracious treatment of her sin. He did not condemn her but released her from the traumatic scene, directing her to sin no more. Jesus treated her differently than the authorities treated her. He cared for her.

How does knowing the depth of God's mercy encourage you to embrace His forgiveness?

_____

_____

_____

_____

THE LORD IS

merciful & gracious,
slow to anger

AND

abounding in steadfast love.

PSALM 103:8

END YOUR STUDY...
Summarize what you learned from this lesson

Reflection

"Holy, holy, holy, is the Lord God Almighty, who was and is and is to come!"

"Worthy are you, our Lord and God, to receive glory and honor and power, for you created all things, and by your will they existed and were created."

REVELATION 4:8b, 11

In "Revelation" song, Jennie Lee Riddle wrote, "With all creation I sing, Praise to the King of Kings; You are my everything, and I will adore You."

Meditate on the above Scripture and the words Riddle penned. Thank God for the depth of His mercy.

─── LESSON 5 ───

Understanding God's Power

In many ways it is impossible to understand God's power because it is so profound.

In Lesson 5 you will get a glimpse of it. The evidence of God's power is everywhere around you, both in the magnitude and majesty of creation as well as in every microscopic detail of your body.

GOD HAS POWER

over all things,

ALL THE TIME

and in all ways!

GOD'S POWER REVEALED IN CREATION

——

REFLECT ON WHAT THE FOLLOWING SCRIPTURES TELL YOU ABOUT GOD'S POWER AS CREATOR.

Read the following Scriptures and underline what you learn about His power.

JEREMIAH 10:12

It is he who made the earth by his power, who established the world by his wisdom, and by his understanding stretched out the heavens.

God made the earth by His power, wisdom, and understanding.

JEREMIAH 32:17

"Ah, Lord GOD! It is you who have made the heavens and the earth by your great power and by your outstretched arm! Nothing is too hard for you."

Nothing is too hard for God.

ROMANS 1:19-20

For what can be known about God is plain to them, because God has shown it to them. For his invisible attributes, namely, his eternal power and divine nature, have been clearly perceived, ever since the creation of the world, in the things that have been made. So they are without excuse.

God's power has been made known to all.

GOD'S POWER EVIDENCED IN THE CREATION OF YOUR BODY

___

I praise you, for I am fearfully and wonderfully made.

PSALM 139:14a

The human body is the most complex, unique organism in the world. Every aspect of the body reveals God's amazing power. Consider the human eye as described by agnostic evolutionist, Robert Jastrow:

"

The eye is a marvelous instrument, resembling a telescope of the highest quality, with a lens, an adjustable focus, a variable diaphragm for controlling the amount of light, and optical corrections for spherical and chromatic aberration. The eye appears to have been designed; no designer of telescopes could have done better. How could this marvelous instrument have evolved by chance, through a succession of random events?[1]

ROBERT JASTROW

HOW DO YOU RESPOND TO THE BEAUTIFUL TRUTH THAT THE CREATOR OF THE UNIVERSE ALSO CREATED EVERY DETAIL OF YOU?

Read the following passage and record your response.

PSALM 139:13-16

For you formed my inward parts; you knitted me together in my mother's womb. I praise you, for I am fearfully and wonderfully made. Wonderful are your works; my soul knows it very well. My frame was not hidden from you, when I was being made in secret, intricately woven in the depths of the earth. Your eyes saw my unformed substance; in your book were written, every one of them, the days that were formed for me, when as yet there was none of them.

FDQ: The word "formed" (Hebrew – *yatsar*) means to form; to fashion; to frame; to mold as in a potter molding clay. God has formed ("ordained" in NASB) not only the length of your days, but also everything each day will hold. God has ordered every event and circumstance of each day of your life.

GOD'S POWER INDWELLS YOU

—

READ AND REFLECT ON SOME OF THE BENEFITS YOU RECEIVE FROM GOD'S INDWELLING POWER THROUGH THE HOLY SPIRIT.

GOD'S POWER ENABLES YOU TO WITNESS BOLDLY.

ACTS 1:8

"But you will receive power when the Holy Spirit has come upon you, and you will be my witnesses in Jerusalem and in all Judea and Samaria, and to the end of the earth."

GOD'S POWER IS EXALTED IN YOUR WEAKNESS.

2 CORINTHIANS 12:9b

"My grace is sufficient for you, for my power is made perfect in weakness." Therefore I will boast all the more gladly of my weaknesses, so that the power of Christ may rest upon me.

GOD'S POWER, THAT WHICH RAISED JESUS FROM THE DEAD, IS AT WORK WITHIN YOU.

EPHESIANS 1:19-20

[W]hat is the immeasurable greatness of his power toward us who believe, according to the working of his great might that he worked in Christ when he raised him from the dead and seated him at his right hand in the heavenly places....

GOD'S POWER IS BEYOND ANYTHING YOU CAN ASK OR IMAGINE AND IS AT WORK WITHIN YOU.

EPHESIANS 3:20

Now to him who is able to do far more abundantly than all that we ask or think, according to the power at work within us....

Where have you seen God's power demonstrated in your life?

_____

_____

_____

_____

"

Well may the saint trust such a God! He is worthy of implicit confidence. Nothing is too hard for Him. If God were stinted in might and had a limit to His strength we might well despair. But seeing that He is clothed with omnipotence, no prayer is too hard for Him to answer, no need too great for Him to supply, no passion too strong for Him to subdue, no temptation too powerful for Him to deliver from, no misery too deep for Him to relieve.[2]

ARTHUR W. PINK

Through the indwelling Holy Spirit, God's power is always available to you and for you. We will discuss the role of the Holy Spirit in more depth in Part 4 Lessons 3 and 4.

In what area(s) of your life is it hardest for you to rely on God's power?

_____

_____

_____

_____

_____

_____

_____

_____

_____

_____

THE STORY OF RAHAB

———

*May the story of Rahab encourage you to recognize and respond to God's power
by deepening your faith in Him.*

A Prostitute Recognizes God's Power
JOSHUA 2:1-16

Rahab was a prostitute living in Jericho, a well-fortified city in Canaan, which God was about to destroy.
Joshua sent two spies to view the land. They entered Rahab's house. When the King was told, he sent
messengers to her house who ordered her to send the spies out. She told them that the spies had already
departed, and she did not know which way they went. They quickly left to find them. Rahab had actually
hidden the spies on her roof. She told them "I know that the LORD has given you the land, and that the
fear of you has fallen upon us....[W]e have heard how the LORD dried up the water of the Red Sea before
you...and what you did to the two kings of the Amorites...whom you devoted to destruction. And as soon
as we heard...our hearts melted...for the Lord your God, he is God in the heavens above and on the earth
beneath" (9-11). Rahab asked the spies to show mercy to her and her family when they returned to destroy
the city. They assured her they would because of the kindness she had shown to them.

• Everyone in the pagan city recognized God's power and was afraid.
• Rahab recognized God's power and acknowledged Him as God of the heavens and earth.
• Rahab responded to God's power by choosing to trust Him and by risking her life to protect His servants.

God Protects Rahab and Her Family
JOSHUA 6:1-5, 20-25

God was faithful to Rahab. When the walls of Jericho fell, Joshua instructed the two spies to go to Rahab's
house and bring her and all her family outside the city to safety. They were all saved from the destruction
and they lived in Israel.

Rahab's Legacy

Rahab's story continues. She is mentioned three times in the New Testament. She was the mother of Boaz,
great-great grandmother to King David (Matthew 1:5). She is listed in the "Hall of Faith." By faith "Rahab
the prostitute did not perish with those who were disobedient, because she had given a friendly welcome
to the spies" (Hebrews 11:31). Lastly she is mentioned in James 2:25: "And in the same way was not also
Rahab the prostitute justified by works when she received the messengers and sent them out by another
way."

Rahab recognized God's power, and she responded in faith, courageously protecting the spies.

In light of knowing the breadth of God's power, what "faith steps" are you taking or do you need to take?

_____

_____

_____

_____

_____

_____

"

God's power is a mighty power, for it brought us from death to life and called us out of darkness into the marvelous light. It is an invincible power, for it subdued our inveterate enmity to God, overcame our stubborn obstinacy, and made us willing to receive Christ as our Lord and King. It is a holy power, for it caused us to repudiate all our righteousness as filthy rags and made us nothing in our own sight. It is a gracious power, for it wrought within us not only when we had no merits of our own but when we had no desire to be subjects of God. It is a glorious power, for by it all our godly affections are sustained and all our acceptable works wrought. It is an infinite power whereby he is able even to subdue all things unto himself (Phil 3:21). God has given us exceeding great and precious promises (2 Peter 1:4). Then there is the exceeding greatness of his power to make them good.[3]

ARTHUR W. PINK

END YOUR STUDY...

Summarize what you learned from this lesson

Reflection

Meditate on God's mighty, invincible, holy, gracious, glorious, infinite power that empowers you as His child.
Record your thoughts.

*Father God, thank You that Your goodness and kindness are always represented in Your sovereignty and power
over all creation and in my life personally. In Jesus' name I pray, Amen.*

PART 3 WORKS CITED

Lesson 1: God is My Perfect Father

1 • Ferguson, Sinclair. Children of the Living God. Banner of Truth, 1989, pgs. 5-6.
2 • Keller, Timothy. Galatians For You. The Good Book Company, North America, 2013, pg. 98.
3 • Keller, Timothy. Galatians For You. The Good Book Company, North America, 2013, pg. 101.

Lesson 2: My Prodigal God

1 • Spurgeon, C.H. "Many Kisses for Returning Sinners, or Prodigal Love for the Prodigal Son." The Spurgeon Archive, Sermon No. 2236, 27 Dec. 1891, http://www.spurgeon.org/sermons/2236.php. Accessed 29 Jan. 2017.
2 • Keller, Timothy. The Prodigal God. Penguin Group, New York, 2008, pg. 24.
3 • Keller, Timothy. The Prodigal God. Penguin Group, New York, 2008, pg. 52.
4 • Keller, Timothy. The Prodigal God. Penguin Group, New York, 2008, pg. 70.

Lesson 3: Understanding God's Sovereignty

1 • Tozer, A.W. The Knowledge of the Holy: The Attributes of God, Their Meaning in the Christian Life. Harper & Row, New York, 1961, pgs. 170-71.
2 • Bridges, Jerry. Trusting God. NavPress, Colorado, 2008, pg. 52.
3 • Piper, John. A Sweet and Bitter Providence: Sex, Race, and the Sovereignty of God. Crossway Books, Wheaton, Illinois, 2010, pgs. 101-102.
4 • Piper, John. "Cancer Is a Parable About Sin." Desiring God, 1 April 2015, http://www.desiringgod.org/articles/cancer-is-a-parable-about-sin. Accessed 29 Jan. 2017.

Lesson 4: Understanding God's Holiness (And His Justice, Wrath & Mercy)

1 • Challies, Tim. "The Holiness of God and the Existence of Hell." https://www.challies.com/articles/the-holiness-of-god-and-the-existence-of-hell/. Accessed 10 July 2018.
2 • Packer, J.I. and Dever, Mark, In My Place Condemned He Stood: Celebrating the Glory of the Atonement, Crossway Books, Wheaton, Illinois, 2007, pg. 35.
3 • Van Groningen, Gerard. "Wrath of God." https://www.biblestudytools.com/dictionaries/bakers-evangelical-dictionary/wrath-of-god.html. Accessed 6 June 2018.
4 • Challies, Tim. "The Patient Mercy of a Holy God." https://www.challies.com/articles/the-patient-mercy-of-a-holy-god/. Accessed 11 June 1018.

Lesson 5: Understanding God's Power

1 • Jastrow, Robert. The Enchanted Loom: Mind in the Universe. Simon and Schuster, New York, 1981, pgs. 96-97.
2 • Pink, Arthur W. The Attributes of God, Baker Books, 2006, Grand Rapids, Michigan, 2006, pg. 51
3 • Pink, Arthur W. Gleanings From Paul. Moody Press, Chicago, Illinois, 1970, pg. 196.

Knowing
JESUS & THE HOLY SPIRIT

PART 4

In Part 3 you marveled at the truth that the Sovereign God is your holy, merciful, and powerful Father who lavishes His love on you. In Part 4 you will learn the unique roles of Jesus and the Holy Spirit in carrying out the Father's will.

—— **LESSON 1** ——

Jesus, Humble Servant

Though Jesus is fully God, He submitted to the Father and chose to humble Himself and become fully human to accomplish His mission.

In Lesson 1 you will discover Jesus' mission and the means by which He accomplished it. Jesus' example is the model of servanthood for your life.

JESUS CHRIST FOREVER EXISTS AS FULLY GOD

He is called God.

HEBREWS 1:8

But of the Son he says, "Your throne, O God, is forever and ever, the scepter of uprightness is the scepter of your kingdom."

He acts like God.

HEBREWS 1:10

"You, Lord, laid the foundation of the earth in the beginning, and the heavens are the work of your hands."

JOHN 1:1-18; COLOSSIANS 1:15-20; HEBREWS 1:1-10

These three passages proclaim Jesus as Creator and Sustainer of the universe.

He is treated as God.

HEBREWS 1:6

And again, when he brings the firstborn into the world, he says, "Let all God's angels worship him."

JOHN 20:28; ACTS 4:12

His disciples treated Jesus as God.

He claims equality with God.

JOHN 5:17-18

But Jesus answered them, "My Father is working until now, and I am working." This was why the Jews were seeking all the more to kill him, because not only was he breaking the Sabbath, but he was even calling God his own Father, making himself equal with God.

MARK 14:61-62; JOHN 8:58; JOHN 10:30

He exists in a state of being God.

COLOSSIANS 2:8-10

See to it that no one takes you captive by philosophy and empty deceit, according to human tradition, according to the elemental spirits of the world, and not according to Christ. For in him the whole fullness of deity dwells bodily, and you have been filled in him, who is the head of all rule and authority.

JOHN 1:1-2

In the beginning was the Word, and the Word was with God, and the Word was God. He was in the beginning with God.

FDQ: What point/passage particularly stood out to you?

Jesus Is

Full Deity & Full Humanity;

No One But Jesus

can make this claim.

JESUS CHRIST BECAME A MAN TO ACCOMPLISH HIS MISSION

"For the Son of Man came to seek and to save the lost."

LUKE 19:10

FDQ: Why did Jesus have to become fully man to accomplish His mission?

Are you convinced that it was the plan from the beginning? (See Ephesians 1:3-14; 1 John 1:1-2; 1 Peter 1:20-21)

Jesus' primary mission was to fulfill God's plan to seek and to save the lost. (See 1 Timothy 1:15; 1 John 3:8b)

To accomplish His mission, Jesus had to become a man and fully experience humanity. If Jesus had not become human, He could not have accomplished what He did on the cross, for God cannot suffer and die, but man can.

JESUS, HUMBLE SERVANT

IN PHILIPPIANS 2, PAUL BEAUTIFULLY DESCRIBES HOW CHRIST'S HUMANITY WAS CHARACTERIZED BY HUMILITY AND SERVANTHOOD.

Read the following Scripture.

PHILIPPIANS 2:1-11

1 So if there is any encouragement in Christ, any comfort from love, any participation in the Spirit, any affection and sympathy,
2 complete my joy by being of the same mind, having the same love, being in full accord and of one mind.
3 Do nothing from selfish ambition or conceit, but in humility count others more significant than yourselves.
4 Let each of you look not only to his own interests, but also to the interests of others.
5 Have this mind among yourselves, which is yours in Christ Jesus,
6 who, though he was in the form of God, did not count equality with God a thing to be grasped,
7 but emptied himself, by taking the form of a servant, being born in the likeness of men.
8 And being found in human form, he humbled himself by becoming obedient to the point of death, even death on a cross.
9 Therefore God has highly exalted him and bestowed on him the name that is above every name,
10 so that at the name of Jesus every knee should bow, in heaven and on earth and under the earth,
11 and every tongue confess that Jesus Christ is Lord, to the glory of God the Father.

In verse 1, Paul states that as a follower of Christ, you are immersed in Him. His presence encourages you; His love comforts you; His Spirit fills you; His affection and sympathy minister to you. In verse 2, Paul states that you are to be of the same mind as Christ (not only thinking but also attaching your emotions).

YOU ARE CALLED TO BE LIKE CHRIST—A LIFE OF HUMILITY AND SACRIFICE

You are to develop and exhibit the same humility, love, and care for others as Jesus has demonstrated toward you.

What is to be your mindset? How are you to think of and care for others? (Philippians 2:3-4)

- I am to humbly serve all people (3).
- I am to do nothing motivated by selfish ambition or conceit (3).
- I am to pursue the good of others and to think of others as more significant than myself (4; 1 Corinthians 10:33).

What does it look like when you are not putting others before yourself?

When I do not put others before myself, I may be:
- Irritable with others, competitive, jealous, demanding, feel sorry for myself.

You have been called to a life marked by humility and sacrifice.

In Philippians 2:6, Paul states that Jesus existed as God in the sense that He was equal with God. The phrase, "in the form of" means that He actually was God. (See also Colossians 2:9 – "For in him the whole fullness of deity dwells bodily," and Hebrews 1:3a – "He is the radiance of the glory of God and the exact imprint of his nature....")

Though His equality with God was a reality, Jesus chose to set aside the independent use of His deity. God gave the Holy Spirit to Jesus without measure (John 3:34). Jesus was completely dependent upon the Holy Spirit for all that He did (Luke 4:1; Matthew 12:28). He did not demand acclaim because it was contrary to His mission. He chose to empty Himself. He emptied Himself by adding something—taking the form of a servant; He became a servant by being human (Philippians 2:7).

""

The expression is not what he emptied himself of; it's an idiomatic way of saying he became a nobody, he humbled himself completely, not only to become a human being, but to go all the way to the ignominy and shame and torture of the cross.... It's talking about the astonishing, unequal, unimaginable, indescribable, self-humiliation in becoming human and then going so far not only to be a slave, but a slave who dies on the cross.[1]

D.A. CARSON

REFERENCE PHILIPPIANS 2:6-8.

Describe how Christ demonstrated absolute humility and sacrifice through His incarnation and death.

- He emptied Himself (7).
- He became a servant (7).
- He became human (8).
- He was willing to die (8).
- He was willing to die on a cross (8).

What was Jesus' mindset?

- Though Christ never relinquished His deity (Colossians 1:19), He did give up the rights and privileges afforded to Him as God (Philippians 2:6; John 17:5).
- Jesus participated in the same flesh and blood as man (Hebrews 2:14).
- The God of creation entered into His creation and assumed the role of servant (John 1:1-4, 14).
- Jesus willingly endured a tortuous death. This was the point of His humanity—to prove humility by voluntary death. This is the ultimate act of humility and sacrifice (Philippians 2:8; Galatians 3:13).

ISAIAH 50:7

"But the Lord God helps me; therefore I have not been disgraced; therefore I have set my face like a flint, and I know that I shall not be put to shame."

LUKE 9:51-56

When the days drew near for him to be taken up, he set his face to go to Jerusalem. And he sent messengers ahead of him, who went and entered a village of the Samaritans, to make preparations for him. But the people did not receive him, because his face was set toward Jerusalem. And when his disciples James and John saw it, they said, "Lord, do you want us to tell fire to come down from heaven and consume them?" But he turned and rebuked them. And they went on to another village.

Jesus was resolved to fulfill His mission, dependent on God and confident of His help.

SO WHAT DID JESUS GIVE UP?

––––

Jesus gave up His privileges and status as God for the benefit of others. In Philippians 2:3-5, Paul exhorts the follower of Christ to live in this same way.

WHAT DO THE FOLLOWING VERSES STATE REGARDING JESUS' HUMILITY?

Read the following Scriptures and record your response.

MATTHEW 11:28-29

"Come to me, all who labor and are heavy laden, and I will give you rest. Take my yoke upon you, and learn from me, for I am gentle and lowly in heart, and you will find rest for your souls."

Jesus is gentle and lowly (humble in station, condition, and nature).

MARK 10:45

"For even the Son of Man came not to be served but to serve, and to give his life as a ransom for many."

Jesus came not to be served but to serve.

JOHN 5:18-19

This was why the Jews were seeking all the more to kill him, because not only was he breaking the Sabbath, but he was even calling God his own Father, making himself equal with God. So Jesus said to them, "Truly, truly, I say to you, the Son can do nothing of his own accord, but only what he sees the Father doing. For whatever the Father does, that the Son does likewise."

Though equal to God, Jesus could do nothing of His own accord, but only what He saw the Father doing.

2 CORINTHIANS 8:9

For you know the grace of our Lord Jesus Christ, that though he was rich, yet for your sake he became poor, so that you by his poverty might become rich.

Though He was rich, for my sake Jesus became poor so that I might become rich.

FDQ: What is the significance of these verses on your life?

In Philippians 2:9-11, Paul proclaims that in Christ's humble obedience, His glory was fully restored and will be proclaimed in the age to come.

Notice the *divine paradox*...

- Jesus humbled Himself. God exalted Him.
- Jesus did not seek a name for Himself. God gave Him a name above all others.
- Jesus bent His knee to serve others. God decrees every knee shall bow to Him.
- Jesus humbly remained silent. God decrees every tongue to confess His lordship.

ANONYMOUS

WHAT DOES IT LOOK LIKE WHEN YOU CHOOSE TO FOLLOW CHRIST'S EXAMPLE AS HUMBLE SERVANT IN YOUR LIFE EACH DAY?

WHAT DOES JESUS STATE REGARDING HUMILITY AND SERVANTHOOD?

Read the following Scriptures and record your response.

JOHN 13:13-17

"You call me Teacher and Lord, and you are right, for so I am. If I then, your Lord and Teacher, have washed your feet, you also ought to wash one another's feet. For I have given you an example, that you also should do just as I have done to you. Truly, truly, I say to you, a servant is not greater than his master, nor is a messenger greater than the one who sent him. If you know these things, blessed are you if you do them."

A servant is not greater than his master.

MATTHEW 23:11-12

"The greatest among you shall be your servant. Whoever exalts himself will be humbled, and whoever humbles himself will be exalted."

A servant is one who is great.... The humble will be exalted.

LUKE 14:7-11

Now he told a parable to those who were invited, when he noticed how they chose the places of honor, saying to them, "When you are invited by someone to a wedding feast, do not sit down in a place of honor, lest someone more distinguished than you be invited by him, and he who invited you both will come and say to you, 'Give your place to this person,' and then you will begin with shame to take the lowest place. But when you are invited, go and sit in the lowest place, so that when your host comes he may say to you, 'Friend, move up higher.' Then you will be honored in the presence of all who sit at table with you. For everyone who exalts himself will be humbled, and he who humbles himself will be exalted."

A servant does not seek recognition.

Is it difficult for you to be "unnoticed"?

How do you respond when others do not notice, appreciate, recognize, or thank you?

In what circumstance is it most difficult for you to serve others?

Is there a person or people you find difficul to serve? Why is that?

WHAT IS TO BE YOUR RESPONSE WHEN YOU ARE MISUNDERSTOOD OR FALSELY ACCUSED?

Read the following Scriptures and record your response.

MATTHEW 5:38-42

"You have heard that it was said, 'An eye for an eye and a tooth for a tooth.' But I say to you, Do not resist the one who is evil. But if anyone slaps you on the right cheek, turn to him the other also. And if anyone would sue you and take your tunic, let him have your cloak as well. And if anyone forces you to go one mile, go with him two miles. Give to the one who begs from you, and do not refuse the one who would borrow from you."

I am not to retaliate against the one who is against me.

1 PETER 2:22-23

He committed no sin, neither was deceit found in his mouth. When he was reviled, he did not revile in return; when he suffered, he did not threaten, but continued entrusting himself to him who judges justly.

I am to follow Christ's example–when I am mistreated, when I am suffering, I am to entrust myself to the Father and remember the Father judges justly.

How do you keep serving a person when his/her disposition is undeserving and disrespectful?

- Recognize that you are not called to entrust your heart to the person (John 2:24-25).
- Pray for them and for your heart and ask God to reveal to you what the person really needs (Matthew 7:3-5; Ephesians 4:29; 1 Thessalonians 5:14-15; James 1:5).
- Recognize that you are serving God and not the other person (1 Corinthians 10:31; Ephesians 4:1-3; Colossians 3:22-24; Hebrews 3:19).

"

[T]he essence of gospel-humility is not thinking more of myself or thinking less of myself, it is thinking of myself less.[2]

TIMOTHY KELLER

END YOUR STUDY...

Summarize what you learned from this lesson

Reflection

What is your heart response to Jesus' humble servanthood? In what areas of servanthood do you need to grow? Ask God for His help.

LESSON 2

Jesus, My High Priest

In Lesson 1 you surveyed Jesus' mission to seek and save the lost by serving those He came to save. Not only is Jesus a humble servant, but He is also High Priest. In service to God, Jesus became both your Priest and your sacrifice.

In Lesson 2 you will discover more about the role and significance of Jesus as the High Priest.

THE HIGH PRIEST'S ROLE IN THE OLD TESTAMENT

———

The office of high priest was hereditary through the Levite tribe. The high priest was the supreme religious leader of the Israelites and his most important duty was to conduct the service on the Day of Atonement. Only he was allowed to enter the Most Holy Place behind the veil to stand before God and offer a sacrifice for himself and for the people, for their sins committed during the past year.

The high priest's role on the Day of Atonement is compared to the ministry of Jesus as High Priest.

HEBREWS 9:11-28

But when Christ appeared as a high priest of the good things that have come, then through the greater and more perfect tent (not made with hands, that is, not of this creation) he entered once for all into the holy places, not by means of the blood of goats and calves but by means of his own blood, thus securing an eternal redemption. For if the blood of goats and bulls, and the sprinkling of defiled persons with the ashes of a heifer, sanctify for the purification of the flesh, how much more will the blood of Christ, who through the eternal Spirit offered himself without blemish to God, purify our conscience from dead works to serve the living God.

Therefore he is the mediator of a new covenant, so that those who are called may receive the promised eternal inheritance, since a death has occurred that redeems them from the transgressions committed under the first covenant. For where a will is involved, the death of the one who made it must be established. For a will takes effect only at death, since it is not in force as long as the one who made it is alive. Therefore not even the first covenant was inaugurated without blood. For when every commandment of the law had been declared by Moses to all the people, he took the blood of calves and goats, with water and scarlet wool and hyssop, and sprinkled both the book itself and all the people, saying, "This is the blood of the covenant that God commanded for you." And in the same way he sprinkled with the blood both the tent and all the vessels used in worship. Indeed, under the law almost everything is purified with blood, and without the shedding of blood there is no forgiveness of sins.

Thus it was necessary for the copies of the heavenly things to be purified with these rites, but the heavenly things themselves with better sacrifices than these. For Christ has entered, not into holy places made with hands, which are copies of the true things, but into heaven itself, now to appear in the presence of God on our behalf. Nor was it to offer himself repeatedly, as the high priest enters the holy places every year with blood not his own, for then he would have had to suffer repeatedly since the foundation of the world. But as it is, he has appeared once for all at the end of the ages to put away sin by the sacrifice of himself. And just as it is appointed for man to die once, and after that comes judgment, so Christ, having been offered once to bear the sins of many, will appear a second time, not to deal with sin but to save those who are eagerly waiting for him.

What did Jesus' role as High Priest entail?

Jesus entered "once for all" into the holy place by means of His own blood and secured eternal redemption (12).
Jesus is the mediator of a new covenant, which secures an eternal inheritance (15).
"Once for all" Jesus put away all sin by the sacrifice of Himself (26).

What is the significance that Jesus' sacrifice was "once for all"?

Jesus' death secured my salvation once and for all.

You do not need another high priest. Jesus made the sacrifice "once for all" (Romans 6:10; Hebrews 7:27; Hebrews 9:12, 26; Hebrews 10:10). Nothing more is needed to make peace with God; Jesus has done it all.

JESUS IS YOUR FAITHFUL HIGH PRIEST

——

Jesus was appointed as High Priest by the Father and in His role as High Priest became the sacrificial Lamb on your behalf. "Therefore, holy brothers, you who share in a heavenly calling, consider Jesus, the apostle and high priest of our confession, who was faithful to him who appointed him" (Hebrews 3:1-2a).

WHAT DO YOU LEARN ABOUT JESUS AS YOUR HIGH PRIEST AND YOUR SACRIFICE?

Read the following Scriptures and record your response.

MATTHEW 20:28

"[T]he Son of Man came...to give his life as a ransom for many."

Jesus knew His mission was to lay down His life as an offering for sin.

ROMANS 5:19

For as by the one man's disobedience the many were made sinners, so by the one man's obedience the many will be made righteous.

Jesus' sacrifice on the cross is what provides cleansing and forgiveness.

HEBREWS 10:10-14

And by that will we have been sanctified through the offering of the body of Jesus Christ once for all. And every priest stands daily at his service, offering repeatedly the same sacrifices, which can never take away sins. But when Christ had offered for all time a single sacrifice for sins, he sat down at the right hand of God, waiting from that time until his enemies should be made a footstool for his feet. For by a single offering he has perfected for all time those who are being sanctified.

Jesus' sacrifice is "once and for all" unlike that of the high priest in the OT who had to sacrifice offerings over and over for the people's sins.

HEBREWS 8:1-2

Now the point in what we are saying is this: we have such a high priest, one who is seated at the right hand of the throne of the Majesty in heaven, a minister in the holy places, in the true tent that the Lord set up, not man.

Jesus is now ministering in the "true tent" in heaven as my high priest.

HEBREWS 7:24

[B]ut he holds his priesthood permanently, because he continues forever.

Jesus' priesthood is permanent and continues forever.

AS YOUR HIGH PRIEST, JESUS SYMPATHIZES WITH YOU

———

Because Jesus took on human nature and lived as a man, Jesus can sympathize with you in all aspects of your life.

REVIEW THE FOUR KEY WAYS JESUS SYMPATHIZES WITH YOU. WHAT DO YOU LEARN?
Read the following Scriptures and record what you learn.

1. *Jesus relates to your deepest longings, desires, and needs.*

Jesus became man and took on all the traits of a human. He understands your needs and longings.

FDQ: How do you respond to the above statements?

HEBREWS 2:17-18

Therefore he had to be made like his brothers in every respect, so that he might become a merciful and faithful high priest in the service of God, to make propitiation for the sins of the people. For because he himself has suffered when tempted, he is able to help those who are being tempted.

Jesus could represent man before God only by becoming a man Himself. He could only turn away God's wrath from guilty sinners by becoming one with them and dying as a substitute for them. He experienced every kind of temptation I have, but He never gave in to temptation.

ISAIAH 53:3-4

He was despised and rejected by men, a man of sorrows and acquainted with grief; and as one from whom men hide their faces he was despised, and we esteemed him not. Surely he has borne our griefs and carried our sorrows; yet we esteemed him stricken, smitten by God, and afflicted.

Jesus is able to sympathize with my grief because He, Himself suffered. Jesus bore my grief, my sins, and my sorrows. He was pierced through for my sins. He was never esteemed.

Take some time to consider and thank Jesus for these truths.

2. Jesus understands your temptations.

Though He never gave in to temptation, Jesus was tempted in every way and thus He understands first-hand what you are facing.

FDQ: How does this statement encourage you?

HEBREWS 4:15-16

For we do not have a high priest who is unable to sympathize with our weaknesses, but one who in every respect has been tempted as we are, yet without sin. Let us then with confidence draw near to the throne of grace, that we may receive mercy and find grace to help in time of need.

Jesus can relate to every one of my temptations and so I can always trust He will receive and understand me. He will give me His grace and mercy to help me in my time of need, and my time of need is always!

HEBREWS 2:14-15

Since therefore the children share in flesh and blood, he himself likewise partook of the same things, that through death he might destroy the one who has the power of death, that is, the devil, and deliver all those who through fear of death were subject to lifelong slavery.

Jesus conquered the enemy that I cannot conquer.

Take some time to consider the ways/areas in which you are currently being tempted.

How does it encourage you to know that Jesus sympathizes with you? Are you in the habit of going to Jesus to receive mercy and grace? Why or why not?

_____

_____

_____

_____

_____

_____

_____

FDQ: Is it difficult for you to consider yourself needy? Are you willing to be needy before God but not people? Or before people and not God? Is it difficult for you to believe that God is enough when you are in need?

You are always to be needy and dependent on God in all situations. You are to intentionally preoccupy yourself with Jesus and rely on the Word and the power of the Holy Spirit to walk in obedience. To depend on God to care for you does not mean you are to be passive. It does not absolve your responsibility to take action when a clear action step is required.

3. Jesus understands your suffering because He experienced ultimate suffering.

LUKE 9:22

"The Son of Man must suffer many things and be rejected by the elders and chief priests and scribes, and be killed, and on the third day be raised."

Jesus suffered many things and was rejected by most people which resulted in his death.

HEBREWS 2:10

For it was fitting that he, for whom and by whom all things exist, in bringing many sons to glory, should make the founder of their salvation perfect through suffering.

Jesus was made perfect through His sufferings. His suffering saved me.

FDQ: What does it mean that Jesus was made "perfect through suffering"?

The Greek word for "perfect" means "to complete, to initiate, to perfect, to qualify. To make Jesus fully qualified as the pioneer of their salvation required passing through suffering (Buchanan; Michel; Weiss; Attridge; Lane; TDNT; EDNT). Christ's perfection may be understood as a vocational process by which He is made complete or fit for His office (Attridge; Moisés Silva, "Perfection and Eschatology in Hebrews," WTJ 39 [1976]: 60—62)," as noted in Linguistic and Exegetical Key to GNT (Greek New Testament), Accordance Software (2018).

Are you going through a challenging time and finding it difficult to trust God?
If so, take comfort in knowing that Jesus understands your suffering.
Acknowledge your need, confess to Him your struggle, and ask Him for help.

4. Jesus is the only mediator between you and God.

Jesus represents you before the Father. You cannot represent yourself because you can do nothing that would be sufficient to mediate between yourself and God. It is only through Jesus' blood that you can stand righteous before God and come before His Throne. Without Jesus, you have no standing or right to come before the Father. That is why you are to pray in Jesus' name.

1 TIMOTHY 2:5

For there is one God, and there is one mediator between God and men, the man Christ Jesus....

Jesus is the mediator between God and me.

HEBREWS 7:25

Consequently, he is able to save to the uttermost those who draw near to God through him, since he always lives to make intercession for them.

Jesus is forever and will always intercede for me before the Father.

JESUS IS YOUR HOPE!

———

Jesus entered the inner place (Hebrews 6:19) that you may have access to God. Jesus, your High Priest, relates to all that you face all the time.

FDQ: You may want to close your lesson by singing or listening to the hymn "Before the Throne of God Above."

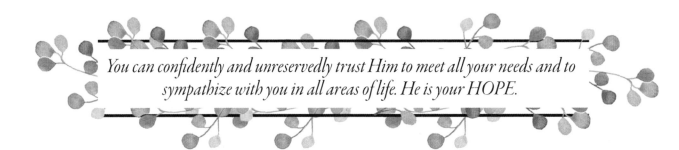

You can confidently and unreservedly trust Him to meet all your needs and to sympathize with you in all areas of life. He is your HOPE.

END YOUR STUDY...

Summarize what you learned from this lesson

High Priest

In Old Testament times, before Christ's great and final sacrifice for us on the cross, priests were appointed by God to offer daily, weekly, and annual blood sacrifices to atone for (or "cover over") the sins of the people. Because sin is so atrocious, an animal had to sacrifice its life as a substitute for the sinner, for "without the shedding of blood there is no forgiveness" (Hebrews 9:22).

"Tens of thousands of animals were ceremonially slaughtered by Jewish priests for centuries, the spilling of their blood vividly illustrat[ing] the deadly seriousness of sin" - Answers in Genesis (www.answersingenesis.org).

These sacrifices were made in the Tabernacle (while the Israelites were wandering in the desert) and in the Temple (during Solomon's time and Jesus' time). The Tabernacle/Temple was divided into various sections, including the Holy Place and the Most Holy Place, which was behind the second curtain/veil (Hebrews 9). The daily and weekly sacrifices were made in the Holy Place, and no one was allowed to go into the Most Holy Place except the High Priest on the Day of Atonement.

The High Priest was appointed from among the Levitical line, and one of his most important jobs was to perform the rites on the annual Day of Atonement. On this day, the High Priest, wearing only a simple robe of white linen instead of his usual priestly garment, would reverently and solemnly enter into the Most Holy Place behind the second veil to sprinkle the blood of the animal sacrifice on the Mercy Seat. This was to take away the sins of the people and himself (see Leviticus 16 and Hebrews 9).

Hebrews 9:11-28 tells us that Jesus came as our High Priest. He entered once for all into the Most Holy Place and secured for us an eternal redemption by putting away all of our sins with the sacrifice of His own blood.

When Christ willingly died for us on the cross, it was as if He entered behind the veil as our High Priest and instead of bringing with Him the blood of an animal sacrifice to sprinkle on the Mercy Seat, He climbed upon the Mercy Seat to spill His own blood to make the perfect or complete atonement for our sins. This was the ultimate and final Day of Atonement. He is indeed able to save us to the "uttermost" (Hebrews 7:25).

At the moment of Jesus' death, the veil separating the Most Holy Place from the Holy Place "was torn in two from top to bottom" (Matthew 27:51a). This tearing of the veil and the tearing of Jesus' body on the cross signify the free access we now have to God. ("[W]e have confidence to enter the holy places by the blood of Jesus, by the new and living way that he opened for us through the curtain, that is, through his flesh...." Hebrews 10:19b-20). This is an incredible privilege and we owe it all to our Lord and Savior, our Great High Priest.

"Since then we have a great high priest who has passed through the heavens, Jesus, the Son of God, let us hold fast our confession. For we do not have a high priest who is unable to sympathize with our weaknesses, but one who in every respect has been tempted as we are, yet without sin. Let us then with confidence draw near to the throne of grace, that we may receive mercy and find grace to help in time of need" (Hebrews 4:14-16).

It is significant that Christ not only acted as our High Priest but that He voluntarily sacrificed Himself as the Lamb of God. "No one takes it from me, but I lay it down of my own accord. I have authority to lay it down, and I have authority to take it up again. This charge I have received from my Father" (John 10:18).

Sources:
gotquestions.org/Jesus-High-Priest
gotquestions.org/animal-sacrifices
www3.telus.net/public/kstam/en/temple/details/day_of_atonement

Let us then with confidence DRAW NEAR to the THRONE OF GRACE, that we may receive MERCY AND FIND GRACE TO HELP in time of need.

HEBREWS 4:16

Reflection

Meditate on Jesus as your perfect High Priest.

—— **LESSON 3** ——

Holy Spirit, My Helper

In Lessons 1-2 you focused on the role of Jesus in carrying out His Father's will. Jesus was both High Priest and the sacrificed Lamb of God.

In Lessons 3 and 4 you will focus on getting to know the third person of the Trinity, the Holy Spirit.

Your relationship with the Holy Spirit is profoundly unique. His presence in the believer's life may seem as unassuming as the whisper of a "still, small voice," yet as all-encompassing as the very air that you breathe and cannot live without. Without the Holy Spirit it would be impossible for you to see the beauty and majesty of Christ. In Lesson 3 you will learn about the Holy Spirit's personal attributes and roles.

AN INTRODUCTION TO THE HOLY SPIRIT

___

WHAT WAS THE ROLE OF THE HOLY SPIRIT IN THE OLD TESTAMENT/OLD COVENANT?

While there is some mystery regarding all of the Holy Spirit's role in the Old Testament, it is certain that He is God and does not change (Malachi 3:6). The Holy Spirit was intimately involved in creation (Genesis 1:2); and He inspired and empowered Old Testament authors and prophets (1 Peter 1:11; 2 Peter 1:21).

The main difference between the Holy Spirit's role in the Old Testament and the New Testament is that in the Old Testament the Holy Spirit only empowered certain individuals at specific times to perform specific tasks regardless of the person's spiritual condition.

The Spirit "came upon" such Old Testament people as Joshua (Numbers 27:18), David (1 Samuel 16:12-13) and even Saul (1 Samuel 10:10). In the book of Judges, we see the Spirit "coming upon" the various judges whom God raised up to deliver Israel from their oppressors.[1]

WHAT IS THE ROLE OF THE HOLY SPIRIT IN THE NEW TESTAMENT/NEW COVENANT?

While the Holy Spirit only empowered certain individuals in the Old Testament for a specific task, after the Pentecost there is a "more powerful, fuller work of the Holy Spirit" in all believers. (For additional teaching on the Holy Spirit, see Wayne Grudem, *Systematic Theology*, page 637ff.)

Joel prophesied that God declared, "And it shall come to pass afterward, that I will pour out my Spirit on all flesh" (Joel 2:28a). The Apostle Peter, quoting Joel, said, "And in the last days it shall be, God declares, that I will pour out my Spirit on all flesh...'" (Acts 2:17a).

We are now living in the "last days," and as of the Pentecost, the Holy Spirit has been poured out fully on all believers. We are now all empowered for ministry and the work of the Kingdom.

"

In the OT, the presence of God was many times manifested in the glory of God and in theophanies [a manifestation of God to a person], and in the gospels Jesus himself manifested the presence of God among men. But after Jesus ascended into heaven, and continuing through the entire church age, the Holy Spirit is now the primary manifestation of the presence of the Trinity among us. He is the one who is the most prominently present with us now.[2]

WAYNE GRUDEM

THE HOLY SPIRIT AND THE FOLLOWER OF CHRIST

———

As a follower of Christ, the Holy Spirit is at the very core of your being. He is the Source of God's power for you to live for His purposes each day and the Revealer of the Father's love that satisfies your every longing.

At this point in your relationship with God, what do you know about the Holy Spirit and who would you say that He is? Take a moment to ask God to deepen your desire and understanding of the Third Person of the Trinity.

THE HOLY SPIRIT'S PERSONAL ATTRIBUTES

———

The Bible clearly teaches that the Holy Spirit is a distinct Person in the Godhead, as much as the Father and the Son are Persons. The following are some fundamental biblical truths about the Holy Spirit's **personal attributes.**

The Holy Spirit is God.

When Jesus was baptized, He saw the Spirit of God descending on Him (Matthew 3:16-17).

Jesus declared the Holy Spirit's deity as He commanded that His followers be baptized in the Name of the Trinity: Father, Son, Holy Spirit (Matthew 28:19).

He is called God. When Ananias and Sapphira sinned against the Holy Spirit, they sinned against God (Acts 5:3-4).

The Holy Spirit is omnipotent, omnipresent, and omniscient.

The Holy Spirit came upon Mary and the power of the Most High overshadowed her, a virgin, to conceive and give birth to the Son of God (Luke 1:35).

The Spirit is present everywhere; there is no place where you can flee from His presence (Psalm 139:7-8).

The Spirit searches all things, even the deep things of God. Only He can know and reveal the thoughts of God that are beyond your comprehension (1 Corinthians 2:9-11).

The Holy Spirit is eternal.

The Lord Jesus promised to send you the Holy Spirit to be your Helper Who will be with you forever (John 14:16).

Through the eternal Spirit, Christ offered Himself unblemished before God so that you may serve the living God (Hebrews 9:14).

The Holy Spirit has emotions.

The Holy Spirit was grieved by the rebellion of His people (Isaiah 63:10).

You are warned against grieving the Holy Spirit of God, with whom you were sealed for the day of redemption (Ephesians 4:30).

The Holy Spirit has an intellect.

The Holy Spirit uses His mind in interceding for the Saints (Romans 8:27).

THE HOLY SPIRIT'S SPECIFIC ROLES

———

The Bible also teaches that the Holy Spirit has **specific roles** in the life of the believer that reveal and glorify the Father and the Son.

WHAT DO YOU LEARN ABOUT THE ROLES OF THE HOLY SPIRIT?

Read the following Scriptures and record your response.

GENESIS 1:26a

Then God said, "Let us make man in our image, after our likeness."
Creator – He took part in creation.

JOHN 14:25-26

"These things I have spoken to you while I am still with you. But the Helper, the Holy Spirit, whom the Father will send in my name, he will teach you all things and bring to your remembrance all that I have said to you."
Helper (Comforter), Teacher.

JOHN 15:26

"But when the Helper comes, whom I will send to you from the Father, the Spirit of truth, who proceeds from the Father, he will bear witness about me."
Witness – bears witness about Jesus; declares and glorifies the Father and the Son.

JOHN 16:13

"When the Spirit of truth comes, he will guide you into all the truth, for he will not speak on his own authority, but whatever he hears he will speak, and he will declare to you the things that are to come."
Guide – leads me in truth.

LUKE 1:35

And the angel answered her, "The Holy Spirit will come upon you, and the power of the Most High will overshadow you; therefore the child to be born will be called holy—the Son of God."
One who generated Jesus' humanity.

ACTS 1:8

"But you will receive power when the Holy Spirit has come upon you, and you will be my witnesses in Jerusalem and in all Judea and Samaria, and to the end of the earth."
Source of Power.

ROMANS 8:11

If the Spirit of him who raised Jesus from the dead dwells in you, he who raised Christ Jesus from the dead will also give life to your mortal bodies through his Spirit who dwells in you.
Life-Giver – spiritual life.

ROMANS 8:16

The Spirit himself bears witness with our spirit that we are children of God....

Witness of my sonship – assures me of my identiy.

ROMANS 8:26-27

Likewise the Spirit helps us in our weakness. For we do not know what to pray for as we ought, but the Spirit himself intercedes for us with groanings too deep for words. And he who searches hearts knows what is the mind of the Spirit, because the Spirit intercedes for the saints according to the will of God.

Intercessor – searches my heart and intercedes on my behalf.

1 CORINTHIANS 2:12-13

Now we have received not the spirit of the world, but the Spirit who is from God, that we might understand the things freely given us by God. And we impart this in words not taught by human wisdom but taught by the Spirit, interpreting spiritual truths to those who are spiritual.

Teacher – the Holy Spirit imparts to me an understanding of the Word.

I CORINTHIANS 12:4-11

Now there are varieties of gifts, but the same Spirit; and there are varieties of service, but the same Lord; and there are varieties of activities, but it is the same God who empowers them all in everyone. To each is given the manifestation of the Spirit for the common good. For to one is given through the Spirit the utterance of wisdom, and to another the utterance of knowledge according to the same Spirit, to another faith by the same Spirit, to another gifts of healing by the one Spirit, to another the working of miracles, to another prophecy, to another the ability to distinguish between spirits, to another various kinds of tongues, to another the interpretation of tongues. All these are empowered by one and the same Spirit, who apportions to each one individually as he wills.

Giver of spiritual gifts.

EPHESIANS 1:13-14

In him you also, when you heard the word of truth, the gospel of your salvation, and believed in him, were sealed with the promised Holy Spirit, who is the guarantee of our inheritance until we acquire possession of it, to the praise of his glory.

Guarantee of my inheritance.

TITUS 3:4-5

But when the goodness and loving kindness of God our Savior appeared, he saved us, not because of works done by us in righteousness, but according to his own mercy, by the washing of regeneration and renewal of the Holy Spirit....

Agent of regeneration and renewal. He passes on the life of God to me.

2 PETER 1:21

For no prophecy was ever produced by the will of man, but men spoke from God as they were carried along by the Holy Spirit.

Co-Author of Scripture.

Which of the Holy Spirit's attribute/role do you find most comforting? Why?

Which attribute/role is new to you or one you would like to experience more fully in your life? Explain.

How does knowing the Holy Spirit's attributes/roles affect your day-to-day walk with God?

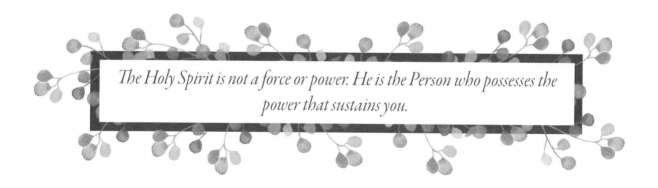

The Holy Spirit is not a force or power. He is the Person who possesses the power that sustains you.

END YOUR STUDY...

Summarize what you learned from this lesson

Reflection

Write a prayer of thanksgiving to God for sending you the gift of Himself, the indwelling Holy Spirit.
Ask God to help you more fully rely on the power of the Holy Spirit in your life.

In Lesson 4, you will examine what it means to walk in the Spirit.

LESSON 4

Walking in the Spirit

In Lesson 3 you learned about the personal attributes and roles of the Holy Spirit. In Lesson 4 you will focus on the Spirit-filled life God desires for you. The Bible teaches that at the point of salvation, the Holy Spirit indwells you and abides in you.

You have been set free to no longer walk in the flesh but rather to walk in the Spirit (Galatians 5:25). You are no longer bound to sin but now you are enslaved to righteousness (Romans 6:18). Obedience to righteousness leads to more righteousness, "sanctification and its end, eternal life" (Romans 6:22). In Lesson 4 you will look at what it means to walk in the Spirit.

HOLY SPIRIT, YOUR HELPER

The promised Holy Spirit is your Helper who guides you into all truth. He reveals to you the beauty of Jesus (John 16:14) and transforms you into His likeness (2 Corinthians 3:18). As you depend upon and cooperate with the Holy Spirit, He grows you in the knowledge and love of God, and He enables you to do the following:

- Exalt God with all that you are as you live your life for His purpose and glory (John 15:8)
- Exhibit the fruit of the Spirit (Galatians 5:22-23)
- Experience the Spirit's power (Ephesians 1:19)
- Exercise the gifts that He has given you to build up and promote unity in the church body (1 Corinthians 12:4-7)
- Extend God's kingdom by being a witness for Jesus everywhere you go (Acts 1:8)

WALKING IN THE SPIRIT

God desires for you to fully enjoy the abundant life He has made available to you in Christ. To experience this you must choose to walk in your new identity—God made you into a new creation; He has regenerated your heart (2 Corinthians 5:17; Titus 3:4-7; Romans 6:11-12). You are no longer enslaved nor are you obligated to sin (Romans 6:6); rather, you are to walk in the Spirit (Galatians 5:25).

In Colossians 3:1-3, Paul writes, "If then you have been raised with Christ, seek the things that are above, where Christ is, seated at the right hand of God. Set your minds on things that are above, not on things that are on earth. For you have died, and your life is hidden with Christ in God."

READ COLOSSIANS 3:5-16.
Read the passage and record what you are to "put to death" and "put on" to keep in step with the Spirit.

Put to death	*Put on*
(5) sexual immorality, impurity, passion, evil desire, and covetousness, which is idolatry	(12) compassionate hearts, kindness, humility, meekness, and patience,
(8) anger, wrath, malice, slander, and obscene talk from your mouth	(13) bearing with one another and, if one has a complaint against another, forgiving each other; as the Lord has forgiven you, so you also must forgive.
(9) telling lies to one another	(14) above all these, [put on] love, which binds everything together in perfect harmony
	(15) the peace of Christ [to] rule in your hearts, to which indeed you were called in one body. And be thankful.
	(16) the word of Christ to dwell in you richly, teaching and admonishing one another in all wisdom, singing psalms and hymns and spiritual songs, with thankfulness in your hearts to God.

Review the list and ask God to help you evaluate and determine the areas of your life where you need to put to death the things of the flesh and put on what is godly. This is not an exhaustive list, and you can find other lists of characteristics or behaviors to "put to death" and/or "put on" in Romans 12, Galatians 5:16-23, Ephesians 4:17-32, Ephesians 5:3-11, and 2 Peter 1.

Galatians 5:16 says, "But I say, walk by the Spirit, and you will not gratify the desires of the flesh." The wisdom, strength, and desire to obey comes from the Helper, the Holy Spirit, Whom the Father has sent to you. Philippians 2:13 says, "for it is God who works in you, both to will and to work for his good pleasure." God longs for you to keep in step with the Holy Spirit always.

"

So then, to walk in the Spirit is achievable when we know the Gospel, believe it to be true (1 John 4:6), and depend on the inward prompting of the Spirit to guide us in that truth (John 16:13).... Really then, the power to walk in the Spirit and turn away from sin begins with decision points we encounter hundreds of times each day. Making the hard choices up front will strengthen one's resolve to be obedient in every thought, word, and deed (Romans 6:11-14). In closing, walking in the Spirit is how we take up our cross, crucify the flesh, die to self, and allow Christ to rise up in our stead (Matthew 16:24-26).[1]

JIM ALLEN

FDQ: What do you do when sin looks good and holiness looks boring or too difficult?

Points to remember:

1. Realize that sin seems like the easiest path initially, but eventually it always becomes a harder path.

2. Realize that you can choose to respond in obedience, even if it means choosing for the next hour and then the next hour.

3. Ask God to renew the desire of your heart toward Christ, your Treasure. Ask God to give you spiritual eyes to see His beauty in these times of temptation.

DO NOT GRIEVE OR QUENCH THE HOLY SPIRIT

———

The Holy Spirit is grieved when a believer lives like an unbeliever and continues to live in the flesh, doing what she knows is wrong.

READ EPHESIANS 4:17-5:5.

In what ways does Paul state that we grieve the Holy Spirit? Make a list.

by being callous (19)

by giving in to sexual temptation (19)

by being greedy and impure (19)

by being deceitful (25)

by being angry (26-27)

by stealing (28)

by cursing and corrupt speech (29)

by being bitter (31)

by being unforgiving (32)

by being sexually immoral (5:3-5)

"

The checks of the Spirit come in the most extraordinarily gentle ways, and if you are not sensitive enough to detect His voice you will quench it, and your personal spiritual life will be impaired. His checks always come as a still small voice, so small that no one but the saint notices them.... Whenever the Spirit checks, call a halt and get the thing right, or you will go on grieving Him without knowing it.[2]

OSWALD CHAMBERS

The Holy Spirit checks your spirit when you are contemplating sin. You have a choice to either obey or ignore His prompting. When you choose to continually ignore the Holy Spirit's warning, you are quenching His voice (I Thessalonians 5:19). When you choose to sin, the Holy Spirit will not be seen in your attitudes and actions. To act out in a sinful manner, whether in thought or deed, grieves the Holy Spirit.

FDQ: How do you recognize the Holy Spirit's prompting in your life?
What does it look or feel like when you are grieving or quenching the Holy Spirit?

WHAT ARE THE CAUSES AND EFFECTS OF QUENCHING AND GRIEVING THE HOLY SPIRIT?

1. You are careless to guard your heart.

This will rob you of your true Treasure: your intimacy with God. Proverbs 4:23 says, "Above all else, guard your heart, for everything you do flows from it" (NIV). You are to be intentional regarding what you allow to influence your heart. If you are careless in guarding your heart, you will find it more difficult to hear the Holy Spirit's promptings. (See Part 6 Lesson 5 – My Guarded Heart)

2. You choose to get distracted by fleshly desires.

This will inevitably lead you astray from God's way. 1 John 2:15-16 says, "Do not love the world or the things in the world. If anyone loves the world, the love of the Father is not in him. For all that is in the world—the desires of the flesh and the desires of the eyes and pride of life—is not from the Father but is from the world." These distractions may seem harmless at first, but when you continue to allow them to preoccupy your mind and influence your actions, you are drifting away from walking with the Spirit.

3. You willfully rebel and disobey the Father's commands.

The Lord Jesus said in John 14:21 and 24, "Whoever has my commandments and keeps them, he it is who loves me, and he who loves me will be loved by my Father, and I will love him and manifest myself to him... Whoever does not love me does not keep my words. And the word that you hear is not mine but the Father's who sent me." Disobedience will cause a separation between you and God.

WHEN HAVE YOU GRIEVED THE HOLY SPIRIT?

Think of a time in your life, past or present, when you grieved the Holy Spirit by being distracted, careless, or rebellious regarding following God's way. Record any thoughts the Holy Spirit brings to mind. Use the My Heart Unveiled chart to process your choice and its outcome.

FDQ: Was it difficult or easy for you to come up with an example? Do you think about the reality that you, at times, grieve the Holy Spirit?

Can you relate to the following example? If no one shares you can read the following example of grieving and quenching the Holy Spirit.

"I was choosing to frequent a local bar 'just to hang out' but was feeling guilty about my choice because I knew it was putting me in a compromising position. I recognized that I liked the attention I was receiving from men but I also knew from past experience what it would lead to. Eventually, I became sexually involved with a guy from the bar and refused to stop seeing him. I made a conscious choice to remain in sin, which resulted in continual guilt. I recognized I had two choices: 1) obey God and stop seeing the man, or 2) bury my guilty feelings and continue to convince myself what I was doing was worth it. I chose to stuff my feelings and continue my actions. Eventually I became dull to the Holy Spirit's prompting.

"Time went by, and I was never satisfied. I am so grateful that the Holy Spirit didn't give up on me. Eventually I shared what I was doing with a mentor and confessed my sin and stopped my sinful actions."

ABOVE ALL ELSE,
guard your heart,
FOR EVERYTHING YOU DO
flows from it.

PROVERBS 4:23

YIELDING TO THE HOLY SPIRIT

———

By God's mercy and grace, He has provided the way for you to get back in step with the Spirit. No matter how far you feel you have fallen, the Father eagerly awaits for you to return. Consider the following steps:

STEP 1: Ask God to search your heart and reveal your heart to you.

PSALM 139:23-24

Search me, O God, and know my heart! Try me and know my thoughts! And see if there be any grievous way in me, and lead me in the way everlasting!

STEP 2: Confess your sin and receive forgiveness.

I JOHN 1:9

If we confess our sins, he is faithful and just to forgive us our sins and to cleanse us from all unrighteousness.

STEP 3: Humble yourself and turn from your sin, confident God will give you His grace.

2 CHRONICLES 7:14

"[I]f my people who are called by my name humble themselves, and pray and seek my face and turn from their wicked ways, then I will hear from heaven and will forgive their sin and heal their land."

JAMES 4:6b

"God opposes the proud, but gives grace to the humble."

STEP 4: Walk by the Spirit in obedience.

GALATIANS 5:16

But I say, walk by the Spirit, and you will not gratify the desires of the flesh.

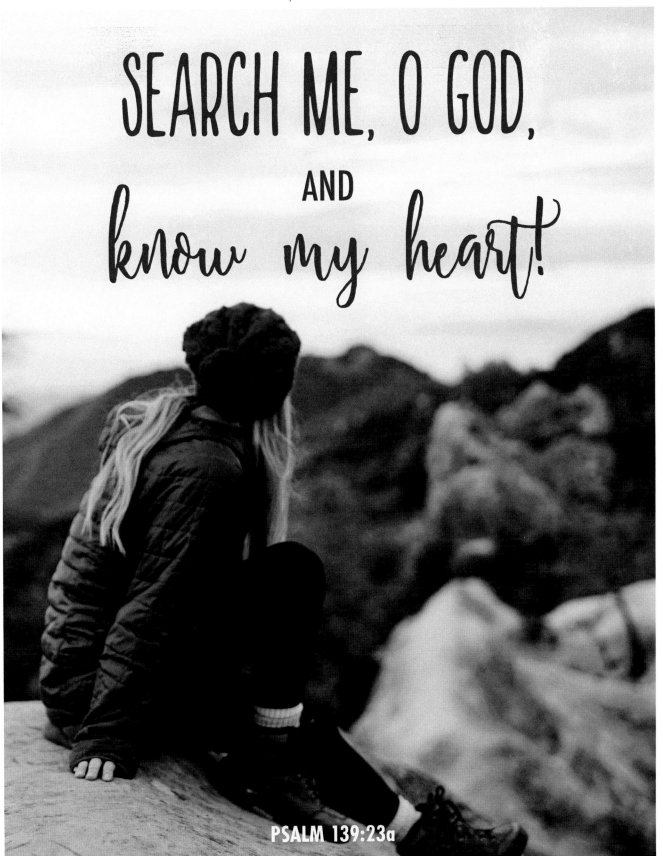

SEARCH ME, O GOD, AND know my heart!

PSALM 139:23a

SPEND TIME IN PRAYER TO CONFESS YOUR SINS TO GOD.

Receive His forgiveness and allow the Spirit to speak to you through God's Word as you meditate on His faithfulness in cleansing you from all unrighteousness. Thank Him for His amazing grace. **Record your thoughts.**

_____

_____

_____

_____

_____

_____

_____

_____

_____

_____

END YOUR STUDY...

Summarize what you learned from this lesson

Reflection

What does it mean to be "slaves of righteousness" (Romans 6:18)?
Thanks be to God that "now that you have been set free from sin and have become slaves of God,
the fruit you get leads to sanctification and its end, eternal life" (Romans 6:22).

—— **LESSON 5** ——

My True Identity

In Lessons 1 and 2 you discovered Jesus as your Humble Servant and High Priest. You can confidently approach God, knowing you are forgiven and stand righteous in His presence.

In Lessons 3 and 4 you learned that the Holy Spirit was active in your new birth and is active in your ongoing daily life, transforming you as you walk in step with Him.

In this lesson you will explore what "identity" is and what it means to live out your new identity in Christ through the Holy Spirit.

WHAT IS "IDENTITY"?

———

Every human being has an identity. Merriam Webster defines "identity" as "who someone is: the name of a person, the qualities, beliefs, etc. that make a particular person different from others." Many things and people influence your **birth identity**—your race, gender, talents, physical looks, physical fitness, personality, relationships, socio-economic standing, career, education, life experiences, roles (daughter, wife, mom, etc.).

You live out of your identity. Your goals, motives, and sense of self-worth or lack of worth come from and are directed by your identity. Your identity will define your outlook on life. More importantly, it will determine what you think, feel, and choose.

When someone asks you to describe yourself, what things typically come to your mind?

When Adam and Eve sinned, spiritual death came to all mankind (Romans 5:12, 18-19), resulting in all people being born into a state of confusion regarding their identity and their purpose (see Part 5 Lesson 1). But thanks be to God, for in Christ, He has redeemed your identity.

YOU WERE GIVEN A NEW IDENTITY WHEN YOU WERE BORN SPIRITUALLY

———

At the point of salvation you were reborn (John 3:3). You were "born of God" (1 John 3:9). You became a new creation. "Therefore, if anyone is in Christ, he is a new creation. The old has passed away; behold, the new has come" (2 Corinthians 5:17). Your **new identity** as a child of God is who you became at the time of your new birth and is who you are now. At the point of your new birth, God's goal for you is to begin to define your worth, motives, goals, values, etc. by your new identity as His child. This is your true identity. Your birth identity becomes secondary to your new identity (Galatians 3:26-29).

"

The most important belief that we possess is a true knowledge of who God is. The second most important belief is who we are as children of God, because we cannot consistently behave in a way that is inconsistent with how we perceive ourselves. And if we do not see ourselves as God sees us, then to that degree we suffer from a wrong identity and a poor image of who we really are. It is not what we do that determines who we are. It is who we are that determines what we do.[1]

NEIL T. ANDERSON

REFLECT ON YOUR TRUE IDENTITY.

What things come to your mind when you think about being a child of God?

_____

_____

_____

Can you think of any immediate changes that took place in your life when you were reborn?

_____

_____

_____

FDQ: If a participant received Christ as a young child, she will more than likely not have a reference point to respond to this question.

Think about and record some of the gradual changes that have taken place in your life since you were reborn. (Some of these may include goals, responses to situations and people, thoughts and feelings, patterns of life, etc.)

_____

_____

_____

_____

_____

YOUR NEW IDENTITY

——

Every child of God has the same identity, which is uniquely expressed through a person's God-given personality, gifts, and skills. In the first two chapters of Ephesians, Paul explains your new identity as a child of God in Christ. This is not an exhaustive list as there are many Scriptures that address this topic, but it is a good start.

READ THROUGH EPHESIANS CHAPTERS 1-2.

List all the things God says you are now. For example: I am blessed with spiritual blessings (1:3).

I am blessed in the heavenly realms with every spiritual blessing (Ephesians 1:3).

I am chosen before the creation of the world (Ephesians 1:4, 11).

I am holy and blameless (Ephesians 1:4).

I am adopted as his child (Ephesians 1:5).

I am given God's glorious grace lavishly and without restriction (Ephesians 1:5,8).

I am in Him (Ephesians 1:7).

I have redemption (Ephesians 1:8).

I am forgiven (Ephesians 1:8).

I have purpose (Ephesians 1:9 & 2:11).

I have hope (Ephesians 1:12).

I am included (Ephesians 1:13).

I am sealed with the promised Holy Spirit (Ephesians 1:13).

I am a saint (Ephesians 1:18).

I have God's power (Ephesians 1:19)

I am alive with Christ (Ephesians 2:5).

I am raised up with Christ (Ephesians 2:6).

I am seated with Christ in the heavenly realms (Ephesians 2:6).

I will be shown the incomparable riches of God's grace (Ephesians 2:7).

I am God's workmanship (Ephesians 2:10).

I have been brought near to God through Christ's blood (Ephesians 2:13).

I have peace (Ephesians 2:14).

I have access to the Father (Ephesians 2:18).

I am a member of God's household (Ephesians 2:19).

I am secure (Ephesians 2:20).

I am a holy temple (Ephesians 2:21).

I am a dwelling for the Holy Spirit (Ephesians 2:22).

Now go back through your Ephesians list. Put a checkmark beside any statements that are meaningful to you right now. Underline any that are difficult for you to believe.

FDQ: Have each woman share one thing for which she is most thankful. How does that truth influence your day-to-day life?

Record one thing for which you are most thankful. How might remembering this truth encourage you on a daily basis?

_____

_____

In what areas is your view and experience of yourself different from who God says you are?

_____

_____

_____

"

Rather than being directed and controlled by emotions, wrong thinking, or even outright lies, we begin to bridge the gap between:
- Our confessional theology (what we claim to believe); and
- Our practical theology (how we actually live).[2]

TARA BARTHEL

Remember, if you interpret any part of your identity through the lens of unbelief, there will be a gap between God's truth and your reality. You "bridge the gap" by choosing to be wholly defined by truth.

GOD DESIRES THAT YOU EXPERIENCE AND WALK IN YOUR NEW IDENTITY

———

Identify one underlined truth from your Ephesians list. What lie are you believing? Write out what is true, personalizing it with your name. Aloud, affirm the truth to yourself and thank God it is true. As needed, renew your mind with this truth.

_____

_____

_____

_____

_____

_____

_____

_____

God's desire for you is to experience and walk in your new identity, the "newness of life" (Romans 6:4b). However, your birth identity will always seek to repress and compete with who you really are in Christ. As you increasingly recognize and embrace God's truth and choose to live it out, you will more fully follow God and enjoy Him. Be encouraged that you are not left alone to accomplish this process. "And I am sure of this, that he who began a good work in you will bring it to completion at the day of Jesus Christ" (Philippians 1:6).

How does knowing that you are chosen and loved by God change the way you view your purpose and mission in your relationships and your roles?

_____

_____

_____

_____

_____

HOW DO YOU WALK IN YOUR NEW IDENTITY?

———

You are empowered to walk in the freedom of your new identity by renewing your mind. (Refer to Part 2 Lesson 4.) "Do not be conformed to this world, but be transformed by the renewal of your mind..." (Romans 12:2a). The word "renew" means to "renovate or restore." You are to renovate your mind by recognizing the faulty thinking of your old identity and replacing it with the life-giving truths of God, just as you practiced in the last exercise. The more you bathe your mind with the truths of God's Word and respond to life situations by walking in these truths, the more you will experience your new identity.

Personal Testimony

"I came to Christ as a child but walked away in my adult life. I lived a double life: one as an upright, single working mom and the other as a promiscuous woman. God in his infinite mercy rescued me from my darkness and drew me back to Himself. I experienced His truly amazing grace. He gave me the power to set right boundaries and live a life aligned to His will; however, I was still plagued with shame and guilt. I was afraid to commit to any ministry because I felt so unworthy. Through two things, reading a book by Robert S. McGee, *The Search for Significance,* and listening to a sermon series on forgiveness, I began to embrace God's forgiveness that I had already received, and I began to believe the truth that I was really a new creation. When I recognized a lie I was believing about myself as a child of God, I would find a Scripture that would tell me the truth and write it out and say it out loud. I now rejoice when I remember what God redeemed me from and what He redeemed me to—a child of God through my precious Savior, Jesus Christ."

RENEW YOUR MIND WITH SCRIPTURES THAT REINFORCE YOUR NEW IDENTITY

———

The Scriptures are rich with the truths that proclaim what God did for you in your new birth and encourage you to walk as His child.

BATHE YOUR MIND IN THE SCRIPTURES BELOW AND HIGHLIGHT THE ONE MOST MEANINGFUL TO YOU AT THIS TIME.

PSALM 103:10-12

He does not deal with us according to our sins, nor repay us according to our iniquities. For as high as the heavens are above the earth, so great is his steadfast love toward those who fear him; as far as the east is from the west, so far does he remove our transgressions from us.

COLOSSIANS 1:21-22

And you, who once were alienated and hostile in mind, doing evil deeds, he has now reconciled in his body of flesh by his death, in order to present you holy and blameless and above reproach before him[.]

1 JOHN 3:1

See what kind of love the Father has given to ("lavished on" NIV) us, that we should be called children of God; and so we are.

ROMANS 8:1

There is therefore now no condemnation for those who are in Christ Jesus.

ROMANS 8:33-34

Who shall bring any charge against God's elect? It is God who justifies. Who is to condemn? Christ Jesus is the one who died—more than that, who was raised—who is at the right hand of God, who indeed is interceding for us.

GALATIANS 5:1

For freedom Christ has set us free; stand firm therefore, and do not submit again to a yoke of slavery.

ROMANS 6:6-8

We know that our old self was crucified with him in order that the body of sin might be brought to nothing, so that we would no longer be enslaved to sin. For one who has died has been set free from sin. Now if we have died with Christ, we believe that we will also live with him.

COLOSSIANS 2:6-7

Therefore, as you received Christ Jesus the Lord, so walk in him, rooted and built up in him and established in the faith, just as you were taught, abounding in thanksgiving.

Write out a Scripture that has helped you embrace your identity as God's child living in Christ through the Holy Spirit.

YOUR ONGOING JOURNEY WALKING IN TRUTH

—

As you walk more and more in light of who you are in Christ, you will be transformed more and more into His image. Your true identity will be increasingly recognizable to both you and to others. "And we all, with unveiled face, beholding the glory of the Lord, are being transformed into the same image from one degree of glory to another. For this comes from the Lord who is the Spirit" (2 Corinthians 3:18). The Holy Spirit makes this a living reality over your lifetime. When Jesus returns, you will be able to see Him and know Him without sin obscuring your vision, and you will fully know who you are in Him.

1 CORINTHIANS 13:9-12

For we know in part and we prophesy in part, but when the perfect comes, the partial will pass away. When I was a child, I spoke like a child, I thought like a child, I reasoned like a child. When I became a man, I gave up childish ways. For now we see in a mirror dimly, but then face to face. Now I know in part; then I shall know fully, even as I have been fully known.

A helpful article on your identity in Christ may be found at the Desiring God website, www.desiringgod.org:
"Know Who You Are Not," by Marshall Segal (December 12, 2018).

END YOUR STUDY...

Summarize what you learned from this lesson

Reflection

The Triune God—God the Father, Christ the Son, and the Holy Spirit—wants you to know how deeply loved you are by Him and to be filled and changed by His love.

Meditate on the following Scripture.

For this reason I bow my knees before the Father, from whom every family in heaven and on earth is named, that according to the riches of his glory he may grant you to be strengthened with power through his Spirit in your inner being, so that Christ may dwell in your hearts through faith—that you, being rooted and grounded in love, may have strength to comprehend with all the saints what is the breadth and length and height and depth, and to know the love of Christ that surpasses knowledge, that you may be filled with all the fullness of God. Now to him who is able to do far more abundantly than all that we ask or think, according to the power at work within us, to him be glory in the church and in Christ Jesus throughout all generations, forever and ever. Amen.

EPHESIANS 3:14-21

PART 4 WORKS CITED

Lesson 1: Jesus, Humble Servant

1 • Carson, D.A. "The Doctrine of the Incarnation, Theology Refresh, Podcast for Christian Leaders." Desiring God, www.desiringgod.org/interviews/the-doctrine-of-the-incarnation. Accessed 20 March 2017.
2 • Keller, Timothy. The Freedom of Self-Forgetfulness, 10 Publishing, 2012.

Lesson 2: Jesus, My High Priest

No works cited.

Lesson 3: Holy Spirit, My Helper

1 • "What was the role of the Holy Spirit in the Old Testament?" Got Questions, www.gotquestions.org/Spirit-Old-Testament.html. Accessed 21 March 2017.
2 • Grudem, Wayne. Systematic Theology. Inter-Varsity Press and Zondervan Publishing, 1994, pg. 637.
3 • Grudem, Wayne. Systematic Theology. Inter-Varsity Press and Zondervan Publishing, 1994, pgs. 634-635.

Lesson 4: Walking in the Spirit

1 • Allen, Jim. "The True Gospel, Part 7: Walk in the Spirit." Blogos, www.blogos.org/keepwatch/gospel7-walk-Spirit.php. Accessed 21 March 2017.
2 • Chambers, Oswald. My Utmost for His Highest. Discovery House, 1992, August 13th devotional.

Lesson 5: My True Identity

1 • Anderson, Neil T. Who I am In Christ. Bethany House Publishers, Minneapolis, Minnesota, 2001, pg. 11.
2 • Barthel, Tara. Living the Gospel in Relationships. Peacemaker Ministries, Billings, Montana, 2007, pg. 16.

MY HEART
Unveiled

PART 5

As you begin Part 5 remind yourself of what you learned in Part 2 Lesson 5—God Desires My Whole Heart.

In Part 5 you will explore the progression from a longing or desire to an idol. You will learn to evaluate and recognize when you are treasuring someone or something more than Christ (Colossians 2:3). You will examine your underlying fears and resulting control-responses and how to surrender your heart to God. In addition, you will understand the roles of grief and worship.

——— LESSON 1 ———

My Longing Heart

At salvation you received a regenerated heart, a new identity, and a redeemed purpose for living—to love God, to enjoy Him, and to live for Him in every area of your life. As you walk in your new identity, your devoted heart will enjoy true freedom in Christ (Galatians 5:1).

WALKING IN FREEDOM

———

Christ's sacrifice on your behalf secured your freedom to walk with Him in obedience. Now you are able to delight in His steadfast love for you (Psalm 136:1).

READ PSALM 86:10-13.

Record David's response to God's steadfast love.

PSALM 86:10-13

"For you are great and do wondrous things; you alone are God. Teach me your way, O LORD, that I may walk in your truth; unite my heart to fear your name. I give thanks to you, O Lord my God, with my whole heart, and I will glorify your name forever. For great is your steadfast love toward me; you have delivered my soul from the depths of Sheol."

As David recognized God's steadfast love, he prayed to be wholehearted toward Him. As you recognize God's faithfulness to you, your desire to honor, please, and obey Him will grow. You will continue to discover that your satisfaction and delight are found in Him.

READ AND REFLECT ON PSALM 36:7-9.

PSALM 36:7-9

"How precious is your steadfast love, O God! The children of mankind take refuge in the shadow of your wings. They feast on the abundance of your house, and you give them drink from the river of your delights. For with you is the fountain of life; in your light do we see light."

What benefits do the "children of mankind" receive as they recognize God's steadfast love?

_____

_____

_____

Can you add to the list from your experience as a child of God?

_____

_____

_____

Pause and thank the Lord for these benefits.

JESUS THE LIVING WATER

––––

When Jesus was in the temple surrounded by the crowd, He spoke of the importance of "living water."

JOHN 7:37-39

On the last day of the feast, the great day, Jesus stood up and cried out, "If anyone thirsts, let him come to me and drink. Whoever believes in me, as the Scripture has said, 'Out of his heart will flow rivers of living water.'" Now this he said about the Spirit, whom those who believed in him were to receive, for as yet the Spirit had not been given, because Jesus was not yet glorified.

Jesus is the source of abundant life (see also John 4:10). The person who comes to Jesus and believes in Him is truly satisfied. Out of her heart overflows delight.

GOD COMMANDS THAT YOU WORSHIP HIM WHOLEHEARTEDLY

––––

The first of the Ten Commandments is "You shall have no other gods before me" (Exodus 20:3); Jesus said that the "great and first commandment" is that "You shall love the Lord your God with all your heart and with all your soul and with all your mind" (Matthew 22:37-38). God has created you to worship Him, and your deepest longings will be satisfied only in worshiping Him. And yet, all hearts are prone to wander, so you will be continually tempted to worship someone or something other than God in your pursuit of happiness.

God is jealous for your allegiance and devotion (Exodus 20:5), which means that He will not tolerate your worship of any other person or thing. His jealousy is righteous because He is right in His assessment that He alone deserves your allegiance and devotion (Isaiah 48:11). God does not command your worship because He is egotistical; He commands your worship because He knows that nothing less will ultimately satisfy you!

What you delight in, you will treasure.

JESUS WARNS AGAINST A DIVIDED HEART

———

When a person is not walking in her true identity, she will be prone to latch on to something else to satisfy her and to deny God's intention to fulfill the longings of her heart that He alone can fulfill.

MATTHEW 6:19-21, 24

"Do not lay up for yourselves treasures on earth, where moth and rust destroy and where thieves break in and steal, but lay up for yourselves treasures in heaven, where neither moth nor rust destroys and where thieves do not break in and steal. For where your treasure is, there your heart will be also…. No one can serve two masters, for either he will hate the one and love the other, or he will be devoted to the one and despise the other. You cannot serve God and money."

What does it look like for you to lay up treasures on earth?

_____

_____

_____

What does it look like or feel like when you try to serve two masters?

_____

_____

_____

As you walk with Jesus, your desires will increasingly align with your chief purpose for living—to love God, to enjoy Him, and to live for Him in every area of your life. If you try to serve two masters, your heart is divided rather than devoted to God. A divided heart will not bring enduring satisfaction, true delight or peace.

JEREMIAH 2:12-13

"Be appalled, O heavens, at this; be shocked, be utterly desolate, declares the LORD, for my people have committed two evils: they have forsaken me, the fountain of living waters, and hewed out cisterns for themselves, broken cisterns that can hold no water."

In Jeremiah 2:12-13, the prophet Jeremiah issues a warning against those who forsake God, the constant Source of all that is good (the "fountain of living waters"), for something of fleeting or no value (cisterns that are broken and cannot hold water).

When you turn from the "living water," your heart becomes divided—something or someone has captured your affections more than God. This is idolatry.

WHAT IS IDOLATRY?

—

Ken Sande of Peacemaker Ministries defines idolatry as...

"Anytime we long for something apart from God, fear something more than God, or trust in something other than God to make us happy, fulfilled, or secure, we worship a false god." [1]

WHAT DO YOU LEARN ABOUT IDOLS?

Read the following Scriptures and record your response.

1 SAMUEL 12:21

"And do not turn aside after empty things that cannot profit or deliver, for they are empty."
It is something empty and will not deliver.

PSALM 16:4a

The sorrows of those who run after another god shall multiply....
If I live for anything other than God, suffering will increase.

PSALM 119:133

Keep steady my steps according to your promise, and let no iniquity get dominion over me.
If sin has dominion over me, it is an indication of an idol.

EPHESIANS 5:5

For you may be sure of this, that everyone who is sexually immoral or impure, or who is covetous (that is, an idolater), has no inheritance in the kingdom of Christ and God.

COLOSSIANS 3:5-6

Put to death therefore what is earthly in you: sexual immorality, impurity, passion, evil desire, and covetousness, which is idolatry. On account of these the wrath of God is coming.
Giving my heart to worldly passions is idolatry and will incur God's wrath.

The Greek word for covetousness is the "desire to have more"—an insatiable greediness and selfishness.

In what sense is covetousness (a desire to have more) considered idolatry? It is when a person sets her heart, her attention, and her devotion to something other than God.

When you give your devotion to anything more than God, you may feel the need to control the person, situation or thing in a sinful way to secure what you feel you must have. This is idolatry. In reality, you are allowing that person or situation to consume your feelings, thoughts, and actions, and you are giving the idol power to control you. In Lesson 2 you will examine what this control looks like and how it manifests itself.

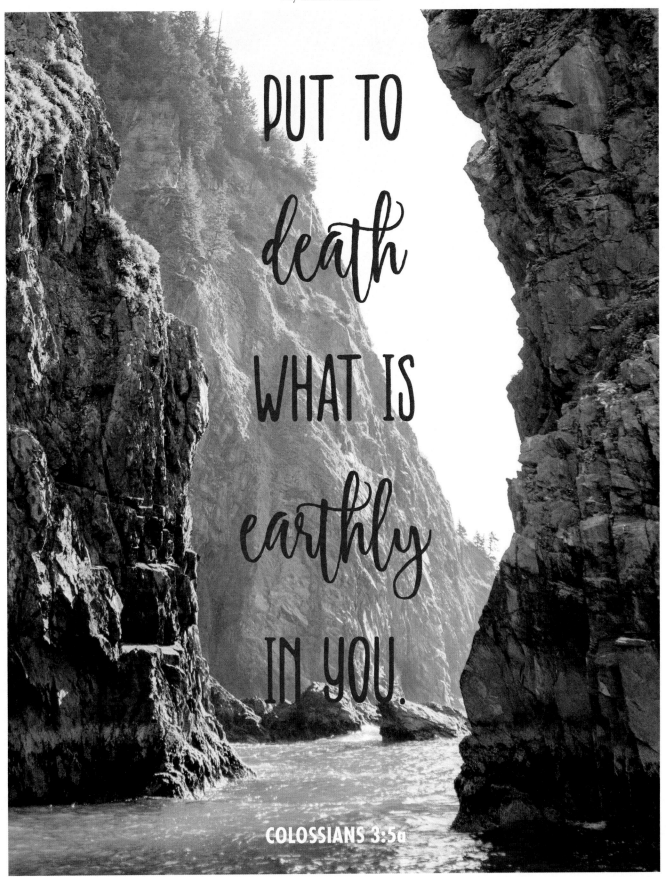

PUT TO death WHAT IS earthly IN YOU.

COLOSSIANS 3:5a

THE SLIPPERY SLOPE FROM DESIRE TO DEMAND

———

I Desire

God has created you with many desires and longings. Your desires are to be submitted to the Father and aligned to His will and purpose, trusting that His desires for you will always result in His glory and your highest quality of life.

Your longings or desires may include:

- Security
- A godly marriage
- Intimacy in marriage
- Children
- A satisfying job/career
- Deep friendships
- Affirmation/validation

- Safety for loved ones
- Salvation for loved ones
- Good health
- A tidy house and order in your home
- Good grades
- To be good, right, or respected
- To be heard, appreciated, loved, or wanted

Review the list above and circle the ones with which you identify.

Do you have desires that are not on this list? Record your thoughts

_____

_____

_____

_____

_____

If a longing or desire (or a real or perceived need) is not being met, it is only natural that you may feel disappointment, hurt, fear, frustration, abandonment, depression, etc. These feelings indicate a struggle in your heart. Your struggle has the potential for two things: 1) to lead you to acknowledge your feelings, to recognize what you desire or feel you need, to surrender this to God in humble dependence, and to trust that He can comfort and satisfy you, or 2) to lead you to believe you deserve what you are desiring to the point of demanding it.

Pause and ask the Lord to align your desires to His.

I Deserve

When the desire/need becomes your focus, it will dictate your choices and behavior and eventually alter your reality. Unmet desires have the potential, if you allow them, to control your life.

When you believe you deserve something, you may view life as "not fair," which results in a grumbling and complaining attitude and reveals your sinful heart.

An "I deserve" attitude may lead to:

- Ingratitude
- Impatience
- Frustration that others do not do or see things your way
- Comparison
- Jealousy

- Blame
- Disbelief that God has your best interest in mind
- Lack of trust in God's plan
- Lack of perseverance through struggles and hardships
- Anger

FDQ: Are you able to identify your response pattern? If so, ask God to help you catch it in the moment of temptation and confess it.

I Demand

A desire has become a demand when you feel and believe you cannot be content—you cannot be fulfilled--unless the desire is met. It is common to justify or legitimize a desire. At this point the desire has progressed to a demand. Although the desire may not be inherently wrong, it has grown so strong that it begins to control your thoughts and your behavior. It has become something you must have. The more you think you are entitled to something, the more convinced you will become that you cannot live without it. The demand has become an idol.

Use the following to assess if a desire has become a demand—an idol:

- I cannot be okay unless _____.
- What is it that I want so much right now that I am willing to offend God in order to get it?
- Am I letting anger fester in my heart? What do I believe is standing in my way of getting something I feel I must have?
- What desire or longing may be taking God's rightful place in my heart right now?
- What is stopping me from loving God with all my heart, mind, soul, and strength?
- How is this desire/longing affecting my relationship with God? My relationship with others?

If you recognize that something other than God has captured your heart, consider praying this prayer:

Create in me a clean heart, O God, and renew a right spirit within me....
Restore to me the joy of your salvation, and uphold me with a willing spirit.

PSALM 51:10, 12

END YOUR STUDY...

Summarize what you learned from this lesson

Reflection

Meditate on the following Scripture:

I love you, O LORD, my strength.
The LORD is my rock and my fortress and my deliverer,
my God, my rock, in whom I take refuge,
my shield, and the horn of my salvation, my stronghold.
I call upon the LORD, who is worthy to be praised,
and I am saved from my enemies.

PSALM 18:1-3

Do you relate to God as your strength, rock, fortress, deliverer, refuge, shield, and horn of salvation? Is God your strength when you are overwhelmed? Is God your rock in difficult times? Is God your refuge when you are afraid? Is God your shield when you are being attacked? If not God, who or what do you run to in these times? This is a great check to identify who or what you are desiring and trusting more than God. Talk to Jesus about this and ask Him to help you make David's prayer in Psalm 18 a reflection of your heart.

LESSON 2

My Controlling Heart

In Lesson 1 you learned that a longing moves from a desire (real or perceived need) to a demand when you must have something or someone to be okay or content. This demand becomes an idol, a functional god, when you give it power to control you. At this point your heart has become divided because you are putting the object of desire in the place of God. When you do, the idol will dictate your beliefs and actions.

A divided heart is not able to fully trust God because it has allowed someone or something to "occupy the place that should be occupied by God alone."[1] In this lesson you will explore your controlling heart—your control responses and their underlying fears that result when your heart is divided.

IDOLS REINFORCE YOUR WRONG BELIEFS

––––

An idol affects your beliefs and your actions, and to the degree it controls you, you will develop control-responses—responses rooted in fear that lead you to control a person or a situation. You may increasingly justify and defend your wrong belief and resist surrendering it to the Lord. In addition, your view of reality will become increasingly distorted.

"

[Your] idols define good and evil in ways contrary to God's definitions. They establish a locus of control that is earth-bound: either in objects (e.g. lust for money), other people (e.g. I need to please my father), or myself (e.g. attainment of my personal goals). Such false gods create false laws, false definitions of success and failure, of values and stigma. Idols promise blessings and warn of curses for those who succeed or fail against the law: "If you get a large enough IRA, you will be secure. If I can get certain people to like and respect me, then my life is valid." [2]

DAVID POWLISON

RECOGNIZING THE STRUGGLE

––––

When you trust in something other than God, you are denying God His proper place in your life. You are not glorifying Him—reflecting an accurate understanding of Him—because you doubt who He is, what He has done, and what He has promised.

Jesus is in control of all people and all things at all times (Ephesians 1:22 – "And he put all things under his feet and gave him as head over all things to the church"). If you do not believe this, you may feel like you must be in charge because you fear God is not. Your fears may lead you to doubt that God is going to come through for you. You doubt that He is going to "get it right." You may work hard to figure out how to coerce God to carry out your plan. You no longer treat God as God. When this happens, self takes charge. The result is you are believing a lie that manifests itself as fear.

FEAR IN ITS MANY FORMS

———

Fear may be an appropriate emotional response in certain situations. In the midst of fear, you may not be able to control your physical symptoms (increased heart rate, sweating, shortness of breath, fuzzy thinking, nauseousness, etc.), but you always have an opportunity to choose to trust God. As fear arises, you remember that everything depends on the Lord, not you. In Psalm 23, David chose to walk with God through his fear. "Even though I walk through the valley of the shadow of death, I will fear no evil, for you are with me; your rod and your staff, they will comfort me" (Psalm 23:4). Even in dark times when evil, danger or uncertainty mark your path, the Lord is your Good Shepherd who is with you, protects you, and comforts you.

"

I don't think it's possible to not worry at all—it's human nature and of course things that we cannot control tend to crowd our thoughts. It's been through the last year and a half that I've realized there is a response to worry that can become worship. In choosing to acknowledge that our fear is a very REAL FEAR but that God is not only in control but FOR US, we can surrender that fear in worship to Him. It's not that the worry has left us, but rather it's found its home. It's found its home with the One who died so we could be with Him. Our worry can be safely handed over to the Overseer of our souls.

ELIZABETH WEHMANN

When fear controls you, you are choosing to believe the lie that God is not in control of the situation. Fear left unchecked grows into dread and terror, and manifests itself in many forms:

- Fear of the unknown
- Fear of the future
- Fear of failure
- Fear of missing out
- Fear of rejection
- Fear of consequences

- Fear of exposure
- Fear of pain and suffering
- Fear of loss (health, financial, relationship, security, reputation)
- _____
- _____

Initially fear may be a helpful response because it signals that you are in some way unsettled or hurting. It provides you an opportunity to check your heart, identify your feelings, and acknowledge you are in a struggle to fight the temptation to sin. In your struggle, you have two choices. You will either humble yourself and yield to the Father, or you will remain prideful and yield to sin (1 Peter 5:6-7).

Sadly, the struggle may lead you to tighten your grip in an attempt to make right the things you feel are not okay. You choose to sin by remaining in control, which feeds your fear and your need to have your way with a person or situation. The influence of culture, Satan, and your flesh (Ephesians 2:1-3) tempt you to believe you can handle life on your own.

Modern western culture promotes self-dependence and the illusion that a person has control over her life, or at the very least her daily decisions. So when something is not okay and she is unable to make it okay, she may become fearful and respond in an attempt to control/fix the person or situation. Her action may work to some degree per her desire. But often her external influence will be limited or will not effectuate a lasting change. And even if it does, it may not truly be what is best for herself or for the other person or situation.

"

If we can't say "thy will be done" from the bottom of our hearts, we will never know any peace. We feel compelled to try to control people and control our environment and make things the way we believe they ought to be. Yet to control life like this is beyond our abilities, and we will just dash ourselves upon the rocks.[3]

TIMOTHY KELLER

CONTROL-RESPONSES

———

A person will rely on control-responses to try to manage her world and protect herself, someone, or something when she is fearful and choosing to not trust God.

The responses fall into two main categories:

- Flight
- Fight

Note: A third response is feeling paralyzed—thinking that you have no control or ability to choose and feeling overwhelmed or hopeless.

IDENTIFY YOUR "GO-TO" CONTROL-RESPONSES.

Review the chart below and **circle** your "go-to" control-responses. If you are unsure, ask the Holy Spirit to help you identify them.

Flight	*Fight*
Withdrawing	Arguing
Hiding	Aggressive
People-pleasing	Manipulating
Minimizing sin	Intimidating
Escaping	Convincing
Denying	Anger
Acting as a martyr/victim	Escaping
Avoiding conflict	Acting as a martyr/victim
Fantasizing	Being negative or critical
Focusing on another's sin	Condemning
Blaming others	Focusing on another's sin
Lying/deceiving	Blaming others
Numbing	Lying/deceiving
	Being passive-aggressive

You will notice "escaping" is on both sides of control-responses. Why is this the case?
Escape is expressed in many ways. A person may escape by turning to excessive behaviors (e.g., exercise, overeat, unhealthy control of food, pleasure) or addictive behavior (e.g., substance abuse, pornography, a sexual encounter or an affair).

FDQ: When a person's control strategies do not appear to work, she may become hopeless. The ultimate escape is suicide.

ASK GOD TO SEARCH YOUR HEART

Acknowledge and confess your sinful behaviors to the Lord, **receive** His forgiveness, and **ask Him** to help you trust Him.

You will notice that the fear and control-responses are listed on the My Heart Unveiled Chart.

It is likely that after considering the flight and fight responses, as well as the list of underlying fears, a situation has come to your mind where you exhibited one or more of these behaviors and felt one or more of these fears. In Lesson 3 - My Surrendered Heart, you will have an opportunity to further process this information using the My Heart Unveiled chart.

END YOUR STUDY...

Summarize what you learned from this lesson

Meditate on the following Scripture:

I know, O Lord, that the way of man is not in himself, that it is not in man who walks to direct his steps.
Correct me, O Lord....

JEREMIAH 10:23-24a

—— **LESSON 3** ——

My Surrendered Heart

In Lesson 2 you were introduced to underlying fears and sinful control-responses that lead a person to try to control someone or something, including self.

In this lesson you will learn what it means to surrender control to God and confidently trust Him, assured that He will care for you in every situation.

WHAT DOES IT MEAN TO SURRENDER TO THE LORD JESUS CHRIST?

———

Jesus is always inviting you to come to Him to receive what you truly need. "Come to me, all who labor and are heavy laden, and I will give you rest. Take my yoke upon you, and learn from me, for I am gentle and lowly in heart, and you will find rest for your souls. For my yoke is easy, and my burden is light" (Matthew 11:28-30).

To "surrender" means saying to the Lord Jesus, "You mean more to me than my desires and my perceived needs. And even if my desires are not fulfilled in this life, You are enough." It is trusting that God uses discontentment to mercifully remind you that the things of this world can never replace God.

"

If I find in myself a desire which no experience in this world can satisfy, the most probable explanation is that I was made for another world. If none of my earthly pleasures satisfy it, that does not prove that the universe is a fraud. Probably earthly pleasures were never meant to satisfy it, but only to arouse it, or suggest the real thing. If that is so, I must take care, on the one hand, never to despise, or be unthankful for, these earthly blessings, and on the other, never to mistake them for the something else of which they are only a kind of copy, or echo, or mirage.[1]

C.S. LEWIS

When you acknowledge your discontentment and feel the struggle and pain, yet choose to believe that God's will is best, you are surrendering to Jesus and setting your eyes on the world that is to come. When Christ returns, all will be made right, and what you were created for will be yours.

"

If we do not aim for the new heaven and the new earth, many of our values and decisions in this world will be myopic, unworthy, tarnished, fundamentally wrongheaded. To put the matter bluntly: Can biblical spirituality survive where Christians are not oriented to the world to come?[2]

D.A. CARSON

Surrender is the practice of humbly submitting your will to His will. Every day, whether all is well in your world or you are going through a crisis or significant temptation, you have an opportunity to submit your will to His and tell the Father, "You mean more to me than everything else. May your will be done on earth as it is in heaven." As you surrender, you hold fast to Jesus by reminding yourself of Who He is and what He has done. He is eager to graciously help you all of the time (Hebrews 4:14-15).

JESUS' EXAMPLE OF SURRENDING TO THE FATHER

——

• *Jesus had a daily practice of going to the Father.*

MARK 1:35

And rising very early in the morning, while it was still dark, he departed and went out to a desolate place, and there he prayed.

LUKE 22:39

And he came out and went, as was his custom, to the Mount of Olives [to pray], and the disciples followed him.

• *Jesus' one goal in life was to do the Father's will.*

JOHN 4:34

Jesus said to them, "My food is to do the will of him who sent me and to accomplish his work."

• *Jesus faithfully ran the race marked out for Him in this life by setting the joy of heaven before Him.*

HEBREWS 12: 2

Jesus, the founder and perfecter of our faith, who for the joy that was set before him endured the cross....

Yet Jesus' human struggle was clearly seen on several occasions. In the Garden of Gethsemane, Jesus' response most clearly demonstrated both His struggle and His resolve to surrender.

READ MATTHEW 26:36-44; MARK 14:32-42; LUKE 22:41-44.

Describe Jesus' struggle and agony. What did He ask of the Father and what did He relinquish? Who did the Father send to help Him? What does this demonstrate?

Jesus asked His disciples to pray (more than once).

Jesus was in agony; He was sorrowful and troubled.

Jesus asked the Father to remove the cup—Jesus asked for another way, a way out.

Jesus prayed earnestly and experienced anguish. While Jesus was in anguish He did not lose hope in the mission or the Father.

The Father sent an angel. This is evidence of Jesus' great need; His Father provided care.

Jesus was resolved to carry out the Father's will.

Jesus acknowledged that all things are possible for Father God.

Hebrews 5:7-9 is a beautiful picture of Jesus' surrendered heart: "In the days of his flesh, Jesus offered up prayers and supplications, with loud cries and tears, to him who was able to save him from death, and he was heard because of his reverence. Although he was a son, he learned obedience through what he suffered. And being made perfect, he became the source of eternal salvation to all who obey him."

- Jesus implored His Father with loud cries and tears.
- Jesus was confident that God heard His cries and would answer Him.
- Jesus learned obedience and submitted to His Father's will.

What does it mean that Jesus "learned obedience"?

Jesus was never disobedient (Hebrews 4:15; 7:26), but his sufferings provided opportunities to demonstrate and practice obedience—the testing ground for Him to be "made perfect" (teleios). In this way "he learned obedience."

Following Jesus' Example

When you are dissatisfied with someone or something, or when you feel overwhelmed and fearful, you will be tempted to control—to manage a person or circumstance. Be aware that it is a struggle to fight temptation and not give in to sin. In these moments, follow Christ's example and bring all your concerns, fears, and requests to the Father. In the practice of going to the Father and casting your cares on Him (1 Peter 5:7; Psalm 55:22), you are choosing to surrender to God and to offer Him your burdens as a sacrifice of praise. This distinguishes one who has a divided, controlling heart from one who is willing to bring every thought, emotion, action under submission to God (2 Corinthians 10:5; John 14:15; Revelations 14:12), trusting that Jesus will care for you in every way.

DEEPEN YOUR DEPENDENCE ON THE FATHER

You bring your emotions under submission to God...

- by expressing them to Him
- by asking God to reveal what you are thinking about the person or situation and how it aligns with His truth
- by renewing your mind in truth
- by obeying His direction

FDQ: Refer to and review the following: Part 2 Lesson 3 – Your ability to think rightly will determine what you feel and choose. Your emotions are a response to your beliefs, longings, desires, and circumstances and serve as a gauge to your inner and outer world. Your right choosing flows from your right thinking. When you choose to follow God's truth, your emotions may not immediately fall in line with the truth, but as you choose to trust God, your feelings will align with your godly choice.

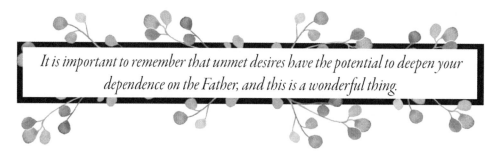

It is important to remember that unmet desires have the potential to deepen your dependence on the Father, and this is a wonderful thing.

Be like Jesus:

- Approach the Father confidently.
- Implore the Father passionately and relentlessly.
- Humble yourself before the Father.
- Pour out your feelings and thoughts to the Father.
- Believe the Father hears your cries and responds.
- Trust and obey the Father completely.
- Know that you will receive grace and mercy to help you in your time of need. (Hebrews 4:16)

What does the alternative look like?

WHAT DO YOU LEARN ABOUT SURRENDER?

Read the following Scriptures and record your response to the questions associated with each verse.

What is the connection between submitting to God and resisting the devil?

JAMES 4:7

Submit yourselves therefore to God. Resist the devil, and he will flee from you.

When I submit to God I am able to resist the devil, and when I resist him, he must flee. God gives me the desire and the power.

What are the two commands? How are they related? What are the promises?

1 PETER 5:6-7

Humble yourselves, therefore, under the mighty hand of God so that at the proper time he may exalt you, casting all your anxieties on him, because he cares for you.

The two commands are to humble myself and to cast my cares on God.

In order to truly cast my cares on God (which means I am turning over my cares to Him – thrusting them on Him), I have to humble myself and acknowledge that I am not in control and acknowledge God is in control and is caring for me all the time in every way. Pride keeps me from casting my cares on God and keeps me believing that I can fix the person or situation.

The promise is that God will exalt me. To exalt means "to lift up." He may exalt me in this life, but definitely when Christ appears (Colossians 3:4).

What does it mean to "crucify the flesh"? Daily, what does this look like?

GALATIANS 5:24

And those who belong to Christ Jesus have crucified the flesh with its passions and desires.

To crucify the flesh means to not let my fleshly desires rule over me, putting to death the sinful desires that still reside in me. This is a continual process that I must engage in daily by asking the Holy Spirit to reveal to me my selfish heart (thoughts and actions), confessing these to the Lord, and asking His help to turn from sin and do what is right.

What should compel you to live for Him instead of yourself?

2 CORINTHIANS 5:14-15

For the love of Christ controls us, because we have concluded this: that one has died for all, therefore all have died; and he died for all, that those who live might no longer live for themselves but for him who for their sake died and was raised.

My love for God is what should always motivate me/compel me to obey God and live for Him.

Ponder

In relinquishing control and surrendering to God, you are opening your hands to Him, trusting Him in what He has for you and placing control where it belongs—in God. How do you know if you are living surrendered to the Father? Consider the following questions. The answers to these questions will help you discern the posture of your heart.

- What am I feeling right now?
- Over what am I feeling anxious?
- Over what am I despairing?
- What or who am I trying to protect?
- Am I spending an excessive amount of time thinking about someone or something?
- Am I spending an excessive amount of money or resources on someone or something?
- What am I seeking for happiness and satisfaction?
- Is there something I desire so much that I am willing to disappoint or hurt someone in order to have it?
- Is there something I desire so much that I am willing to sin because I do not have it?
- What am I loving, serving, trusting, and worshiping?
- What do I fear more than I fear sinning against God?
- Whose opinion am I valuing over God's?
- How do I respond when I am criticized or corrected? (You can judge how much you value and worship other people's opinions by your honest response to this question.)
- How much self-justifying am I doing to approve of myself or to gain the approval of others?

Be aware, you can become idolatrous about your own ability to diagnose yourself. Be careful of spending too much time digging around your heart or believing that if you get it all figured out, you will be free from sin. Remember—you have been justified and given a perfect record by the only One in the universe whose opinion matters.

MY HEART UNVEILED CHART EXERCISE

Think of a situation and complete the My Heart Unveiled chart, specifically considering your fear and control-responses. The next time you meet with your discipleship group, you will be given an opportunity to discuss your completed chart with the goal of revealing your self-protecting strategies and uncovering what a surrendered heart might look like.

END YOUR STUDY...

Summarize what you learned from this lesson

My Heart Unveiled

My situation

_____

_____

_____

My response

FEELING	THINKING	CHOOSING

Why am I responding this way?

PERCEIVED NEED/DESIRE	CONTROL-RESPONSES	UNDERLYING BELIEF/FEARS

Steps to walk in obedience

GOD'S TRUTH	ACTION STEPS

(Refer to My Heart Unveiled Instructions on p. 118)

My Heart Unveiled

Common Control-Responses & Fears

CONTROL-RESPONSES:

Flight	*Fight*
Withdrawing	Arguing
Hiding	Manipulating
People-pleasing	Intimidating
Minimizing sin	Convincing
Escaping	Anger
Denying	Escaping
Acting as a martyr/victim	Acting as a martyr/victim
Avoiding conflict	Being negative or critical
Fantasizing	Condemning
Focusing on another's sin	Focusing on another's sin
Blaming others	Blaming others
Lying/deceiving	Lying/deceiving
Numbing	Being passive-agressive
Denying	

UNDERLYING BELIEFS/FEARS:

- Fear of the unknown
- Fear of the future
- Fear of failure
- Fear of missing out
- Fear of rejection

- Fear of consequences
- Fear of exposure
- Fear of pain and suffering
- Fear of loss (health, financial, relationship, security, reputation)

Meditate on the following Scripture:

Therefore, since we are surrounded by so great a cloud of witnesses, let us also lay aside every weight, and sin which clings so closely, and let us run with endurance the race that is set before us, looking to Jesus, the founder and perfecter of our faith, who for the joy that was set before him endured the cross, despising the shame, and is seated at the right hand of the throne of God. Consider him who endured from sinners such hostility against himself, so that you may not grow weary or fainthearted.

HEBREWS 12:1-3

LESSON 4

My Grieving Heart

As you discovered in Lesson 1, a desire (real or perceived need) has the potential to control your life. The person or object of your longing becomes an idol once you fixate on it and believe you must have it. At this point the idol controls and enslaves you while you desperately try to control it.

In Lesson 2 you identified underlying fears and resulting control-responses—things you do to try to control and protect your world or the world of someone you love.

Next, in Lesson 3 you learned that as you surrender your control and entrust the person or situation to God, you are confessing your need for God and choosing to trust Him. It is important to acknowledge and address the reality that as you relinquish control, you may experience deep loss, pain, and sorrow. In this lesson you will examine how to walk through the pain of unmet longings and painful losses.

As you practice a surrendered life, you will need to surrender your control of some very difficult situations as well as some less grievous ones. In either case, the sense of loss may be significant, and in order to truly trust God it will be necessary for you to recognize your pain. Allow yourself to mourn even if and when the pain seems disproportionate to the situation. Never minimize your pain.

For example: Your adult child is choosing to use drugs. You cannot stop him or effectively control him, yet you witness his life spiraling out-of-control. Though there may be some helpful things you can do, truly you know that you cannot change him. But God can, so you surrender your son's life and his choices one by one to the Lord. This is at times an agonizing moment-by-moment process, one in which you may fear the loss of your reputation as a parent. You may experience the loss of dreams for your child, the loss of hope for him, the loss of relationship with him. You may even fear the loss of his very life. In this painful process of surrender you are experiencing various losses that result in grief.

GRIEVING AND MOURNING

——

Many situations in your life may cause grief or pain. Perhaps you have lost a close relationship, or a position, or your health, or a home, or something else of value to you. Perhaps you have been sinned against. Your losses and hurts result in great pain and an array of feelings such as abandonment, fear, anger, hurt, sadness, shame, disappointment or despair. Whatever the reason, it is important to mourn (lament) your pain. To lament is to feel and express sorrow or regret or grief.

As you grieve you must allow yourself to mourn/lament. It is not enough to only feel the pain. Grief is the emotional response to loss. Mourning is the behavioral response, the act of actually sorrowing or lamenting in response to the grief. If you do not allow yourself to mourn, the grief will build up and express itself in harmful ways. Christian Psychologist, Freda Crews, once stated, "Grief demands satisfaction."[1] If you push down the pain of loss, it will eventually come out physically, emotionally or relationally. Anxiety and depression can result from unexpressed grief.

The Mourning/Lamenting Process

Your grief does not have a timeline. Contemporary research no longer supports the theory that grief occurs in five easily defined stages. This means your grief may take different forms at different times, resulting in varied and at times intense emotion. Your painful emotions must find expression. Acknowledge your pain. Allow yourself to feel your pain. Express your pain with tears. Do not hold them back. Pray out loud to God, expressing your feelings to Him. Do not be afraid to express your disappointment, frustration, helplessness, hopelessness, sadness, fear, confusion, sense of feeling overwhelmed or betrayed, as well as your anger. By expressing your anger, you are able to release it to God. Otherwise a root of bitterness may grow toward God or toward another person.

Victoria Alexander, a prominent grief educator, concluded that grief has three needs.

A need to:

1. Find words to express loss.

2. Say words aloud.

3. Know your words have been heard.[2]

In praying your pain out loud to your Father, you are accomplishing these three things, knowing your Father hears and cares.

Examples in Scripture

Scripture is filled with lament. Habakkuk cried out to God regarding the coming judgment of Israel. "O Lord, how long shall I cry for help, and you will not hear? Or cry to you 'Violence!' and you will not save?" (Habakkuk 1:2). The book of Lamentations is one long lament. "Arise, cry out in the night at the beginning of the night watches! Pour out your heart like water before the presence of the Lord!" (Lamentations 2:19a). Our Savior, too, cried out in lament on many occasions. As Jesus approached Jerusalem (the triumphal entry), Jesus grieved the Jews' rejection of Him and what that would mean for their future. "And when he [Jesus] drew near and saw the city, he wept over it, saying, 'Would that you, even you, had known on this day the things that make for peace! But now they are hidden from your eyes'" (Luke 19:41-42).

The lament psalms are more in number than any other category of psalms (about 40%) and express the heartfelt cries and honest pleas of the troubled, hurting psalmists to God whom they trusted and chose to praise. You can do the same—cry out to God, ask Him for help, and choose to trust and praise Him.

WHAT EMOTIONS ARE EXPRESSED?

Read the following Scriptures and record your response.

PSALM 22:1-3

My God, my God, why have you forsaken me? Why are you so far from saving me, from the words of my groaning? O my God, I cry by day, but you do not answer, and by night, but I find no rest. Yet you are holy, enthroned on the praises of Israel.

PSALM 44:23-25

Awake! Why are you sleeping, O LORD? Rouse yourself! Do not reject us forever! Why do you hide your face? Why do you forget our affliction and oppression? For our soul is bowed down to the dust; our belly clings to the ground.

The Psalmist feels as if God is not listening to his cries. He may be feeling desperate, angry, and/or frustrated.

PSALM 13:1-2; 5-6

How long, O LORD? Will you forget me forever? How long will you hide your face from me? How long must I take counsel in my soul and have sorrow in my heart all the day?...But I have trusted in your steadfast love; my heart shall rejoice in your salvation. I will sing to the Lord, because he has dealt bountifully with me.

The Psalmist feels the Lord has turned his back on him. He feels cut off from the Lord. He may be feeling hopelessness, sadness, and/or despondency since he has no peace.

PSALM 57:1-4

Be merciful to me, O God, be merciful to me, for in you my soul takes refuge; in the shadow of your wings I will take refuge, till the storms of destruction pass by. I cry out to God Most High, to God who fulfills his purpose for me. He will send from heaven and save me; he will put to shame him who tramples on me. Selah God will send out his steadfast love and his faithfulness! My soul is in the midst of lions; I lie down amid fiery beasts—the children of man, whose teeth are spears and arrows, whose tongues are sharp swords.

You may be surprised by some of the emotions expressed in the above prayers. You may also be surprised by some of your emotions as you express your pain to God in prayer; however, God is not surprised nor is He put-off by your emotions or your expression of pain. He is near to the broken-hearted.

Keep in mind that you can mourn a loss, expressing all your emotions to God, and yet not surrender the situation or person to God. By not surrendering the situation or person for which you still feel the need to control, you are not able to access God's resources of peace, comfort, and direction in the mourning process. Also, be aware that surrender is not usually a one-time action. In a season of mourning you may need to surrender over and again, each time the painful emotions come up. Continual surrender is an important part of mourning "well." Mourning "well" means to allow yourself to feel your emotions, to surrender them to the Lord, and to continue to move through the painful season without getting stuck in the pain.

Are you presently in a season of grief? Have you surrendered it to God? If not, take time now to do so.

_____

_____

_____

_____

_____

_____

_____

_____

_____

FDQ: If you have experienced a significant loss, would you be willing to share your grieving and mourning experience?

ENGAGING YOUR WILL AND YOUR MIND
―――

As you mourn, honestly expressing your feelings to God, it is important to also engage your will (your ability to choose) and your mind (your thinking). In Timothy Keller's book, *Walking With God Through Pain and Suffering*, Keller describes how Paul tells his readers in Philippians 4:8 to "think (*logizdomai*) about these things" and Romans 8:18 to "consider (*logizdomai*) that the sufferings of this present time are not worth comparing with the glory that is to be revealed to us."[1] The word *logizdomai* is an accounting word sometimes translated "to reckon" or "to count up." Paul is telling his readers to "count up" the truths of God. This is a response of the will and the mind even if the emotions do not seem to agree.

HOW DID THE PSALMIST AND JEREMIAH COUNT GOD'S TRUTHS IN THE MIDDLE OF PAIN?
Read the following Psalm and record your response.

PSALM 42:3-5
My tears have been my food day and night, while they say to me all the day long, "Where is your God?" These things I remember, as I pour out my soul: how I would go with the throng and lead them in procession to the house of God with glad shouts and songs of praise, a multitude keeping festival. Why are you cast down, O my soul, and why are you in turmoil within me? Hope in God; for I shall again praise him, my salvation and my God.

The Psalmist remembers God's faithfulness and goodness in his past.
The Psalmist hopes in God as he looks to the future.
The Psalmist acknowledges God as his salvation.
The Psalmist speaks these truths to himself (his soul).

LAMENTATIONS 3:17-25
My soul is bereft of peace; I have forgotten what happiness is; so I say, "My endurance has perished; so has my hope from the Lord." Remember my affliction and wanderings, the wormwood and the gall! My soul continually remembers it and is bowed down within me. But this I call to mind, and therefore I have hope: The steadfast love of the Lord never ceases; his mercies never come to an end; they are new every morning; great is your faithfulness. "The Lord is my portion," says my soul, "therefore I will hope in him." The Lord is good to those who wait for him, to the soul who seeks him.

Jeremiah also "counted up" God's truths when he chose to call to his mind God's faithfulness and steadfast love even as he expressed his pain.

COUNT UP GOD'S WONDERFUL TRUTHS

———

Read the following Scriptures as reminders to "count up" God's wonderful truths. They will bring comfort to your soul in your times of grief.

PSALM 3:3

But you, O LORD, are a shield about me, my glory, and the lifter of my head.

PSALM 27:13-14

I believe that I shall look upon the goodness of the LORD in the land of the living! Wait for the Lord; be strong, and let your heart take courage; wait for the LORD!

PSALM 34:18

The LORD is near to the brokenhearted and saves the crushed in spirit.

PSALM 40:5

You have multiplied, O LORD my God, your wondrous deeds and your thoughts toward us; none can compare with you! I will proclaim and tell of them, yet they are more than can be told.

PSALM 56:8

You have kept count of my tossings; put my tears in your bottle. Are they not in your book?

2 CORINTHIANS 1:3-4a

Blessed be the God and Father of our Lord Jesus Christ, the Father of mercies and God of all comfort, who comforts us in all our affliction....

FDQ: Is there a Scripture that has encouraged you during your grief?

END YOUR STUDY...

Summarize what you learned from this lesson

"GRIEVING"

———

A personal testimony

My firstborn turns 8 years old this fall. I had hoped we would've conceived at least two more precious littles by this time in our journey. There's a cloud of sadness that follows me around, in my not-yet-met longing for more children. The sadness cloud swells and rains when certain dates or markers are reached, and still our family hasn't grown beyond the three of us. Sometimes there are triggers that catch me off guard. The past several years, filing our tax return, of all things, has been a trigger of grief for me. One question is a fill-in of the anticipated number of children to be claimed as dependents for the following tax year. It hurts my heart to keep filling in a "1" year after year.

One challenge in my grief that I didn't anticipate are the days when my daughter is teary because of her not-yet-met longing for siblings. One such day came after swim class. Dripping and wrapped in a towel, she looked up at me with distress in her eyes and a quivering lower lip, "Mama?" she said with a shaky voice, "When will you have a baby? It seems like everyone at swim school has a brother or sister in another class that they get to wave to and make faces at across the pool...everyone but me. I want a sister to wave to so bad." Her chin dropped to her chest and she began to cry.

My heart ached as I enveloped her in a hug and held her there for a short time before responding. "I want more children in our family, too, and I often feel sad about it. But it's really important to me that you know—at the exact same time that I feel sad, I also deeply trust the story that God is writing for our family. I have trusted and followed Jesus since I was a little girl like you, and all my life I've watched how His plans, His ways, and His timing have always been best. He's never ultimately disappointed me in decades of following Him. I'm sad like you that God hasn't yet grown our family, but I really, really do trust Him."

Reflection

Think of a time of grief in your life. Perhaps you have never acknowledged and thanked God for His faithfulness to meet you in your pain. Take time now to do so. Even if you have thanked Him in the past, once again recall His kindness and provision, and praise Him for His faithfulness.

LESSON 5

My Worshiping Heart

You learned in Lessons 1-3 that you must surrender your fears, demands, and control in order to have a whole heart toward God. A whole heart toward God allows you to see Him for who He is. It frees you to worship Him.

WORSHIP DEFINED

———

The Hebrew word for worship is *shachah* (Strong's number 7812), and the Greek word is *proskuneo* (Strong's number 4505). Both words mean "to bow down."

To "bow down" before God is not just a physical posture but a heart posture, one of humility.

The word "worship" comes from the word "worthy." True worship comes from a reverent, humble heart toward God. It affirms that God has worth and that He is worthy of our complete adoration and devotion. In corporate worship we exalt God together—we speak and sing about how good, beautiful, wonderful, and awesome God is. He is worthy. The same attitude of worship should be a part of our daily lives.

According to Webster's Dictionary (1828), worship is "to honor with extravagant love and extreme submission. Worship "express[es] the beauty of holiness through an extravagant or exaggerated love for God, and you...live in extreme or excessive submission to God."[1]

As you more and more behold the glory of God, your desire to honor Him and to show Him extravagant love will grow.

"

The glory of God also means his supreme importance. The Hebrew word for "glory" is "kabod", which means "weight,"—literally God's weightiness.... When the Bible says that God is glorious, it means he should matter, and does matter, more than anything else or anyone else. And if anything matters to you more than God, you are not acknowledging his glory. You are giving glory to something else.[2]

TIMOTHY KELLER

Having a right view of God—rightly understanding the fear of God—is essential to true worship.

The Fear of the Lord

There are more than 150 references to "fear of the Lord" in the Bible.

WHAT DOES IT MEAN TO FEAR THE LORD?

The fear of the Lord is "that indefinable mixture of reverence, fear, pleasure, joy and awe which fills our hearts when we realize who God is and what He has done for us."[3] The fear of the Lord gives you the right understanding of God in order to truly worship Him. You will have a firmer grasp of what Psalm 111:10a means when it states "[t]he fear of the Lord is the beginning of wisdom." When you do not understand who God is, and what it means to fear Him, you may be prone to be complacent or cavalier about your sins and sinful patterns.

"

"Safe?" said Mr. Beaver; "don't you hear what Mrs. Beaver tells you? Who said anything about safe? 'Course he isn't safe. But he's good. He's the King, I tell you."

C.S. LEWIS, *The Lion, the Witch, and the Wardrobe*

WHAT DO YOU LEARN ABOUT THE FEAR OF THE LORD?

Write out the following verses and record your response.

PROVERBS 1:7

The fear of the Lord is the beginning of knowledge; fools despise wisdom and instruction.

PSALM 86:11

Teach me your way, O Lord, that I may walk in your truth; unite my heart to fear your name.

MATTHEW 10:28

And do not fear those who kill the body but cannot kill the soul. Rather fear him who can destroy both soul and body in hell.

The word "fear" in both the Hebrew (*yir-a*) and the Greek (*phobos*) means "to have terror" or "causing fear." It also means "respect, reverence and a sense of awe."

CC

These two common uses of the word "fear" in the vocabulary of the people of biblical times (and also in some measure in our vocabulary) are both included in the biblical notion of the fear of God.

There is a legitimate sense in which the fear of God involves being afraid of God, being gripped with terror and dread. Though this is not the dominant thought in Scripture, it is there nonetheless.

The second aspect of fear, which is peculiar to the true children of God, is the fear of veneration, honor, and awe with which we regard our God. It is a fear that leads us not to run from Him but to draw near to Him through Jesus Christ and gladly submit to Him in faith, love, and obedience.[3]

ALBERT MARTIN

THE GOSPEL AND THE FEAR OF THE LORD

——

Because of the punishment that Christ endured for you on the cross, if you have put your faith and trust in Him, you need not fear God for "the day of wrath when God's righteous judgment will be revealed" (Romans 2:5).

JEREMIAH 17:14, 17

Heal me, O Lord, and I shall be healed; save me and I shall be saved, for you are my praise…. Be not a terror to me; you are my refuge in the day of disaster.

When you truly understand the gospel message, how without God's plan of redemption to "heal" and "save" you from the "day of disaster," you cannot help but marvel and tremble at God's "spotless holiness, inflexible justice, incomprehensible wisdom, omnipotent power, and holy love."[5] Seeing the infinite beauty and excellence of God causes you to respond in gratitude and worship.

CC

Nothing is so well fitted to put the fear of God—which will preserve men from offending him— into the heart, as an enlightened view of the cross of Christ…. Nowhere does justice appear so awful, mercy so amiable, or wisdom so profound.[6]

JOHN BROWN

As you mature, is your gaze increasingly set on the cross?
In your daily life, how do you recall/remember what God has done for you?

ACCEPTABLE WORSHIP IS IN SPIRIT AND TRUTH

WHAT KIND OF WORSHIPERS IS THE FATHER SEEKING?

Read the following verses and record your response.

JOHN 4:23-24

"But the hour is coming, and is now here, when the true worshipers will worship the Father in spirit and truth, for the Father is seeking such people to worship him. God is spirit, and those who worship him must worship in spirit and truth."

ROMANS 12:1

I appeal to you therefore, brothers, by the mercies of God, to present your bodies as a living sacrifice, holy and acceptable to God, which is your spiritual worship.

HEBREWS 12:28-29

Therefore let us be grateful for receiving a kingdom that cannot be shaken, and thus let us offer to God acceptable worship, with reverence and awe, for our God is a consuming fire.

God desires that I worship Him in a genuine way—in spirit and truth. He desires my worship to be marked by reverence and awe.

In your own words explain what it means to worship God in spirit and in truth?

What is unacceptable worship?

Worshiping God in spirit is only possible for the follower of Christ because God's Spirit makes your spirit alive and ignites and energizes your spirit to worship Him.

Worshiping God in truth is worshiping Him in His fullness, not taking only a part of Him. Worshiping God in truth is to have a proper view of Him based in His Word—to understand the fullness of all of God's characteristics. Seeing God rightly for who He is will propel you, motivate you, and challenge you to resist making yourself the lord of your life and demanding your way. Instead you will gladly submit and surrender to the God who is holy and mighty because you understand He is worthy of your adoration and love.

What might your worship look like if you do not understand or accept God for who He truly is?

I am not really worshiping God because I am defining God by what is acceptable to me rather than seeing Him for who He is.

How is worshiping God in spirit and in truth related to what you have learned about idolatry?

I cannot worship God in spirit and in truth if I will not release my idols. Lessons 1-3 explain that when I do not release my idols, I am worshiping them.

WORSHIP GOD AS YOU READ AND MEDITATE ON THE SCRIPTURES WRITTEN BELOW.

PSALM 95:6-7a

O come, let us worship and bow down; let us kneel before the Lord, our Maker! For he is our God, and we are the people of His pasture, and the sheep of his hand.

PSALM 103:1

Bless the Lord, O my soul, and all that is within me, bless His holy name!

2 SAMUEL 7:22

Therefore you are great, O LORD God. For there is none like you, and there is no God besides you, according to all that we have heard with our ears.

REVELATION 4:11

"Worthy are you, our Lord and God, to receive glory and honor and power, for you created all things, and by your will they existed and were created."

JUDE 1:25

[T]o the only God, our Savior, through Jesus Christ our Lord, be glory, majesty, dominion, and authority, before all time and now and forever. Amen.

END YOUR STUDY...

Summarize what you learned from this lesson

Reflection

Read, reflect upon, and pray through Psalm 16 and write your thoughts/prayer below.

FDQ: To end your lesson, you may want to read Psalm 16 aloud in unison.

PART 5 WORKS CITED

Lesson 1: My Longing Heart

1 • Sande, Ken. The Peacemaker. Baker Books, Grand Rapids, Michigan, 2004, pgs. 109, 204.

Lesson 2: My Controlling Heart

1 • As defined by DM Lloyd-Jones in Idolatry in Life in God: Studies in 1 John.
2 • Powlison, David. "Idols of the Heart and Vanity Fair." The Journal of Biblical Counseling, Volume 13, Number 2, Winter 1995.
3 • Keller, Timothy. Prayer — Experiencing Awe and Intimacy with God. Dutton, New York, New York, 2014, pg. 113.

Lesson 3: My Surrendered Heart

1 • Lewis, C.S. Mere Christianity. Harper One, New York, New York, 1952, pgs. 136-137.
2 • Carson, D.A. Praying With Paul: A Call to Spiritual Reformation. LifeWay Press, Nashville, Tennessee, 2014, pg. 31.

Lesson 4: My Grieving Heart

1 • Source Unknown.
2 • Source Unknown.
3 • Keller, Timothy. Walking With God Through Pain and Suffering. Dutton, New York, New York, 2013, pg. 298.

Lesson 5: My Worshiping Heart

1 • Kennebrew, Delesslyn A. "What is True Worship?" Christianity Today, www.christianitytoday.com/biblestudies/bible-answers/spirituallife/what-is-true-worship.html. Accessed 21 March 2017.
2 • Keller, Timothy. Walking With God Through Pain and Suffering. Dutton, New York, New York, 2013, pgs. 168-169.
3 • By Sinclair Ferguson as quoted by Jerry Bridges in I Give You Glory Oh God. WaterBrook, 2002, pg. 48.
4 • Martin, Albert. The Forgotten Fear. Reformation Heritage Books, 2015, pg. 27.
5 • By John Brown (1851) as quoted by Jerry Bridges in The Joy of Fearing God. WaterBrook, 2004, pg. 76.
6 • By John Brown (1851) as quoted by Jerry Bridges in The Joy of Fearing God. WaterBrook, 2004, pg. 76.

Attitudes
OF THE HEART

PART 6

In Part 5 you learned that your heart is divided when you put anything or anyone above God. You also learned that you must surrender these things or persons to God, along with your fears and your perceived need/desire to control.

In Part 6 you will examine "Attitudes of the Heart."

---- **LESSON 1** ----

My Forgiving and Confessing Heart

In Part 5 you discovered the ways your heart can be divided when you try to control a situation or person in order to protect yourself. In this lesson, My Forgiving and Confessing Heart, you will discover that unforgiveness also divides your heart. It stands in the way of doing what God calls you to do—to forgive as He forgives.

When your heart has been injured by someone (whether intentional or not), it is also divided or fractured. Pain lingers in your heart. In My Grieving Heart (Part 5 Lesson 4), you learned you must mourn your pain in order to release it. As you choose to forgive, you can open your injured heart to receive God's comfort and healing.

YOU ARE FORGIVEN AND THUS YOU ARE TO FORGIVE OTHERS

———

The definition for *forgiveness* is "to pardon; to renounce anger, resentment or punishment against; to absolve from payment."[1]

You have been forgiven by God your great debt against Him. It is only in response to how much you have been forgiven that you are able to forgive others. Remembering that you are undeserving of God's forgiveness gives you the right perspective when you need to forgive someone. As God initiated His forgiveness toward you while you were yet His enemy (Romans 5:10), so you must forgive your offender regardless of her posture. A forgiving heart is the only loving and obedient response to God's command to forgive others.

THINK ABOUT THE WONDERFUL SALVATION YOU HAVE RECEIVED.

Read the following verses.

TITUS 3:3-5
For we ourselves were once foolish, disobedient, led astray, slaves to various passions and pleasures, passing our days in malice and envy, hated by others and hating one another. But when the goodness and loving kindness of God our Savior appeared, He saved us, not because of works done by us in righteousness, but according to his own mercy, by the washing of regeneration and renewal of the Holy Spirit....

EPHESIANS 1:7-8
In him we have redemption through his blood, the forgiveness of our trespasses, according to the riches of his grace, which he lavished upon us, in all wisdom and insight....

2 CORINTHIANS 5:21
For our sake he made him to be sin who knew no sin, so that in him we might become the righteousness of God.

You may have been deeply hurt by someone's sin(s) against you; however, as you choose to forgive, God will bring healing to your heart. This may be immediate, or it may be a process over a long period. You may need to grieve the loss of someone dear or something you never had (e.g., love of a parent or spouse) as part of the process of healing, but you can trust the great Healer to heal your heart. *Forgiveness is releasing the offender and the offense to God, and if you have been deeply hurt, forgiveness is an avenue to release your deep hurt to God* (review Part 5 Lesson 4 - My Grieving Heart).

FDQ: Ask if anyone would like to share how choosing to forgive someone brought healing to her heart.

HOW DOES JESUS' EXAMPLE OF FORGIVING OTHERS AND ENDURING UNJUST SUFFERING IMPACT AND ENCOURAGE YOU?

Read the following verses and record your response.

LUKE 23:34a

And Jesus said, "Father, forgive them, for they know not what they do."

1 PETER 2:23-24

When he was reviled, he did not revile in return; when he suffered, he did not threaten, but continued entrusting himself to him who judges justly. He himself bore our sins in his body on the tree, that we might die to sin and live to righteousness. By his wounds you have been healed.

What do you think it means to entrust your heart to the Father?

_____

_____

_____

_____

FDQ: See John 2:23-25 for a fuller picture of what it means that Jesus entrusted His heart to no one but the Father.

TO FORGIVE IS A COMMAND

———

There is no Scripture that gives you permission to withhold forgiveness from a person, whether she is a follower of Christ or not. Offering forgiveness to others is a gracious response to God's forgiveness of you. Extending forgiveness is not based on a feeling. It cannot be withheld until you feel like forgiving. Extending forgiveness is a choice of the will and an act of obedience. Our horizontal relationship with others reveals the nature of our vertical relationship with God. Because the Holy Spirit resides within you, you have His power to make a right decision to forgive. Again, forgiveness is a loving and obedient response to the forgiveness you have received from God.

WHAT SCRIPTURE SAYS ABOUT FORGIVENESS AND UNFORGIVENESS

———

WHAT IS THE COMMAND TO FORGIVE? AND WHAT IS THE CONSEQUENCE OF NOT FORGIVING?

Read the following verses and record your response.

MATTHEW 18:21-35

Then Peter came up and said to him, "Lord, how often will my brother sin against me, and I forgive him? As many as seven times?" Jesus said to him, "I do not say to you seven times, but seventy-seven times. "Therefore the kingdom of heaven may be compared to a king who wished to settle accounts with his servants. When he began to settle, one was brought to him who owed him ten thousand talents. And since he could not pay, his master ordered him to be sold, with his wife and children and all that he had, and payment to be made. So the servant fell on his knees, imploring him, 'Have patience with me, and I will pay you everything.' And out of pity for him, the master of that servant released him and forgave him the debt. But when that same servant went out, he found one of his fellow servants who owed him a hundred denarii, and seizing him, he began to choke him, saying, 'Pay what you owe.' So his fellow servant fell down and pleaded with him, 'Have patience with me, and I will pay you.' He refused and went and put him in prison until he should pay the debt. When his fellow servants saw what had taken place, they were greatly distressed, and they went and reported to their master all that had taken place. Then his master summoned him and said to him, 'You wicked servant! I forgave you all that debt because you pleaded with me. And should not you have had mercy on your fellow servant, as I had mercy on you?' And in anger his master delivered him to the jailers, until he should pay all his debt. So also my heavenly Father will do to every one of you, if you do not forgive your brother from your heart."

Command: forgive 77 times (many other translations state "70 times 7")
Consequence: the forgiven yet ungrateful servant who withheld forgiveness was thrown into jail. Unforgiveness leads to bondage.

MARK 11:25

"And whenever you stand praying, forgive, if you have anything against anyone, so that your Father also who is in heaven may forgive you your trespasses."

Command: the forgiven must forgive
Consequence: sin that keeps my heart divided so that I cannot be at peace with God; it separates me from experiencing God's peace and fellowship with God.

The two passages above indicate that the Father does not forgive the one who will not forgive. What does this mean?

_____

_____

_____

_____

FDQ: People who have a pattern of unforgiveness demonstrate that they may not have truly received God's forgiveness and may not be regenerated. This always gives us an opportunity to examine our hearts before the Lord.

Our gratitude for God's mercy to us will be reflected in how merciful we are toward those who "owe" us. Forgiveness always requires a price. Christ paid the ultimate price in order to forgive us. There is a price in forgiving others. These costs may include giving up the right to be right, the right to be vindicated, the right to be repaid, and the right to have justice.

EPHESIANS 4:30-32

And do not grieve the Holy Spirit of God, by whom you were sealed for the day of redemption. Let all bitterness and wrath and anger and clamor and slander be put away from you, along with all malice. Be kind to one another, tenderhearted, forgiving one another, as God in Christ forgave you.

Command: forgive as Christ forgives

Consequence: it grieves the Holy Spirit; an attitude of bitterness, wrath, anger, clamor, slander, and malice can result from an unforgiving heart.

COLOSSIANS 3:12-14

Put on then, as God's chosen ones, holy and beloved, compassionate hearts, kindness, humility, meekness, and patience, bearing with one another and, if one has a complaint against another, forgiving each other; as the Lord has forgiven you, so you also must forgive. And above all these put on love, which binds everything together in perfect harmony.

Command: the forgiven must forgive; Out of a heart of kindness, humility and patience I am called to bear with one another, forgive, and love. All these attributes are fruit of the Holy Spirit (Galatians 5:22).

What forgiveness looks like:

- Not bringing up the wrong with the other person.

- Not bringing it up with others.

- Not bringing it up in your own thoughts.

- Not dwelling on the hurt.

- Not wishing ill on the other person.

- Praying for the other person.

- Living out the fruit of the Spirit toward that person.

THE BURDEN OF UNFORGIVENESS

Being unwilling to forgive is a burden to you. It separates you from fellowship with God. According to Hebrews 12:15 it not only affects you but it also affects others. "See to it that no one fails to obtain the grace of God; that no root of bitterness springs up and causes trouble, and by it many become defiled." A bitter root of unforgiveness will continue to grow in your heart and negatively affect you and others unless it is completely cut off by your choice to forgive. Manifestations of a bitter heart include anger or frustration when you see or think about the offender or the desire (need) to withdraw from the offender. As you choose to forgive, you release the burden of an unforgiving heart to God and experience His grace once again.

What forgiveness is not:

- Forgiveness is not minimizing the sin or making excuses for the sin.

- Forgiveness is not the absence of anger at the sin.

- Forgiveness does not make an abusive offender a safe or trustworthy person. You are not commanded to trust an untrustworthy person.

- Forgiveness does not mean there are no consequences for sin.

- Forgiveness is not dependent on the response of the offender or whether justice is served.

- Forgiveness is not self-blame, although you are required to take responsibility for your part.

- Forgiveness is not remaining silent and refusing to confront when necessary.

- Forgiveness is not forgetting.

FDQ: Be sure to review this list and ask if there are questions. It is important that there is accurate understanding of these points.

If you are forgiving a person who you feel is abusive, it is wise to seek godly counsel to determine if any form of relationship should continue.

STEPS TO FORGIVENESS

———

Take some time now to allow God to speak to your heart. Is there anyone you need to forgive? Work through the following steps to release the burden of an unforgiving heart to God. (If you do not presently have a person that comes to your mind, practice this exercise with someone you have forgiven in the past.) At the next meeting you will pray through your forgiveness and confession lists with a partner. If you are struggling to begin the forgiveness process, ask God to show you your fears.

Practical Steps to Forgiveness: [2]

Step 1: Make a list of all the ways the person has sinned against you or hurt you.

The list may include things that were not intentional wrongs against you. The list may also include habits or actions that in themselves are not sins, but you may be harboring resentment or experiencing pain nevertheless.

Step 2: The focus of the list may relate to a specific situation, or it may relate to an entire relationship over a long period.

Step 3: Allow yourself to experience your feelings during this process.

By allowing yourself to feel the feelings that come during this process (e.g., abandonment, loss, rage, sadness, fear or even physical symptoms), you are beginning to mourn your pain.

Step 4: After you have completed the list, pray out loud telling God you are choosing to forgive the offender for every offense (specifically naming each one).

In this process you are continuing to mourn your pain as you release the offense to God. It may be helpful to pray through this list with a trusted person.

Step 5: Tear up the list.

Take a moment to thank Jesus that you can place your burden at the foot of His cross. Thank Him for the forgiveness He enables you to extend to your offender. Thank Him that He is able to lift the burden of unforgiveness and the pain you have carried.

Step 6: Continue to walk in forgiveness.

Remember that thoughts and feelings resulting from the sin committed against you may continue to come up in your memory. Also, your offender may continue to sin against you. Each time, choose in that moment to forgive again (Matthew 18:22). Remind yourself that you have placed the offense and the offender at the cross. You no longer have to carry this burden.

FDQ: If you are facilitating someone praying her forgiveness list, ask God to help you and protect you as you enter into her pain. You may hear some very difficult things, so you may also need to forgive the offender in the moment the offense is being verbalized. God does not want you to take on the burden that is being released to Him in this process.

STEPS TO CONFESSION

The Webster's 1828 dictionary defines "confession" as "the acknowledgment of a crime, fault or something to one's disadvantage; open declaration of guilt, failure, debt, accusation, etc."

Forgiveness and confession should always go hand-in-hand.

Step 1: Ask God to reveal ways you may have sinned in attitudes, actions or patterns against the person you are choosing to forgive.

You may have been sinned against in horrific ways. Your sin might be your unforgiveness toward the offender or the ways you have allowed the sin against you to control certain areas of your life.

PSALM 139:23-24

Search me, O God, and know my heart. Try me and know my thoughts! And see if there be any grievous way in me, and lead me in the way everlasting!

MATTHEW 7:3-4

"Why do you see the speck that is in your brother's eye, but do not notice the log that is in your own eye? Or how can you say to your brother, 'Let me take the speck out of your eye,' when there is the log in your own eye?"

Step 2: If you are in a conflict with the person, ask God to reveal how you may have contributed to the conflict.

JAMES 4:1

What causes quarrels and what causes fights among you? Is it not this, that your passions are at war within you?

Step 3: Now make a list of the things God has revealed to you: attitudes, actions or patterns; and if there was a conflict, ways you contributed to it.

FDQ: Instruct your group to retain their confession lists for Lesson 2.

IS THERE ANOTHER STEP?

___

Consider which scenario describes your situation:

- If you have sinned against someone and she has something against you (Matthew 5:23-24), the next step is to go and ask for forgiveness. See Lesson 2.

- Sometimes, however, your confession is only vertical before God because the other person is not aware that you have sinned against her.

- If you are in a conflict with another person, regardless of whose sin caused the conflict, if possible, go and seek reconciliation (Romans 12:18).

- If a person has sinned against you, you must forgive her vertically before God. If she has not sought forgiveness from you, you are not to extend it prematurely (see Luke 17:3). However, there may be an opportunity for restoration of the relationship if you keep a posture of grace toward the person. You may never hear a "please forgive me" from the other person. In this situation, you must surrender your requirement for justice (to be heard, to be understood, or an acknowledgement from the other person how she hurt you). Remember, grace is undeserved favor from God toward you and underserved favor you extend to others. Entrust your heart to God's protection.

"

Although followers of Jesus never have a right to refuse forgiveness, let alone to take revenge, we are not permitted to cheapen forgiveness by offering it prematurely when there has been no repentance…. The incentive to peace-making is love, but it degenerates into appeasement whenever justice is ignored. To forgive and to ask for forgiveness are both costly exercises. All authentic Christian peace-making exhibits the love and justice—and so the pain—of the cross.[3]

JOHN STOTT

FDQ: Break up your group into pairs and instruct them to each pray through their forgiveness and confession lists aloud to one another. After praying, each participant should tear up her forgiveness list. She has forgiven the offender and is choosing to "keep no record of wrongs" (1 Corinthians 13:5). She has released them to the Father.

_____

_____

_____

_____

_____

_____

_____

_____

_____

_____

_____

_____

_____

_____

_____

_____

_____

_____

END YOUR STUDY...

Summarize what you learned from this lesson

TRY ME

and know my thoughts!

AND SEE IF THERE BE

any grievous way in me,

AND LEAD ME IN THE

way everlasting!

PSALM 139:23b-24

Reflection

Write a prayer of thanksgiving in response to the truth that you can entrust the safety and care of your heart to the Father, despite the pain you may have experienced from someone's sin against you.

— LESSON 2 —

My Reconciling Heart

In Lesson 1 you learned that extending forgiveness is a choice of the will based on recognizing how much God has forgiven you. Luke 6:36 tells you to "be merciful, even as your Father is merciful." The American Heritage dictionary defines "mercy" in very practical terms as follows: the kind and compassionate treatment of an offender with a disposition to be forgiving.

When you forgive someone who has offended you and confess your sin against her, God grants you the ability to extend mercy and to seek reconciliation.

RECONCILIATION DEFINED

―――

The following definitions of "reconciliation" give a good understanding of its meaning:

AMERICAN HERITAGE DICTIONARY
To re-establish friendship between; to settle or resolve, as a dispute

THE FREE DICTIONARY
To cause to become friendly or peaceable again; to bring back into agreement or harmony

OXFORD DICTIONARY
To restore friendly relationships between

Note: Even if a relationship is extremely abusive, you are still called to forgive; however, it may not be wise to re-establish the relationship.

FDQ: If a woman is in an abusive situation, encourage her to seek Godly counsel from the leadership of her church.

A LOOK AT SCRIPTURE

―――

Scripture also has much to say about reconciliation. The following verses confirm the need to pursue peace and reconciliation with others.

WHAT DO YOU LEARN ABOUT RECONCILIATION?
Read the following verses and record your response.

MATTHEW 5:23-24
So if you are offering your gift at the altar and there remember that your brother has something against you, leave your gift there before the altar and go. First be reconciled to your brother, and then come and offer your gift.

If I recognize I have offended a brother or sister, if they are holding something against me, then I am to go and be reconciled. I must make it right before God accepts my offering of worship.

ROMANS 14:19
So then let us pursue what makes for peace and for mutual upbuilding.

I am to pursue peace and encourage others.

ROMANS 12:16
Live in harmony with one another. Do not be haughty, but associate with the lowly. Never be wise in your own sight.

I am to live in humility and in harmony with others.

EPHESIANS 4:1-3
I therefore, a prisoner for the Lord, urge you to walk in a manner worthy of the calling to which you have been called, with all humility and gentleness, with patience, bearing with one another in love, eager to maintain the unity of the Spirit in the bond of peace.

Paul urges me to walk in a manner worthy of my calling, with humility, gentleness, and patience, bearing with one another in love and eager to maintain unity and peace.

THE RECONCILIATION PROCESS

——

Steps to Reconciliation:

Step 1: *Forgive*

Choose to forgive your offender as described in Lesson 1.

Step 2: *Confess your sin or your part of the conflict*

Choose to confess your own sins as described in Lesson 1. Consider the following as you continue to evaluate how you may have contributed to the conflict:

"

Confession isn't merely an admission of where we may have gone wrong. It's an acknowledgment of how our actions may have hurt someone else. When we are willing to confess our faults, and then go a step further by admitting how our actions have been hurtful, there is greater opportunity to go beyond clearing the air and actually establishing a new connection with that person.[1]

DALE PYNE

Step 3: *Create a reconciliation list*

Using your confession list, create a reconciliation list of the things for which you need to ask forgiveness. Eventually you will use this list to reconcile with the other person involved in the conflict. If your confession is lengthy, limit the number of items to no more than eight. More than that could be overwhelming to the listener. Include items that will be most encouraging, helpful, and healing for the other person to hear.

FDQ: You may want the women to complete and/or review their reconciliation lists in class. Be sure you give the ladies opportunity to talk through a difficult relationship but do this privately, apart from the group. Some relationships have been unsafe—not only hurt feelings but a pattern of abuse in some form.

If someone in your group was abused as a child and she is uncertain regarding her responsibility toward her offender, encourage her to seek counsel from her church leaders. It may not be appropriate to discuss these issues in the group.

The reconciliation process with an abuser is not an attempt to re-establish relationship if the relationship has been broken. It is specifically the process of recognizing your own sin in the relationship and asking for forgiveness. It is dealing biblically with your own sin, not theirs. It may not be safe to meet with an abuser in person. A phone call may be sufficient. You may also want to have a trusted person with you when you make a call.

There may be times in a difficult relationship, or any relationship for that matter, when it is necessary to confront the situation and the person. Scriptural guidelines for admonishing will be addressed in Part 7 Lesson 3.

Step 4: *Go and be reconciled*

As God is faithful in revealing your attitudes and actions that contributed to the conflict, and you are faithful in confessing your part and creating a reconciliation list, it is important to take the next step in the reconciliation process. It may be helpful for you to meet face-to-face with the person to verbally confess your part and ask for forgiveness. If meeting in person is not possible, try to talk by phone. As a last resort, communicate in written form.

Don't	*Do*
• Bring up the way the person sinned against or offended you.	• Confess or admit what you did to contribute to the conflict.
• Make excuses for your actions against the person.	• Acknowledge the pain or hurt you caused.
• Seek justice for yourself.	• Ask for forgiveness.
• Require the other person to acknowledge how you were sinned against or offended.	• If appropriate to the circumstance, ask how you could have done it differently or how you can do it differently in the future.
• Demand reconciliation if the other person is not willing.	• Make restitution, if necessary.

KEEP THE FOLLOWING SCRIPTURES IN MIND AS YOU APPROACH THE OTHER PERSON:

PHILIPPIANS 2:3-4

Do nothing from selfish ambition or conceit, but in humility count others more significant than yourselves. Let each of you look not only to his own interests, but also to the interest of others.

EPHESIANS 4:29

Let no corrupting talk come out of your mouths, but only such as is good for building up, as fits the occasion, that it may give grace to those who hear.

WHAT HAPPENS IF THE OTHER PERSON DOES NOT WANT TO MEET OR TO RECONCILE?

It is your responsibility to do what God calls you to do in the reconciliation process, all of which are described above. It is not your responsibility to convince the other person to reconcile. It is not your responsibility to change the other person's heart. Only the Holy Spirit can do that. If the other person is not willing to reconcile, continue praying for the other person's heart, continue praying for opportunities to extend mercy and grace, and continue praying for reconciliation.

If the other person not only refuses to reconcile but appears to have become an enemy by her words or actions, let Romans 12:17-19 guide your attitude and actions.

Repay no one evil for evil, but give thought to do what is honorable in the sight of all. If possible, so far as it depends on you, live peaceably with all. Beloved, never avenge yourselves, but leave it to the wrath of God, for it is written, "Vengeance is mine, I will repay, says the Lord." To the contrary, "if your enemy is hungry, feed him; if he is thirsty, give him something to drink; for by so doing so you will heap burning coals* on his head." Do not be overcome by evil, but overcome evil with good.

ROMANS 12:17-19

In ancient times when a person was remorseful and repentant, they would show it by putting a container of coals or ashes on their heads.

END YOUR STUDY...
Summarize what you learned from this lesson

Read John 13:34-35 and 1 John 4:19-21. Meditate on these Scriptures. Ask God to show you how to love in your relationships.

LESSON 3

My Trusting Heart

As you have worked through the My Heart Unveiled lessons, you have had many opportunities to learn about and practice trusting God. Trust is a choice. Trust is not a one-time decision but an active, moment-by-moment choosing to walk in the Spirit (see Part 4 Lesson 4).

You have learned that it is your choice (a wise choice) to do the following:
- invite the Spirit to search your heart (My Heart Unveiled Chart)
- find your identity and satisfaction in God (Part 2 Lesson 1; Part 4 Lesson 5)
- surrender your way and embrace His way (Part 5)
- forgive instead of harboring bitterness (Part 6 Lesson 1)

FDQ: How does the above list connect with a trusting heart?

GOD IS TRUSTWORTHY

———

God's character and His commitment to you as His child is absolutely trustworthy; therefore, you can have confidence in His perfect integrity, strength, ability, and faithfulness.

Integrity of God: *God is honest, good, and honorable.*

NUMBERS 23:19
"God is not man, that he should lie, or a son of man, that he should change his mind. Has he said, and will he not do it? Or has he spoken, and will he not fulfill it?"

Strength of God: *God is all-powerful.*

MATTHEW 8:27b
"What sort of man is this, that even winds and sea obey him?"

EPHESIANS 1:19-20
[A]nd what is the immeasurable greatness of his power toward us who believe, according to the working of his great might that he worked in Christ when he raised him from the dead and seated him at his right hand in the heavenly places....

Ability of God: *God is qualified, capable, competent, intelligent, and skillful.*

ISAIAH 40:13-14, 18
Who has measured the Spirit of the LORD, or what man shows him his counsel? Whom did he consult, and who made him understand? Who taught him the path of justice, and taught him knowledge, and showed him the way of understanding?... To whom then will you liken God, or what likeness compare with him?

JUDE 1:24-25
Now to him who is able to keep you from stumbling and to present you blameless before the presence of his glory with great joy, to the only God, our Savior, through Jesus Christ our Lord, be glory, majesty, dominion, and authority, before all time and now and forever. Amen.

Faithfulness of God: *God is unchangeable, secure, dependable, and loyal.*

HEBREWS 10:23
Let us hold fast the confession of our hope without wavering, for he who promised is faithful.

HEBREWS 13:5b
[H]e has said, "I will never leave you nor forsake you."

Which of the above traits would be helpful for you to remember when you face a dilemma?

HINDRANCES TO TRUSTING

———

These wonderful truths regarding God's trustworthiness are encouraging and comforting. However, when you face difficult situations, you may be tempted to doubt, worry, deny or toil.

Take a closer look at what each of these words mean:

DOUBT (VERB)

To be uncertain about; consider questionable or unlikely; hesitate to believe.

WORRY (VERB)

Allowing one's mind to dwell on difficulty or troubles; to torment oneself; to give way to unease or anxiety.

DENY (VERB)

To avoid; to refuse to recognize or acknowledge.

TOIL (VERB)

To labor; to work; to exert strength with pain and fatigue of body or mind, particularly of the body, with efforts of some continuance or duration.

This may result in you choosing to keep busy, analyzing a situation in order to control it, or trying to accomplish something in your own strength rather than relying on God.

What do you find yourself most tempted to do?

_____

_____

_____

_____

FDQ: Can you think of other indicators of an untrusting heart?

The above are indicators of an unsettled heart which, when left unchecked, may lead to anxiety, depression, and despair.

You also learned in Part 5 Lesson 4 "My Grieving Heart" that anxiety and depression can come from unexpressed grief.

ANXIETY

———

Anxiety may be described as "a thin stream of fear trickling through the mind. If encouraged, it cuts a channel into which all other thoughts are drained." [1] Anxiety can be your mind's constant background noise, or it can push itself forward to a full-blown panic attack.

Although anxiety can be a symptom of doubt and worry, it may also be caused by physiological factors such as illness or hormones (particularly around menstrual cycles or menopause). Regardless of the reasons for anxiety and panic attacks, it is important to set the Lord before you (Psalm 16:8) and to ask Him to help you, for He is always present and a constant help. Choose to renew your mind with God's truth. His truth is a steady anchor, even during a panic attack.

PAUL'S ANTIDOTE FOR ANXIETY

———

Paul wrote his letter to the Philippian church when he was under house arrest in Rome, aware that he was probably facing execution. Though in a dire situation, Paul exhorted his readers in Philippians 4:4-8 to focus not on their troubles but to take the following actions:

Verse 4: *Rejoice in the Lord always; again I will say, rejoice.*

When you are worrying and anxious, the focus is on you, the situation, a real or imagined fear, or a perceived outcome. Paul tells his readers to adjust their focus to the Lord and rejoice in Him—praise and worship Him. "Rejoice" means "joyful, cheerful, glad." You can rejoice because the object of your focus is the character of God, His good and steadfast love that will never fail regardless of the circumstance. So despite how you are feeling, you can choose to rejoice in Him.

FDQ: Why does Paul repeat the word "rejoice"?

Verse 5: *Let your reasonableness be known to everyone. The Lord is at hand.*

The Lord is at hand. He is present in your fear, panic, and distress. You can be reasonable and gentle in your response to the situation because the Holy Spirit empowers you and comforts you. You do not need to toil or strive. You must recall that He is with you and rest in His presence.

FDQ: What does it mean to "be reasonable"?
To be reasonable in judging. The word signifies a humble patient steadfastness which is able to submit to injustice, disgrace, and maltreatment without hatred and malice, trusting in God in spite of it all. Linguistic and Exegetical Key to GNT (Greek New Testament). Accordance Software (2018).

Verse 6: *Do not be anxious about anything, but in everything by prayer and supplication with thanksgiving let your requests be made known to God.*

Again Paul instructs his readers to not only focus on God but also to pray about three things. First, he tells them to pray about everything on their minds. You can pray about the things that are disturbing, worrisome, and fearful. Second, He instructs them to make supplication. The word "supplication" means to beg for something earnestly or plead humbly with another, either for yourself or another person. You can pour out your heart in supplication to the Lord, for He hears and He cares. Third, Paul says to pray with thanksgiving. Thanksgiving is an expression of gratitude. Praying with gratitude is accepting by faith God's faithful work on your behalf.

Verse 7: *And the peace of God, which surpasses all understanding, will guard your hearts and your minds in Christ Jesus.*

Paul wisely assures his readers of the wonderful result of renewing their minds. When you shift your focus from self or a situation to Him, and when you surrender your self-sufficiency and humble yourself before God, He fills you with His peace. This peace comes whether or not the problem is resolved. This peace guards and protects your heart and truly is beyond your human understanding.

FDQ: "surpasses" means "is superior to."
"guard" is a military term picturing soldiers standing on guard duty at the city gate protecting from a hostile invasion or controlling who went out.

Verse 8: *Finally, brothers, whatever is true, whatever is honorable, whatever is just, whatever is pure, whatever is lovely, whatever is commendable, if there is any excellence, if there is anything worthy of praise, think about these things.*

Paul specifically states the characteristics of the things on which you are to place your thoughts. This shifts your focus and encourages your gratitude.

FDQ: This is an important passage (Philippians 4:4-8) to memorize to combat anxiety.

Share a time in your life when you used this Scripture or another to calm your anxious heart. Record the Scripture and the situation.

_____

_____

_____

_____

_____

_____

_____

See Appendix B for a list of verses to help you in your battle against anxiety.

DEPRESSION AND DESPAIR

—

Depression is the feeling of gloom and severe despondency, an attitude of hopelessness or joylessness. Despair is the complete loss of hope. Despair and depression are symptoms of doubt and worry (not trusting God); however, depression may have a physiological component if the body chemistry becomes imbalanced. This can happen in periods of high stress, illness, as well as post-partum.

You may need to consult a doctor to determine if there is a chemical imbalance. Sometimes medication may be helpful; however, renewing your mind with God's truth and calling out to Him are invaluable in all situations. Reminding yourself of God's goodness and faithfulness is especially important when you are suffering from depression.

FDQ: Martin Luther, Charles Spurgeon, and John Piper to name a few are individuals who regularly suffer(ed) with depression.

HOW ASAPH DEALS WITH DESPAIR

—

PSALM 77:3-4

When I remember God, I moan; when I meditate, my spirit faints. You hold my eyelids open; I am so troubled that I cannot speak.

Asaph's words indicate that he is in despair. Though the Psalm does not reveal the specific situation, it clearly expresses his many doubts concerning God's trustworthiness.

RECORD ALL OF ASAPH'S DOUBTS IN YOUR OWN WORDS.

PSALM 77:7-9

"Will the Lord spurn forever, and never again be favorable? Has his steadfast love forever ceased? Are his promises at an end for all time? Has God forgotten to be gracious? Has he in anger shut up his compassion?"

Will the Lord reject forever?
And will He never be favorable again?
Has His lovingkindness ceased forever?

Have His promises come to an end forever?
Has God forgotten to be gracious or has He in anger withdrawn His compassion?

WHAT DID ASAPH CHOOSE TO DO NEXT?

PSALM 77:10

Selah. Then I said, "I will appeal to this, to the years of the right hand of the Most High."
He chose to stop dwelling on his many doubts concerning God's faithfulness and chose to remember God's faithfulness.

IN VERSES 11-15 ASAPH REMEMBERED, PONDERED, AND MEDITATED UPON GOD'S MIGHTY DEEDS. HE RENEWED HIS MIND.

Underline the specific things Asaph remembered.

PSALM 77:11-15

I will remember the deeds of the Lord; yes, I will remember your wonders of old. I will ponder all your work, and meditate on your mighty deeds. Your way, O God, is holy. What god is great like our God? You are the God who works wonders; you have made known your might among the peoples. You with your arm redeemed your people, the children of Jacob and Joseph.

RESOLVE TO TAKE STEPS OF OBEDIENCE

The ongoing act of renewing your mind keeps you focused and dependent on God and enables you to do whatever it is He is calling you to do, which may involve taking a difficult action step. At this point you may still be fearful; however, you are resolved to obey.

BELOW ARE SOME VERSES THAT MAY ENCOURAGE YOU TO TAKE THE NEXT STEP.

PSALM 56:3-4

When I am afraid, I put my trust in you. In God, whose word I praise, in God I trust; I shall not be afraid. What can flesh do to me?
See also, Psalm 27:1

PROVERBS 3:5-6

Trust in the Lord with all your heart, and do not lean on your own understanding. In all your ways acknowledge him, and he will make straight your paths.

ISAIAH 26:3-4

You keep him in perfect peace whose mind is stayed on you, because he trusts in you. Trust in the Lord forever, for the Lord God is an everlasting rock.

What you keep your mind on is what you are trusting in.

See Appendix C—"Do the Next Thing," a poem beautifully quoted by Elisabeth Elliot.

END YOUR STUDY...

Summarize what you learned from this lesson

Reflection

Remember your sacred history. Recall the ways in which God has shown His integrity, strength, ability, and faithfulness in your life.

LESSON 4
My Grateful Heart

In Lesson 3 you were reminded that God is trustworthy and His devotion to you is unwavering. He can be trusted always in all situations because His presence is a constant in your life. This knowledge is the springboard for a grateful heart. Gratitude is not just a happy feeling. It is a heartfelt acknowledgement and appreciation to God in response to who He is, His grace (unmerited favor) toward you, and His faithful provision.

EXPRESSING GRATITUDE TO GOD FOR WHO HE IS

———

Scripture is full of expressions of praise and thanksgiving to Him who is worthy of all praise. As you read the following Scriptures, personalize each one in a prayer of thanksgiving.

PSALM 18:3a

I call upon the LORD, who is worthy to be praised....

PSALM 107:1

Oh give thanks to the LORD, for he is good, for his steadfast love endures forever!

PSALM 145:3

Great is the LORD, and greatly to be praised, and his greatness is unsearchable.

PSALM 145:13a

Your kingdom is an everlasting kingdom, and your dominion endures throughout all generations.

PSALM 145:17

The LORD is righteous in all his ways and kind in all his works.

PSALM 96:4-9

For great is the LORD, and greatly to be praised; he is to be feared above all gods. For all the gods of the peoples are worthless idols, but the LORD made the heavens. Splendor and majesty are before him; strength and beauty are in his sanctuary. Ascribe to the LORD, O families of the peoples, ascribe to the LORD glory and strength! Ascribe to the LORD the glory due his name; bring an offering, and come into his courts! Worship the LORD in the splendor of holiness; tremble before him, all the earth!

1 CHRONICLES 29:11-13

Yours, O LORD, is the greatness and the power and the glory and the victory and the majesty, for all that is in the heavens and in the earth is yours. Yours is the kingdom, O LORD, and you are exalted as head above all. Both riches and honor come from you, and you rule over all. In your hand are power and might, and in your hand it is to make great and to give strength to all. And now we thank you, our God, and praise your glorious name.

REVELATION 5:9b-10

"Worthy are you to take the scroll and to open its seals, for you were slain, and by your blood you ransomed people for God from every tribe and language and people and nation, and you have made them a kingdom and priests to our God, and they shall reign on the earth."

REVELATION 5:13b

"To him who sits on the throne and to the Lamb be blessing and honor and glory and might forever and ever!"

EXTRAVAGANT GRATITUDE FROM A SINFUL WOMAN

——

A grateful heart is characterized by awe at the great contrast between a woman's own unworthiness and the incredible lavishness of God's grace toward her.

Luke 7:36-50 tells the story of a sinful woman from the city who hears Jesus is in a Pharisee's home. She went uninvited to the house, bringing with her an alabaster flask of ointment, and "standing behind him at his feet, weeping, she began to wet his feet with her tears and wiped them with the hair of her head and kissed his feet and anointed them with the ointment" (38). Her extravagant expression of love was in response to how much she had been forgiven. She was not timid or ashamed to show her gratitude in such a demonstrative way, even though she was in the presence of the judgmental Pharisee. Jesus had something to say to the Pharisee in this story. "[Y]ou gave me no water for my feet.... You gave me no kiss.... You did not anoint my head with oil.... I tell you, her sins, which are many, are forgiven—for she loved much. But he who is forgiven little, loves little" (44-47).

A lavish expression of gratitude is a beautiful response to recognizing both the depth of your need and the depth to which the Father has forgiven you through Christ Jesus.

FDQ: There is a similar event occurring at a different time in Jesus' ministry as recorded in Matthew 26:6-13; Mark 14:3-9; and John 12:1-8.

GOD'S EXTRAVAGANT GIFTS TO YOU

——

If God's only gift to you was the forgiveness of your sins, it would truly be enough to keep you grateful for the rest of your life here on earth and throughout eternity. A grateful heart sees God for who He is and recognizes His unmerited grace poured out in her salvation. Out of that heart she views all aspects of her life as God's good gifts, for "in him we live and move and have our being" (Acts 17:28).

God the Father, God the Son, and God the Holy Spirit are always present, always responding on your behalf, and always working in you and for your good, keeping you, empowering you, and bringing you eventually to your heavenly home. All blessings come from your good and loving triune God.

FDQ: In your group time take two minutes and have each woman make a personal list of what she is thankful for from her day. Ask the ladies if they would like to share their list.

THE POSTURE OF A GRATEFUL HEART

——

A grateful heart humbly recognizes that all things, big or small, wonderful, mundane, and even difficult, are from Him, and in response she is eager and purposeful to thank Him for all things.

EPHESIANS 5:20

[G]iving thanks always and for everything to God the Father in the name of our Lord Jesus Christ....

1 THESSALONIANS 5:18

[G]ive thanks in all circumstances; for this is the will of God in Christ Jesus for you.

HEBREWS 13:15

Through him then let us continually offer up a sacrifice of praise to God, that is, the fruit of lips that acknowledge his name.

Considering the previous verses, what things might you give thanks for that you have not yet acknowledged as gifts from the Father?

Everything: the good and the difficult, and blessings and the trials.

What do you think it means to offer a "sacrifice" of praise? In your own life, when is offering praise a sacrifice?

Thank and praise God even when I do not feel like it or even when the situation is difficult.

What is the connection between humility and gratefulness?

Humility focuses on God in order to remember that everything I have comes from God. If my heart is not humble, it is prideful, and pride is not able to see God for who He is or recognize His faithfulness and goodness to me.

Which of God's gifts do you tend to take for granted? How can you develop gratitude for these specific things?

"

Gratitude is the overflow of a humble heart, just as surely as an ungrateful, complaining spirit flows out of a proud heart.[1]

NANCY LEIGH DeMOSS

A GRATEFUL HEART PROTECTS AND GUARDS YOU FROM COMPLACENCY AND GRUMBLING

God desires for you to cultivate a grateful heart because He knows that sin is borne out of ingratitude. Ingratitude reveals itself in a complacent or grumbling attitude.

The Danger of a Complacent Heart

According to Dictionary.com, "Complacency" is defined as being "pleased, especially with oneself or one's merits, advantages, situation, etc., often without awareness of some potential danger or defect; self-satisfied."

When the Christ-follower is complacent, she is living self-sufficiently. Whether things are going well or not, she relies on her own strength and ability to get through each day seldom thinking about God. Often this is not intentional; she simply does what she is capable to do. So it is easy for her to take for granted God's faithful presence and provision and neglect to give Him thanks.

Do you find yourself at times going through your day seldom thinking about God or giving Him thanks? Why do you think this is so?

The Danger of a Grumbling Heart

A grumbling heart cheats God of His glory (Psalm 50:23a), and it cheats you from recognizing God's faithfulness and provision in your daily life.

What are some characteristics of a grumbling heart?

pride, discontent, complaining, entitlement, feeling sorry for oneself, bitterness, discouragement, resentment.

The Israelites often grumbled (Exodus 14:11-12; 15:24;16:2-3; and 17:1-7). By Exodus 17 the Israelites had experienced crossing the Red Sea on dry land, they had watched their enemies drown in the Red Sea, they had drunk bitter water turned sweet by a miracle, they had been guided and protected in the wilderness by a cloud during the day and a pillar of fire during the night, and they had been nourished by manna. Yet they quarreled with Moses (17:2) and grumbled against him, declaring, "Why did you bring us up out of Egypt, to kill us and our children and our livestock with thirst?" (17:3). They continued, "Is the Lord among us or not?" (17:7). God graciously provided water for them again even though they grumbled and tested God. Moses called the name of this place Massah (test) and Meribah (quarrel).

In Psalm 95:8-9 the psalmist states, "[D]o not harden your hearts, as at Meribah, as on the day at Massah in the wilderness, when your fathers put me to the test and put me to the proof, though they had seen my work."

According to these verses what resulted from the Israelites' grumbling hearts?
Their hearts were hardened.

What does a hardened heart look like?
A hardened heart misses the grace of God; it remains bitter and prideful.

What had they failed to see?
They failed to see how God had provided for them.

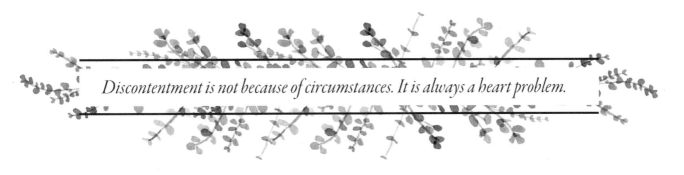

Discontentment is not because of circumstances. It is always a heart problem.

THE GRATEFUL HEART IS A CONTENTED HEART

"

I have learned that in every circumstance that comes my way, I can choose to respond in one of two ways: I can whine or I can worship! And I can't worship without giving thanks. It just isn't possible. When we choose the pathway of worship and giving thanks, especially in the midst of difficult circumstances, there is a fragrance, a radiance, that issues forth out of our lives to bless the Lord and others.[2]

NANCY LEIGH DeMOSS

Practicing gratefulness grows a contented heart. A biblical definition of contentment (*autarkeias*) is "to be satisfied, sufficient; to be free from care because of satisfaction with what is already one's own." For most people being content does not come naturally, but as you daily practice giving thanks for what you have and do not have, you will increasingly see all these things as God's gifts to you.

"

He knows exactly what we need and He gives us everything that is appropriate to the job He wants to do. Understanding this we can say, "Yes Lord, I'll take it. Thank you." [3]

ELISABETH ELLIOT

1 TIMOTHY 6:6-8
But godliness with contentment is great gain, for we brought nothing into the world, and we cannot take anything out of the world. But if we have food and clothing, with these we will be content.

1 TIMOTHY 6:17
As for the rich in this present age, charge them not to be haughty, nor to set their hopes on the uncertainty of riches, but on God, who richly provides us with everything to enjoy.

CULTIVATING A GRATEFUL HEART: MORNING, NOON, AND NIGHT
——

You must be intentional to cultivate a grateful heart by choosing to take time to consider and remember the undeserved gifts that come from God, the Extravagant Giver. Consider incorporating one or more of the following practices into your life to develop a more grateful heart:

• Filter everything in your day through God, recognizing that He is intimately involved in every detail of your life.

• Choose to look for and recognize His specific gifts including "trials of various kinds" (James 1:2), because you are confident that "[e]very good gift and every perfect gift is from above, coming down from the Father of lights with whom there is no variation or shadow due to change" (James 1:17).

• Delight in His gifts. Receive the enjoyment of these things, recognizing they are from God.

FOR WE BROUGHT

NOTHING

into this world,

AND WE CANNOT TAKE

ANYTHING

out of the world.

1 TIMOTHY 6:7

- Remember, every morning is a new opportunity to see God's steadfast love and mercy. "The steadfast love of the Lord never ceases; his mercies never come to an end" (Lamentations 3:22).

- At the end of the day, recall what He has done. What was the special gift of the day?

- Be intentional in recognizing God in creation, and specifically thank Him for the ways it thrills you.

- Tell others how you see God working in your life.

- Guard against replaying in your mind the "if only" or the "what if" so that you will not miss God's present blessings.

- Keep grounded in the knowledge that this fallen world is passing away, and your hope is kept for you in heaven (1 Peter 1:4). This eternal perspective balances the ups and downs of this life.

- Start a "Thanksgiving List" and take some time each day to add a line or two to your list.

Which of the above practices would you like to incorporate? Do you have other ideas?

END YOUR STUDY...
Summarize what you learned from this lesson

Ask the Lord to reveal to you if you have a complacent and/or grumbling heart. If so, confess these sins to the Lord and receive His forgiveness. Ask God to show you specific things for which to be grateful. Meditate on the following verses.

Oh come, let us worship and bow down;
let us kneel before the Lord, our Maker!
For he is our God, and we are the people of his pasture,
and the sheep of his hand.

PSALM 95:6-7a

LESSON 5

My Guarded Heart

So far in Part 6 you have learned the importance of cultivating healthy heart attitudes in the areas of forgiveness, confession, reconciliation, trust, and gratefulness. In this lesson you will consider the final attitude, guarding your heart.

What comes to mind when you think of guarding something? What do you guard? Why do people guard things?

What a person values, she guards. When Shirley was growing up she lived on a farm where her parents raised livestock. They also had a beautiful vegetable garden and several fruit trees. A small room off the front porch housed a large deep freezer where they stored their meat, vegetables, and fruit to keep their family of five well-fed. Though her parents would not always lock the house doors, they always locked the freezer! Clearly, the product of their toil was of great value.

In Proverbs 4:23 (NASB) Solomon instructs, "Watch over your heart with all diligence, for from it flow the springs of life."

What do you find yourself guarding?

_____

_____

_____

_____

_____

WHAT DOES IT MEAN TO GUARD YOUR HEART?

———

The word "guard" means "to watch over in order to protect or control, to keep an eye on, keep safe, be alert to." Some synonyms include "secure, protect, shield." You are to watch over your heart to keep it safe from harmful influences so that you may serve God and others purely and honorably.

"

Guard is not an impenetrable shield in which we do not let anything in.

ALLISON AUSER

People often think guarding the heart means guarding it from pain or hurt. The goal is not to avoid pain and hurt. If this is your goal, you will miss God's provision and direction through the difficult circumstance or relationship.

C. S. Lewis encourages:

Of all arguments against love none makes so strong an appeal to my nature as "Careful! This might lead you to suffering."

To my nature, my temperament, yes. Not to my conscience. When I respond to that appeal I seem to myself to be a thousand miles away from Christ. If I am sure of anything I am sure that His teaching was never meant to confirm my congenital preference for safe investments and limited liabilities....

There is no safe investment. To love at all is to be vulnerable. Love anything, and your heart will certainly be wrung and possibly be broken. If you want to make sure of keeping it intact, you must give your heart to no one, not even to an animal. Wrap it carefully round with hobbies and little luxuries; avoid all entanglements; lock it up safe in the casket or coffin of your selfishness. But in that casket—safe, dark, motionless, airless—it will change. It will not be broken; it will become unbreakable, impenetrable, irredeemable. The alternative to tragedy, or at least to the risk of tragedy, is damnation. The only place outside Heaven where you can be perfectly safe from all the dangers and perturbations of love is Hell.[1]

Have you ever guarded your heart from pain or hurt? In what ways have you tried to protect your heart? Are you able to connect this to any underlying fear(s)?

_____

_____

_____

_____

GUARDING YOUR HEART FROM UNGODLY INFLUENCES

———

To love and serve God and others honorably you must guard and protect your heart against ungodly influences—those that are contrary to God's nature and purposes. Your heart will be trained either by the Word of God or by the world. Both external and internal influences will directly impact what flows from your heart, so you must keep a watchful eye on its musings and inclinations. Evaluate your go-to's when you are bored, depressed, or tired because often these are times of temptation.

"

Sin has its residence in that which is inconstant, changing, and habitually deceitful, i.e., in our hearts. This means that we must be on constant vigil for its actings; we must be in a perpetual state of watchfulness (not fearfulness or hyper-activity). If we were fighting against an enemy who presented himself in the open, that would be one thing; we could rest in peace knowing that he was far away at times or incapable of striking at others. But we wrestle not against such a foe. Sin living in the heart is deceitful, deals treacherously, and often comes by stealth. Therefore, we must be vigilant; we must watch and pray as the Lord himself repeatedly taught us.[2]

JOHN OWEN

Take a few minutes to ask the Holy Spirit to reveal to you what is most influencing your heart right now. Brainstorm a list and ask yourself if each of these people/things is influencing your heart toward God or away from God?

———————————————————

———————————————————

———————————————————

———————————————————

GOD'S WORD IS YOUR STANDARD

To guard her heart a woman thoughtfully considers what is influencing it. She filters what she is thinking, feeling, and choosing through the grid of God's Word.

DO NOT IMBIBE A WAY OF THINKING THAT IS CONTRARY TO THE WORD OF GOD!

God's Word is the final authority, so be careful not to allow culture (secular or Christian) a stronger voice. Christian podcasts, blogposts, speakers, books or devotionals may be helpful tools but only to the degree that they are submitted to the authority of God's Word.

WHAT IS THE CONNECTION BETWEEN KNOWING GOD'S WORD AND GUARDING YOUR HEART?

Read the following passage and record your response.

PSALM 119:9-11

How can a young man [woman] keep his way pure? By guarding it according to your word. With my whole heart I seek you; let me not wander from your commandments! I have stored up your word in my heart, that I might not sin against you.

I guard my heart with the Word. I am to treasure the Word and memorize and meditate on it. This will keep me from sinning.

READY PROVERBS 2:1-10.

Circle the verbs that indicate your part and underline the verbs that indicate God's response.

PROVERBS 2:1-10

My son, if you receive my words and treasure up my commandments with you, making your ear attentive to wisdom and inclining your heart to understanding; yes, if you call out for insight and raise your voice for understanding, if you seek it like silver and search for it as for hidden treasures, then you will understand the fear of the LORD and find the knowledge of God. For the LORD gives wisdom; from his mouth come knowledge and understanding; he stores up sound wisdom for the upright; he is a shield to those who walk in integrity, guarding the paths of justice and watching over the way of his saints. Then you will understand righteousness and justice and equity, every good path; for wisdom will come into your heart, and knowledge will be pleasant to your soul[.]

What are God's promises to those who seek and treasure His Word?

He will give wisdom, knowledge, and understanding. He is a shield, guarding your paths and watching over your way.

GUARD YOUR HEART WITH DILIGENCE AND DISCERNMENT

————

You are to guard your heart diligently (Proverbs 4:23).

LOOK UP THE DEFINITION OF "DILIGENT" AND WRITE IT BELOW:

Attentive and persistent in doing anything; constant and careful effort.

As a follower of Christ you are indwelled by the Holy Spirit, Who is eager to give understanding and discernment to those who ask Him. "Now we have received not the spirit of the world, but the Spirit who is from God, that we might understand the things freely given us by God. And we impart this in words not taught by human wisdom but taught by the Spirit, interpreting spiritual truths to those who are spiritual. The natural person does not accept the things of the Spirit of God, for they are folly to him, and he is not able to understand them because they are spiritually discerned" (1 Corinthians: 2:12-14).

Humbly ask the Lord to grow your understanding of His word and diligence to obey it.

BEWARE OF FALSE TEACHING

————

HOW IS FALSE TEACHING DESCRIBED IN THE FOLLOWING SCRIPTURES? WHAT HAPPENS WHEN YOU CHOOSE TO FOLLOW FALSE TEACHING?

Read the following Scriptures and record your response.

GALATIANS 1:6-9

I am astonished that you are so quickly deserting him who called you in the grace of Christ and are turning to a different gospel—not that there is another one, but there are some who trouble you and want to distort the gospel of Christ. But even if we or an angel from heaven should preach to you a gospel contrary to the one we preached to you, let him be accursed. As we have said before, so now I say again: If anyone is preaching to you a gospel contrary to the one you received, let him be accursed.

I must be aware of false teaching that presents a different gospel message. It may deny, diminish, or distort Truth by altering the Word.

COLOSSIANS 2:8

See to it that no one takes you captive by philosophy and empty deceit, according to human tradition, according to the elemental spirits of the world, and not according to Christ.

False teaching is empty and deceitful and is based on the things of the world, not on Christ. If I follow it I am held captive by it.

FDQ: How is the culture at large influencing the church in a negative way?
What are some examples of false teaching in the church?

2 TIMOTHY 4:3-5a

For the time is coming when people will not endure sound teaching, but having itching ears they will accumulate for themselves teachers to suit their own passions, and will turn away from listening to the truth and wander off into myths. As for you, always be sober-minded....

1 PETER 1:13

Therefore, preparing your minds for action, and being sober-minded, set your hope fully on the grace that will be brought to you at the revelation of Jesus Christ.

What does it mean to be "sober-minded"?

νήφοντες pres. act. part. νήφω (G3768) to be sober. In the NT the word generally denotes self-control and the clarity of mind which goes with it (Kelly; s. 2 Tim. 4:5; 1 Thess. 5:6). Linguistic and Exegetical Key to GNT (Greek New Testament), Accordance Software (2018).

"

Bible literacy matters because it protects us from falling into error. Both the false teacher and the secular humanist rely on biblical ignorance for their messages to take root, and the modern church has proven fertile ground for those messages. Because we do not know our Bibles, we crumble at the most basic challenges to our worldview. Disillusionment and apathy eat away at our ranks.[3]

JEN WILKIN

INFLUENCES THAT DIMINISH HOLINESS

You are to protect yourself from influences that diminish holiness.

WHAT DO THE FOLLOWING SCRIPTURES ADVISE?

Read the following Scriptures and record your response.

1 CORINTHIANS 15:33

Do not be deceived: "Bad company ruins good morals."

I am foolish to think that the world will not directly influence me. Taking delight in the company of those with worldly morals puts me at risk of being influenced by their behavior, their language, and their habits.

It does not mean I am to stay away from non-Christians.

PSALM 1:1-2

Blessed is the man who walks not in the counsel of the wicked, nor stands in the way of sinners, nor sits in the seat of scoffers; but his delight is in the law of the LORD, and on his law he meditates day and night.

I am to not be influenced or counseled by ungodly people, or join in, participate in or mimic their behavior. If I associate with or delight in the company of those who are not followers of Christ, it is more likely that I will be influenced by them rather than be a godly influence on them.

2 TIMOTHY 2:14-17a

Remind them of these things, and charge them before God not to quarrel about words, which does no good, but only ruins the hearers. Do your best to present yourself to God as one approved, a worker who has no need to be ashamed, rightly handling the word of truth. But avoid irreverent babble, for it will lead people into more and more ungodliness, and their talk will spread like gangrene.

I am to take seriously how I handle the Word and avoid empty or vain talking.
To "handle" in Greek: ὀρθοτομοῦντα pres. act. part. ὀρθοτομέω (G3982) to cut along a straight line, to cut a straight road, to handle correctly (TLNT). The metaphor could be that of plowing a straight furrow, or of a road foreman making his road straight, or of a mason squaring and cutting a stone to fit in its proper place, or the cutting of a sacrifice or household food (Lock; EGT ; Kelly; Spicq; MM). As noted in Linguistic and Exegetical Key to GNT (Greek New Testament), Accordance Software (2018).

PSALM 101:2b-3a

I will walk with integrity of heart within my house; I will not set before my eyes anything that is worthless.

I am to be careful what I set my eyes on, for it will affect my heart.

PSALM 119:37

Turn my eyes from looking at worthless things; and give me life in your ways.

I am to ask God to help me protect my eyes from evil.

I WILL NOT

set before my eyes

ANYTHING

that is worthless.

PSALM 101:3a

HEART CARE

—

Practical Tips for Heart Care:

1. Incorporate God's Word in your daily life. (Part 7 Lesson 1 will address this in more detail.)

2. Talk to God about what is on your heart. Take some time daily (or more often!) to do a "heart check" asking God to reveal to you any ways you are not walking in light of His Word.
- Am I dissatisfied? What am I looking at or listening to that is breeding dissatisfaction?
- Can I eliminate these things?
- Am I comparing myself and my life to others?
- Is what I am choosing life-giving?
- In light of eternity, does this matter?

3. Invite God into your daily routines.

4. Remain in Christian community. Seek out a trusted friend to share your struggle, pray together, and keep each other accountable. In a social media world, you must be intentional to build authentic relationships and real community. The right relationships point you to God, sharpen you, encourage you, and hold you accountable. Strong mutual Christian support among family and friends is essential for keeping your heart guarded in the middle of life's challenges.

5. Take time to care for yourself as you are more likely to let down your heart-filter when you are tired, hungry, worn out, etc.

What are other practical ways you can care for your heart?

_____

_____

_____

_____

_____

_____

_____

_____

_____

_____

And it is my prayer that your love may abound more and more, with knowledge and all discernment, so that you may approve what is excellent, and so be pure and blameless for the day of Christ, filled with the fruit of righteousness that comes through Jesus Christ, to the glory and praise of God.

PHILIPPIANS 1:9-11

END YOUR STUDY...
Summarize what you learned from this lesson

Reflection

Meditate on the heart attitudes you explored in Part 6. Is there one in which you would particularly like to grow? Talk to the Lord about it in prayer.

PART 6 WORKS CITED

Lesson 1: My Forgiving and Confessing Heart

1 • As defined by the American Heritage Dictionary.
2 • Adapted from Called to Obedience Ministries.
3 • Stott, John R.W. The Cross of Christ, Downers Grove, Illinois, 2006, pg.289.

Lesson 2: My Reconciling Heart

1 • Pyne, Dale. "The Path of a Peacemaker: Have I Hurt You?" Peacemaker, http://blog.peacemaker.net/?p=4259. Accessed 22 March 2017.

Lesson 3: My Trusting Heart

1 • Roche, Arthur, Reader's Digest (June 1998), pg. 64.

Lesson 4: My Grateful Heart

1 • DeMoss, Nancy, "Gratitude and Humility," October 5, 2009. BillyGraham.org.
2 • DeMoss, Nancy Leigh. Choosing Gratitude: Your Journey to Joy. Moody, Chicago, Illinois, 2011, pgs. 23-24.
3 • Citation unknown.

Lesson 5: My Guarded Heart

1 • Lewis, C.S. The Inspirational Writings of C.S. Lewis: The Four Loves. Nelson, Nashville, Tennessee, 2004, pgs. 278-279.
2 • Owen, John. The Works of John Owen, Vol. 6: Temptation and Sin. Goold, Banner of Truth, 1967, pg. 175.
3 • Wilkin, Jen. Women of the Word: How to Study the Bible with Both Our Hearts and Our Minds. Crossway, Wheaton, Illinois, 2014, pg. 45.

MY
Abiding
HEART

PART 7

In Part 7 you will look afresh at five spiritual disciplines: Abiding in the Word, Prayer, Community, Suffering, and the Hope of Heaven.

LESSON 1

Abiding in the Word

FDQ: Why did we title Part 7 "My Abiding Heart" instead of "Disciplines of the Heart" or "Habits of the Heart"?

In Lesson 1 you will see how abiding in God's Word and beholding His glory changes you into His likeness.

Spiritual habits/disciplines do not change you; they create space for you to connect and engage with God. Spiritual habits/disciplines encourage your heart to be sensitive to the Holy Spirit and train your heart (what you think, feel, and choose) to seek Jesus and look for Him in all things with expectation.

FDQ: What is the significance of abiding? What are other words that come to your mind for "abiding"?

ABIDING BRINGS JOY

——

ABIDE

To stay in, continue in, and remain in

According to John 15 those who abide in Christ:

1. Reveal the true nature of the living God (John 15:8; 1:18; 8:12).

2. Bear fruit (John 15:8) and point to the reality of a relationship with God.

3. Live as people loved by God and as people loving one another (John 15:9-10; 12-15)

4. Experience joy and delight because of loving Jesus and obeying His commandments (John 15:10).

5. Influence others for Christ (John 15:16).

6. Ask for the right things and receive them (because they are the right things) (John 15:7, 16).

Jesus delights in hanging out with His people as friends relating to each other. Jesus is the Word (logos: John 1:1,14), the personification of God Himself, who has made His home in you and who wants you to be fully at home in Him.

BEHOLD THE GLORY OF THE LORD

——

In Part 7 you will explore spiritual disciplines God has given you to draw near to Him and behold Him. In 2 Corinthians 3:18a Paul writes, "And we all, with unveiled faces, beholding the glory of the Lord, are being transformed into the same image from one degree of glory to another."

Beholding the glory of the Lord means that you are to think about Jesus by giving your strong, reflective thinking to thoughts about the Savior. You can divide this thinking into two categories: (1) what the Bible says about Jesus as a Person (who He is, what He is like), and (2) what the Bible says about what Jesus has done (accomplished), what He is doing, and what He will do in the future.

As you behold the glory of the Lord you will know Him, enjoy Him, and exalt Him; and as you do, you will become like Him and experience the abundant life He has planned for you. Abiding brings joy!

One essential way to behold the glory of the Lord is to read, study, meditate on, and memorize the Word. The Word reveals God—His character and His work--to man. Beholding the glory of the Lord through the Word will change you. As it energizes your heart, the truth will set you free. "If you abide in my word, you are truly my disciples, and you will know the truth, and the truth will set you free" (John 8:31-32). As you see God and treasure Him above all else, your deepest longings will align with His will and be satisfied. Everything that comes out of your heart will be different! In this lesson you will realize the connection between abiding in the Word of God and treasuring Him.

The heart
CANNOT LOVE
-WHAT-
the mind
DOES NOT KNOW.

JEN WILKIN

OPEN THE EYES OF MY HEART

In Ephesians 1:18 Paul prays that his listeners will have "the eyes of your hearts enlightened, that you may know what is the hope to which he has called you, what are the riches of his glorious inheritance in the saints." To know God is to experience the reality of God. When you open the Word, ask the Lord to open the eyes of your heart that you might see Him.

It is important to remember that the Spirit and the flesh are at war against each other (Galatians 5:17). The culture, Satan, and your flesh get in the way and block your ability to understand the Word and your desire for it. So you must ask the Holy Spirit to help you understand Scripture and to increase your desire and ability to know and believe God. The Holy Spirit promises to interpret spiritual truths to you (1 Corinthians 2:12-13).

IN ADDITION TO EPHESIANS 1:18, YOU MAY WANT TO PRAY ONE OF THE FOLLOWING VERSES BEFORE YOU READ OR LISTEN TO THE WORD.

Look up the following Scriptures and write out each verse.

PSALM 119:18

Open my eyes, that I may behold wondrous things out of your law.

PSALM 86:11

Teach me your way, O Lord, that I may walk in your truth; unite my heart to fear your name.

Come to the Word with **expectation**. Though you cannot have expectations of others, you can have expectations of the Word.

How do you approach the Word with expectation? Pay attention to any and all reactions you have with the Scriptures.

- What surprises you?
- What confronts you? Confrontation reveals what is in your heart, the good things you are missing. It is not to condemn but to reveal your heart so that you may enjoy Him more fully.
- How is God drawing you into deeper relationship with Him? What are new insights to familiar passages?

Engage with God and ask Him to give you His perspective as you read the Word. If necessary, engage with God to give you a change of heart.

DAILY INTAKE OF THE WORD NOURISHES YOUR FAITH

———

Paul writes in Romans 10:17, "So faith comes from hearing, and hearing through the word of Christ." For your faith to grow, you must be in the Word.

HOW DOES THE WORD NOURISH YOUR FAITH?

Psalm 119 has 176 verses, the longest chapter in the Bible. In almost every verse, the Word of God is mentioned (eight different terms). Psalm 119 beautifully declares not only the character of the Scriptures but also the character of God. All of the attributes of the Word are attributes of God.

"Blessed are those who keep his testimonies, who seek him with their whole heart" (Psalm 119:2). With a humble heart, you are to develop a practical habit which seeks to know God and His will in order to keep it.

READ THE BELOW TEN BEAUTIFUL TRUTHS REGARDING GOD'S WORD.

God's Word is wonderful.

PSALM 119:18

Open my eyes, that I may behold wondrous things out of your law.

God's Word gives strength.

PSALM 119:28

My soul melts away for sorrow; strengthen me according to your word!

God's Word is good.

PSALM 119:39

Turn away the reproach that I dread, for your rules are good.

God's Word gives comfort.

PSALM 119:50

This is my comfort in my affliction, that your promise gives me life.

God's Word gives life.

PSALM 119:93

I will never forget your precepts, for by them you have given me life.

God's Word is sweet.

PSALM 119:103

How sweet are your words to my taste, sweeter than honey to my mouth!

God's Word is light.

PSALM 119:105

Your word is a lamp to my feet and a light to my path.

God's Word is precious.

PSALM 119:127

Therefore I love your commandments above gold, above fine gold.

God's Word is right.

PSALM 119:137

Righteous are you, O Lord, and right are your rules.

God's Word is true.

PSALM 119:160

The sum of your word is truth, and every one of your righteous rules endure forever.

FDQ: Break your group into pairs. Assign stanzas to each pair.
How is the Word described? What are the benefits of believing and obeying the Word? Choose 1-2 to share with the group.

*Over the next several days read through Psalm 119 in short sections. Reflect upon and record some
of the characteristics of the Word that particularly encourage and challenge you.*

TREASURE THE WORD

—

FDQ: What do you treasure and why?

God's Word is designed to gradually free you from sin's hold on you. The Psalmist said it this way: "I have stored up your word in my heart, that I might not sin against you" (Psalm 119:11). Note the cause and effect: God's Word is "stored up." Why? to stop sin.

This Hebrew word "stored up" is also translated "treasured." The NASB translates Psalm 119:11 accordingly: "Your word I have treasured in my heart." You consider God's Word as a treasure by internalizing it as such. Treasuring the Word leads to transformation.

Proverbs 2 uses vivid language to depict how the believer is to treasure God's Word. "Wisdom" is speaking and is viewed as a person. You are wisdom's daughter.

HOW DOES WISDOM ENTREAT YOU TO PURSUE HER?

Read the following passage.

PROVERBS 2:1-4

My son, if you receive my words and treasure up my commandments with you, making your ear attentive to wisdom and inclining your heart to understanding; yes, if you call out for insight and raise your voice for understanding, if you seek it like silver and search for it as for hidden treasures....

receive, treasure up (same as in Ps 119:11), make your ear attentive, incline your heart, call out, raise your voice, seek like silver, and search as for hidden treasure.

FDQ: How does a person become wise?
- TREASURE — store up Scripture in your mind.
- BE ATTENTIVE, INCLINE — meditate on Scripture.
- CALL OUT — pray for insight.

God is eager to give us the free, merciful gift of wisdom.

This list of activities addresses both the internal issues and motives of the heart, as well as the external efforts (both mental and physical). Wisdom's urgent plea points to this: whatever is necessary, expend all energies in your pursuit of Wisdom!

Proverbs 2:5 continues, "then you will understand the fear of the Lord and find the knowledge of God." The remaining verses (Proverbs 2:5-15) describe the benefits that come to you when you develop the pattern of pursuing wisdom.

BE A WOMAN OF THE WORD

——

How then are you to engage with God's Word so that you can experience personal transformation and growth?

Read the Bible Regularly

One of the most important things you can do is to regularly read (or listen to) the Bible. There is no replacement. Becoming familiar with the whole counsel of God is essential and profitable (2 Timothy 3:16), for all Scripture reveals to you who God is, what He has promised, and how He has worked and is working. "For whatever was written in former days was written for our instruction, that through endurance and through the encouragement of the Scriptures we might have hope" (Romans 15:4).

To "endure" is to remain under pressure an extended period of time. Endurance requires focusing on the promises of God (not focusing on unmet desires). God makes promises to His people and He wants His people to trust in these promises. Through "endurance" and the "encouragement of the Scriptures," your hope grows.

Do you have a regular time in the Word? What does it look like for you?

What keeps you from being in the Word, both inward attitudes and outward obstacles?

What are you willing to sacrifice to be in the Word?

FDQ: Do you spend more time reading or listening to things about the Bible than you spend actually reading or listening to the Bible?

A personal testimony

I sacrifice to be in the Word. I can't study the Word at night because that is my time to spend with my husband and my kids. So I choose to wake up early before everyone else is awake so I can have some quiet time to read the Word and to pray. I sacrifice sleep, watching TV, looking at my phone—checking email and social media. But I love the Word, so it is well worth it.

The Word is at Work in You and Energizes You

1 THESSALONIANS 2:13

And we also thank God constantly for this, that when you received the word of God, which you heard from us, you accepted it not as the word of men but as what it really is, the word of God, which is at work in you believers.

2 PETER 1:3

His divine power has granted to us all things that pertain to life and godliness, through the knowledge of him who called us to his own glory and excellence....

The author of Hebrews writes, "For the word of God is living and active, sharper than any two-edged sword, piercing to the division of soul and spirit, of joints and marrow, and discerning the thoughts and intentions of the heart" (Hebrews 4:12). The Bible is alive and powerful, so every time you read it, it can, if you allow, work in your heart with surprising precision to discern your thoughts and motives. It will convict, instruct, and revive you, and as it does you will behold God's glory.

Have you been experiencing Scripture alive and active in your life? Give an example.

In no more than fifteen minutes a day you can read through (or listen to) the entire Bible in less than one year! So pick a time in your day that you can commit to read (listen to) the Word and to pray, and do it. Ask the Lord to help you guard this time. If you miss a day or two, or a week or two, or a month or two, do not become defeated. That is just what the enemy desires. Keep at it.

One favorite reading plan is the 5 Day Bible Reading Program. This is a chronological reading plan with five readings a week allowing for catch-up days. (See www.BibleClassMaterial.com for the schedule as well as a companion study guide.)

In addition, the ESV Chronological Podcast by Crossway is an excellent option for listening through the Bible.

MEDITATE ON THE WORD

—

FDQ: How does biblical meditation differ from other forms of meditation?

Throughout Scripture the importance of meditating on the Word is instructed. Donald S. Whitney in his book *Spiritual Disciplines for the Christian Life* defines meditation as "deep thinking on the truths and spiritual realities revealed in Scripture for the purposes of understanding, application, and prayer."[1] God has designed you to stop and ponder His truths so that you are not only familiar with the Word but captivated by it and build your life on it.

As the Psalmist declares, "Blessed is the man... [whose] delight is in the law of the LORD, and on his law he meditates day and night" (Psalm 1:2). The blessed one, the happy one, is the one who loves the Word of God.

FDQ: Review Psalm 1. Delighting on the law parallels meditating on the law. What does it mean to delight in something? Give an example. Delighting in the Word leads us to think on the Word which increases our delight of the Word.

V 3 — What is the blessed person like? The tree represents life. The water represents God's Word. Why does the tree flourish? Because it is planted near water—its life source. The imagery is beautiful. Israel is a semi-desert region with almost no rain from May to October. For a tree to flourish it must be planted intentionally by water.

Likewise, the Scripture is living water for our thirsty souls. We must be intentional to read and meditate upon the Word. How are you being intentional to think on the Word throughout the day?

HOW ARE YOU TO MEDITATE ON THE WORD?

Read the following Scriptures and record your response.

PSALM 119:15

I will meditate on your precepts and fix my eyes on your ways.

I am to fix my eyes, focus on the Word and tune out distractions.

PSALM 119:27

Make me understand the way of your precepts, and I will meditate on your wondrous works.

I am to ask God to help me understand His ways.

PSALM 143:5

I remember the days of old; I meditate on all that you have done; I ponder the work of your hands.

I am to remember what God has done from beginning to end in the world and in my life.

In your daily Bible reading you may come across a verse or passage that catches your attention. Spend some intentional time at different points in your day thoughtfully considering the Scripture. Whitney suggests several ways to think on the passage (pages 56-68 from his book). A few of his suggestions include:

1. Emphasize different words in the text. Ponder every word and what it brings to the meaning of the sentence.

2. Rewrite the text in your own words.

3. Ask: What does it teach about God, Jesus, the Gospel?

4. Ask: What question is answered or what problem is solved?

5. Ask: Is there a command for me to follow or a sin for me to avoid?

6. Pray through the text.

7. Memorize the text.

NOTICE HOW MEDITATION IS PRECIOUS TO THE PSALMIST.

Review the following meditations recorded in Psalm 119.

- "on your precepts" (15, 78)
- "on your statutes" (23, 48)
- "on your wondrous works" (27)
- "Your testimonies are my meditation" (99)
- "Oh how I love your law! It is my meditation all the day" (97)

MEMORIZE THE WORD

—

Though the Bible does not command Scripture memorization, the Christ-follower is to know, remember, store-up, and keep God's Word. Memorizing Scripture is an aid to meditation. Janet Pope, who has memorized 17 books of the Bible, advocates memorizing passages and books instead of scattered verses.

"

By memorizing sequential verses you avoid wrong thinking, which leads to wrong application.... A better approach involves memorizing them in their context, which keeps the focus on God and greatly enhances our learning in the process.[2]

JANET POPE

Every person can memorize, and every person has the choice to memorize. Perhaps you need some incentive. What are some benefits of memorizing the Word?

As you gaze upon God:

1. You will become more like Him and enjoy Him more fully.

2. You will be better able to renew your mind.

3. You will be better equipped to fight temptation with God's truth.

4. You will be better able to comfort and care for others.

5. You will be better equipped to share the gospel with others.

''

I know of no other single practice in the Christian life more rewarding, practically speaking, than memorizing Scripture.... No other single exercise pays greater spiritual dividends! Your prayer life will be strengthened. Your witnessing will be sharper and much more effective. Your attitudes and outlook will begin to change. Your mind will become alert and observant. Your confidence and assurance will be enhanced. Your faith will be solidified.[3]

CHUCK SWINDOLL

If you are not in the habit of memorizing the Word, begin by memorizing Psalm 1. It is only six verses and can be recited and reviewed in less than one minute. Why not memorize Psalm 1:1 today?

Tips for Memorizing:

- Choose a Bible version you like and stick to this version.
- Write out the passage on a 4 x 6 card and/or use a Bible app (like www.fighterverses.com).
- Begin by repeating the first verse 10x in a row. The next day review the first verse and continue with the next one, repeating it 10x in a row. Continue in this pattern.
- Use the time—when you are driving, doing dishes, folding laundry, brushing your teeth, etc. to recite and review.
- Be sure to review at least twice every day, in the morning and evening.
- Create a review schedule.
- Have an accountability partner and check in once a week with each other.

OBEY THE WORD
—

Reading, meditating upon, and memorizing the Word should always result in your obeying it. Obeying the Word brings blessing—your faith grows, your character becomes more Christ-like, and your joy increases.

JAMES 1:22-25

But be doers of the word, and not hearers only, deceiving yourselves. For if anyone is a hearer of the word and not a doer, he is like a man who looks intently at his natural face in a mirror. For he looks at himself and goes away and at once forgets what he was like. But the one who looks into the perfect law, the law of liberty, and perseveres, being no hearer who forgets but a doer who acts, he will be blessed in his doing.

ABIDE IN THE LORD AND BEHOLD HIS GLORY

——

Perhaps you are feeling discouraged because you do not treasure God's Word. Or you feel you have tried to develop a regular time in the Word to read, pray, and meditate but it never lasts long. Remember, there is a war going on for your heart every day. So ask the Lord, plead with Him, to teach you (Psalm 119:33) and to increase your understanding of His Word (Psalm 119:34) that you might taste and see that He is good. Then choose each day to keep your date with Him. Abiding in the Lord by beholding the glory of the Lord through His Word changes you into His likeness. A woman who wants to be transformed must see the glory of the Lord over and over again.

Sanctify them in the truth; your word is truth.

JOHN 17:17

END YOUR STUDY...

Summarize what you learned from this lesson

"ABIDING IN THE WORD"

———

A personal testimony

About five years ago I joined a women's Bible study. We were led through Scripture verse-by-verse by a very enthusiastic teacher who had a heart for leading women through the Bible. When I started the study (to be honest) I was just excited to be with my friends! I was not expecting how God's Word was going to change me and my spiritual walk.

I was thankful for the opportunity to study Scripture and I had good intentions to know God, but I was a little nervous to open the Word and jump in. For me the Bible was a little intimidating to read. For starters...it's a pretty long book! I had a difficult time understanding some of the words and terminology. I also wanted to know everything now. But over time and through several different studies, God increased my love for Him and my desire to know Him grew. The Bible is no longer intimidating to me. It has become welcome, familiar, and a constant reminder to me of God's promises.

1 Peter 1:22-2:3 is a great section to sum up my experience over the past few years.

1 PETER 1:22-2:3

Having purified your souls by your obedience to the truth for a sincere brotherly love, love one another earnestly from a pure heart, since you have been born again, not of perishable seed but of imperishable, through the living and abiding word of God; for "All flesh is like grass and all its glory like the flower of grass. The grass withers, and the flower falls, but the word of the Lord remains forever." And this word is the good news that was preached to you. So put away all malice and all deceit and hypocrisy and envy and all slander. Like newborn infants, long for the pure spiritual milk, that by it you may grow up into salvation—if indeed you have tasted that the Lord is good.

As a believer, you have the Spirit and the Word of God to help you through this crazy world. Reading the Word of God and choosing to obey the Spirit will equip you and nourish you spiritually. The more you are exposed to the truths of God, the more you will desire to know them and live by them.

Are you willing to allow God to do His work in you?

"MEMORIZING THE WORD"

A personal testimony

My thoughts, I've realized, can be extremely destructive. Whether I'm driving, going to bed or simply bored, my mind can easily wander to useless or sinful things. A while back I decided to start memorizing Colossians. From that point on, whenever I got in my car or was trying to fall asleep at night, I would immediately start working on my verses and would recite them over and over again. I was literally consuming my mind with God's Word.

Because my thoughts were turned more to the Lord, I noticed that my emotions were affected as well. For example, a few weeks ago I was disappointed by someone close to me. In the past I would have allowed something like this to make me cry and/or hide out and fall into self-pity. As I walked away from this disappointing conversation, I was flooded with verses that I had been memorizing. Colossians 1:15-17 says, "He is the image of the Invisible God, the firstborn of all creation. For by Him all things were created, in Heaven and on Earth, visible and invisible—whether thrones or dominions or rulers or authorities—all things were created through him and for him. And he is before all things, and in him all things hold together." I was able to praise God knowing that He is intimately involved in EVERYTHING. He holds everything together and I can trust that He was involved in that circumstance too! When I got in my car I was filled with peace and even joy! I laughed and said, "Well I guess I'll just keep living my life!"

There are days when I don't necessarily want to go over verses. It is so easy to do nothing and be tempted by our own desires and to let them consume us. But I found that when I trust that the Holy Spirit is going to produce fruit through my efforts of discipline, it is incredible to see the crazy awesome things He does. We can expect Him to move and that should excite us and make us want to do some of those things that may go against our flesh nature!

Ask the Father to open the eyes of your heart that you may behold wondrous things from His Word (Psalm 119:18). Write your prayer below. What is one thing you would like to commit to doing to abide in the Word? Share this with a friend.

— LESSON 2 —

Abiding in Prayer

Prayer is an important part of abiding in Christ; it is an intentional way to recognize and acknowledge God's greatness. "Prayer is a spiritual practice of the presence of God. It is a way we become aware of and experience God's presence and character, allowing us to become aware of our desperate need for Him."[1] As a child of God you have access to the Father through prayer every moment of every day. He is eager for you to pour out your heart to Him in small and great matters (Psalm 62:8; Lamentations 2:19). Prayer is a command (Ephesians 6:18; Romans 12:12), but more than that, it is your awesome privilege as a follower of Christ. In this lesson you will examine what it looks like to develop the habit of prayer.

COME INTO THE FATHER'S PRESENCE

—

Prayer is an invitation to come into the presence of God your Father and share your heart.

God invites.

JEREMIAH 33:3

"Call to me and I will answer you, and will tell you great and hidden things that you have not known."

Jesus provides access.

EPHESIANS 2:18

For through him we both have access in one Spirit to the Father.

Holy Spirit intercedes.

ROMANS 8:27b

[T]he Spirit intercedes for the saints according to the will of God.

In His presence there is great joy knowing that your heavenly Father hears, cares, and responds. So come to Him whether you are grieving, happy, burdened, needy, joyful or downcast.

FDQ: You know intellectually that you can approach God as Father, but how does it make you feel? It will encourage some participants, but others may struggle because they do not have a nurturing earthly father. Encourage them to ask God to reveal Himself as a loving father to them as they go through this lesson.

A PRAYING LIFE

—

Paul Miller, in his book, *A Praying Life* [2], shares that God taught him much about prayer as he sought to love and care for his severely autistic daughter. It became Miller's great joy to receive his daughter when she learned to run to him with her needs, joys, tears, laughter, and as she communicated in her own childlike, sometimes frustrated, way. Miller began to understand this was a picture of how we are to come to our Heavenly Father in prayer. It brings God great joy when His children run to Him just as they are, sharing everything. Miller's encouragement includes the following:

• Prayer does not offer us a less busy life; it offers us a less busy heart.
• Do not try to get prayer right; just tell God where you are and what is on your mind. Do not be embarrassed by how needy your heart is.
• Learned desperation is at the heart of a praying life.
• Live in your Father's story. Prayer helps you watch God weave His patterns in the story of your life. When the story is not going your way, ask yourself, "What is God doing?"

CONSTANT AND INTENTIONAL PRAYER

It is important to have both an intentional, focused prayer time each day as well as an attitude of prayer throughout your day.

Constant Prayer

What do you think it means that you are to "pray without ceasing" (1 Thessalonians 5:17)?

As a child of God I am indwelled by the Spirit to live every moment in the knowledge and attitude of being in the Father's presence. I can talk to Him at any point in my day.

Praying without ceasing means you can keep in step with the Spirit. So as the Spirit convicts, you are able to recognize it and offer a prayer of confession. It means when you are in the midst of a conflict or dilemma, you can offer a quick prayer for help—a "breath" prayer. It means that you can "multi-task" (i.e., work and pray at the same time). You can praise God in the middle of whatever you are doing.

Intentional Prayer

It is also important that you are intentional about setting aside time in your day for focused prayer. Read the Scriptures below and answer the questions.

PSALM 5:3
O Lord, in the morning you hear my voice: in the morning I prepare a sacrifice for you and watch.

LUKE 5:16 (NIV)
But Jesus often withdrew to lonely places and prayed.

Do you have an intentional prayer time(s) in your day?

_____

_____

What things have you learned that are helpful in keeping intentional prayer in your day?

_____

_____

_____

CONNECTING IN PRAYER

___

LIST THE ATTITUDES OF THE HEART THAT MAY PREVENT YOU FROM CONNECTING WITH THE FATHER IN PRAYER.

Read the following passage and list your response.

JAMES 4:2-6

You desire and do not have, so you murder. You covet and cannot obtain, so you fight and quarrel. You do not have, because you do not ask. You ask and do not receive, because you ask wrongly, to spend it on your passions. You adulterous people! Do you not know that friendship with the world is enmity with God? Therefore whoever wishes to be a friend of the world makes himself an enemy of God. Or do you suppose it is to no purpose that the Scripture says, "He yearns jealously over the spirit that he has made to dwell in us"? But he gives more grace. Therefore it says, "God opposes the proud, but gives grace to the humble."

Trying to get something by your own means

Not asking God

Asking with wrong motives

Living with a divided heart (friendship with world)

Pride

Forgetting the Holy Spirit indwells you

HINDRANCES TO PRAYER.

Read the following verse and record your responses to the questions below.

PSALM 66:18

If I had cherished iniquity in my heart, the Lord would not have listened.

Loving sin

FDQ: What does it mean to cherish iniquity in your heart? Can you share a time you realized something you cherished was a sin or had become a sin/idol to you?

List some of the things that hinder you or challenge you in praying.

Being tired or busy, being discouraged because I do not see answers to long-standing prayers for others, feeling like it is dry, feeling like I am following a formula instead of connecting with God.

FDQ: In this section encourage your participants to discuss their personal hindrances in prayer. You may need to start the discussion by sharing the hindrances you have been challenged with. Encourage them to brainstorm ways to overcome those hindrances. Be sure to discuss practical hindrances such as scheduling a prayer time in your life (where, when, for what to pray, how to consistently pray for those people I say I will pray for, etc.)

What can you do differently?

Make it a time of worship. Remind myself of my relationship with the Father in prayer so that it comes from my heart and not from a "formula." Pray (long or short, depending on the circumstance) first thing in the morning, whether it is a breath prayer or a prayer time and Scripture reading, with a cup of coffee or a brisk walk, or worship music. Ask God to show me how my heart best connects with Him in a scheduled way that becomes part of my daily life.

FDQ: Have participants share their ideas.

STRUGGLES IN PRAYER

――

The Psalms teach you to pour out your heart to the Lord. Jesus said, "If you abide in me, and my words abide in you, ask whatever you wish, and it will be done for you" (John 15:7). You may ask for healing or for a loved one to be saved or for your marriage to be restored. You may not believe that God answered you because you may not see the answer as you requested. However, God answers all your requests, either in His own way or in a "no." But remember, the Father's heart is for you, and He is faithful to you. Jesus, in the Garden of Gethsemane, asked His Father to take the cup of the cross from Him. The Father's answer was "no." Jesus' submission to the Father's will is described in Part 5 Lesson 3, including the Scriptures. Second Corinthians 12:7-10 describes Paul's prayer-- to have his "thorn in the flesh" removed. Three times Paul pleaded with the Lord. The Lord's answer was, "My grace is sufficient for you, for my power is made perfect in weakness." Paul determined to "boast all the more gladly of [his] weaknesses, so that the power of Christ may rest upon [him]." Christ was more important to Paul than the specific answer Paul had asked for. In both situations God provided what they needed even though they didn't get the answer they requested. Luke 22:43 describes the help the Father gave to Jesus. He sent an angel to strengthen Him. Hebrews 4:16 tells you to come confidently to the throne of grace "that [you] many receive mercy and find grace to help in time of need." God always gives you what you need if you are coming to Him.

RIGHT ATTITUDES OF PRAYER

――

As you overcome hindrances in your prayer life and make prayer a daily habit, your heart will become more and more aligned to God's heart. Prayer will change your attitude toward situations and persons. It will humble you and help you see God more clearly and accurately. The most precious gift you will receive in prayer is God Himself—knowing Him more intimately.

Have a right view of God

1 CHRONICLES 29:10-13

Therefore David blessed the LORD in the presence of all the assembly. And David said: "Blessed are you, O LORD, the God of Israel our father, forever and ever. Yours, O LORD, is the greatness and the power and the glory and the victory and the majesty, for all that is in the heavens and in the earth is yours. Yours is the kingdom, O LORD, and you are exalted as head above all. Both riches and honor come from you, and you rule over all. In your hand are power and might, and in your hand it is to make great and to give strength to all. And now we thank you, our God, and praise your glorious name."

Are there any heart changes you need to make to see God the way David does?

I know these things intellectually, but I need to spend more prayer and meditation time actually worshiping God.

Be steadfast, watchful, and thankful

COLOSSIANS 4:2
Continue steadfastly in prayer, being watchful in it with thanksgiving.

What does it mean to be steadfast in prayer?

To be consistent, devoted, not giving up in prayer, praying with your whole heart undivided; praying expectantly.

What does it mean to be watchful in prayer?

To be alert, taking prayer seriously, asking God to show me my motive. Also, watchful (i.e., looking for how God is working in the situation). I am to pray expectantly even if I pray the same prayer for years (e.g., someone's salvation).

When you do not see an answer to prayer, how can you be thankful (i.e., have a heart of gratitude)?

I can have confidence that God hears and God responds. It may not be on my timetable, and it may not be answered the way I envision, but if I am asking with right motives, He will respond. I can also continue to count the blessings God is daily providing.

Seek an undivided heart

PSALM 86:11b-12a
[U]nite my heart to fear your name. I give thanks to you, O Lord my God, with my whole heart....

Have a humble heart

JAMES 4:10
Humble yourselves before the Lord, and He will exalt you.

Acknowledge your need for God and ask Him to unite your heart to His.

FDQ: God responds to our prayers when they are asked with the right motive (James 4:3), but His answer may be "no" or may be different than we anticipate. Can you share a time when God answered "no" or He responded differently than you hoped, and you now see the benefit of His answer? Can you think of a time you prayed for something and God answered in a way that far exceeded your expectations? "Now to him who is able to do far more abundantly than all that we ask or think, according to the power at work within us, to Him be the glory in the church and in Christ Jesus throughout all generations, forever and ever. Amen" (Ephesians 3:20-21).

PRAYING THE SCRIPTURES

Personalizing and praying Scripture is a powerful and encouraging way to communicate with God and to allow Him to communicate with you. Several examples are listed below:

FDQ: Do you pray the Scriptures? How have you found it helpful?

HEBREWS 13:20-21

Now may the God of peace who brought again from the dead our Lord Jesus, the great shepherd of the sheep, by the blood of the eternal covenant, equip you with everything good that you may do his will, working in us that which is pleasing in his sight, through Jesus Christ, to whom be glory forever and ever. Amen.

HEBREWS 13:20-21 *Personalized*

Thank you that you are a God of peace and that you brought Jesus back to life to be my peace and to be my Great Shepherd. Thank you that you keep your promises for all eternity. Thank you that you equip me with every good thing so that I am able to do your will. Help me recognize the ways you are equipping me in the situation I am now dealing with. Help me to do your will. Work in me what is pleasing and honoring to you. May the Lord Jesus Christ be glorified in my life now and forever and ever. Amen!

PSALM 62:1-2

For God alone my soul waits in silence; from him comes my salvation. He alone is my rock and my salvation, my fortress; I shall not be greatly shaken.

PSALM 62:1-2 *Personalized*

Thank you Lord that you alone are my salvation for all eternity. You are my salvation even now, when my soul is distressed, when my soul is evaluating other sources of comfort. Thank you for reminding me of the truth I already know, that you alone satisfy my soul!

NOW READ THE FOLLOWING SCRIPTURES AND WRITE A PERSONAL PRAYER FOR EACH ONE.

HEBREWS 12:1-2

Therefore, since we are surrounded by so great a cloud of witnesses, let us also lay aside every weight, and sin which clings so closely, and let us run with endurance the race that is set before us, looking to Jesus, the founder and perfecter of our faith, who for the joy that was set before him endured the cross, despising the shame, and is seated at the right hand of the throne of God.

HEBREWS 12:1-2 *Personalized*

PSALM 31:14-16

But I trust in you, O LORD; I say, "You are my God." My times are in your hand; rescue me from the hand of my enemies and from my persecutors! Make your face shine on your servant; save me in your steadfast love!

PSALM 31:14-16 *Personalized*

Praying Scripture may be a new concept for you. If so, as you read the Word each day, pause as you come across something that stands out to you or "speaks to you." Pray this back to the Lord. It can be very encouraging to keep a journal of all your prayer Scriptures. Date them. They will be reminders of God's intimate presence in your life throughout all the seasons of your life.

FOR WHAT SHALL I PRAY?

—

Different types of prayers are listed below. This is not an exhaustive list.

Thanksgiving

PSALM 118:1

Oh give thanks to the LORD, for he is good; for his steadfast love endures forever!

Guidance

PSALM 25:4-5

Make me to know your ways, O LORD; teach me your paths. Lead me in your truth and teach me, for you are the God of my salvation; for you I wait all the day long.

Anxiety

PSALM 94:19

When the cares of my heart are many, your consolations cheer my soul. (ESV)
When anxiety was great within me, your consolation brought me joy. (NIV)

Surrender

JOHN 12:27-28a

"Now is my soul troubled. And what shall I say? 'Father, save me from this hour'? But for this purpose I have come to this hour. Father, glorify your name."

Confession

PSALM 51:1

Have mercy on me, O God, according to your steadfast love; according to your abundant mercy blot out my transgressions.

Supplication, petition, intercession

COLOSSIANS 1:9-11

And so, from the day we heard, we have not ceased to pray for you, asking that you may be filled with the knowledge of his will in all spiritual wisdom and understanding, so as to walk in a manner worthy of the Lord, fully pleasing to him, bearing fruit in every good work and increasing in the knowledge of God. May you be strengthened with all power, according to His glorious might, for all endurance and patience with joy....

Adoration and Praise

JUDE 24-25

Now to him who is able to keep you from stumbling and to present you blameless before the presence of his glory with great joy, to the only God, our Savior, through Jesus Christ our Lord, be glory, majesty, dominion, and authority, before all time and now and forever. Amen.

Scripture provides many wonderful lessons on prayer, but learning about prayer is not the same as actually praying. D. A. Carson gives this reminder: "Effective prayer is the fruit of a relationship with God, not a technique for acquiring blessings."[3] As you abide in the Lord may your communion with the Lord through prayer grow rich, meaningful roots.

END YOUR STUDY...

Summarize what you learned from this lesson

JESUS INSTRUCTED US TO

"pray then like this:

Our Father in heaven, hallowed be your name.

Your kingdom come, your will be done, on earth as it is in heaven.

Give us this day our daily bread,

And forgive us our debts, as we also have forgiven our debtors.

And lead us not into temptation, but deliver us from evil."

MATTHEW 6:9-13

The Lord's Prayer

"Our Father in heaven, hallowed be your name."

What a beautiful declaration. Through Jesus our meditator, we have access to come before our loving Father (Romans 5:2; Ephesians 2:18; 1 Peter 2:24). We need not fear approaching God in prayer because He loves us and calls us His own.

He is not only our Father but also our Supreme King for He is sacred and ultimate (hallowed). So we are to ask God to help us honor, esteem, revere, value, treasure, and love the name of God in our hearts, and we are to ask Him to cause His name to be treasured above all things everywhere in the world. (There are more than 900 names of God in the Bible!)

DEUTERONOMY 32:3-4
"For I will proclaim the name of the LORD; ascribe greatness to our God! The Rock, his work is perfect, for all his ways are justice. A God of faithfulness and without iniquity, just and upright is he."

"Your Kingdom come, your will be done, on earth as it is in heaven."

Next, Jesus instructs us to pray that God's reign will expand and come to fullness, to completion. "But according to his promise we are waiting for new heavens and a new earth in which righteousness dwells" (2 Peter 3:13). We are to hunger for God's kingdom to come in all its righteousness.

Because God is our loving Father who faithfully cares for our every need, because He is our Holy God who is above all things and worthy of all our praise, we can cry out to Him in surrender, "Your will be done." We are to ask Him to fully rule, and we are to seek to follow Him with our whole hearts.

What God commands in heaven the angels are eager and joyful to carry it out. This is to be our disposition. We are to ask God to help us live each day mindful and eager to obey Him and to do His will.

In these first petitions the focus is on the expansion of His glory and His kingdom. What follows are the petitions a child of God prays for herself and for others.

"Give us this day our daily bread."

In this brief sentence, Jesus teaches us to pray for our needs. He is not teaching us to necessarily pray for extravagant things—rather we are to pray regarding even the mundane and very ordinary aspects of our lives. We need daily food to survive and thrive, and in asking to God to provide for this basic necessity, we are acknowledging and trusting Him as the Giver of all things.

"If God doesn't rule your mundane, then he doesn't rule you. Because that's where you live."–Paul Tripp (as quoted in *Glimpses of Grace: Treasuring the Gospel in Your Home* by Gloria Furman, p.27).

Notice also that in praying only for today's needs ("daily bread"), we are compelled to rely on Him for tomorrow's needs, trusting that He will provide again when the needs arise. Just as the Israelites were commanded to gather just enough manna for the day and trust that God will provide manna for the next day, we are to trust Him for our needs day-by-day.

"Therefore do not be anxious about tomorrow..."–Jesus in Matthew 6:34a.

Another significant aspect of this prayer is the connection between "daily bread" and Jesus, who called Himself "the Bread of Life" (John 6:35, 41, 48). Just as we need physical bread, we need to daily feed on (i.e., love, treasure, and obey) the True Bread.

"It is written, 'Man shall not live by bread alone, but by every word that comes from the mouth of God'"–Jesus in Matthew 4:4.

"And forgive us our debts, as we also have forgiven our debtors."

Jesus wants us to understand that we need forgiveness for the ways we daily sin, and we need to daily forgive those who sin against us.

Ephesians 1:7-8 says, "In him (Christ) we have redemption through his blood, the forgiveness of our trespasses, according to the riches of his grace, which he lavished upon us." Our forgiveness from God through Christ is ongoing and covers every trespass—all the ways we cross the line with God. This ongoing forgiveness was accomplished once for all at the cross, when Jesus took on our sins, and it was imparted to us when we were "born again."

Now because of our rebirth, Jesus tells us we are to forgive others in the same way He forgives us. We are to have an ongoing attitude of forgiveness toward those who sin against us. "[B]earing with one another and, if one has a complaint against another, forgiving each other, as the Lord has forgiven you, so you also must forgive" (Colossians 3:13). Through Christ's forgiveness we have both the command and the ability to forgive others.

"And lead us not into temptation, but deliver us from evil."

In the final petition Jesus instructs us to ask the Father to help us not fall victim to temptation and to rescue us from evil.

All things that come into our lives, both good and bad, have the potential, depending on what we believe and choose, to draw us to the Father or to propel us away from Him.

As we pray, we are to appeal to the Father to keep us from the prospect of giving into temptation and sin. We are to view everything that comes into our lives as from the Father's hand and respond accordingly. If we do, we will choose to trust and obey Him. If we do not view things in this way, we may not recognize God or we will find it difficult to trust and obey God, and we will likely give in to temptation and sin.

ALL our experiences are both tests from God and temptations from Satan. In every experience, both pleasant and painful, we have a choice either to acknowledge God and respond in humble dependence and gratitude, or we have a choice to forsake our allegiance to God, give in to temptation, and respond in prideful disobedience.

In pleasant experiences the

- test is – Will we recognize God and thank Him for His care and provision?
- temptation is – Will we idolize the experience? Will we become complacent and not acknowledge God or thank Him? Will we take credit or take things for granted?

In painful experiences the

- test is – Will we trust God? Do we believe that through the experience, God desires to refine us into His likeness and increase our dependency on Him and our intimacy with Him?
- temptation is – Will we curse God and blame Him? Will we turn away from Him to the things of the world? Will we seek control of the situation or person?

What are the keys to resisting temptation?

1. God's Word is our best defense. The better we know His Word, the easier it will be to victoriously fight in our daily struggles.
2. Remember what Jesus endured. Jesus endured the torture of the cross and God's wrath on our behalf (Romans 5:8). How much does the love of Jesus occupy our hearts?
3. Keep watch and pray. Jesus warned in the Garden of Gethsemane, "Watch and pray that you may not enter into temptation. The spirit indeed is willing, but the flesh is weak" (Matthew 26:41).

Take some time now to pray about whatever is on your heart.

O LORD, I call upon you; hasten to me!
Give ear to my voice when I call to you!
Let my prayer be counted as incense before you,
and the lifting up of my hands as the evening sacrifice!

PSALM 141:1-2

LESSON 3

Abiding in Community

Scripture gives a beautiful picture of the role of the church in the spread of the gospel as well as the growth and care of Christ-followers. In Lesson 3 you will explore the role of the local church in the life of a believer. To begin you will look at the gathering of the first church described in Acts 2:42-47.

ABIDING IN COMMUNITY

REVIEW THE ACTIVITIES OF THE EARLY CHURCH BELIEVERS. WHAT WAS THEIR ATTITUDE TOWARD THE GOSPEL AND TOWARD ONE ANOTHER?

Read the following passage and record your response.

ACTS 2:42-47

And they devoted themselves to the apostles' teaching and the fellowship, to the breaking of bread and the prayers. And awe came upon every soul, and many wonders and signs were being done through the apostles. And all who believed were together and had all things in common. And they were selling their possessions and belongings and distributing the proceeds to all, as any had need. And day by day, attending the temple together and breaking bread in their homes, they received their food with glad and generous hearts, praising God and having favor with all the people. And the Lord added to their number day by day those who were being saved.

They were devoted to the apostles' teaching, devoted to fellowship with each other, awed by evidence of God's presence in signs and wonders. They had all things in common, sold their possessions to provide for those in need, daily attended temple together, broke bread together in their homes, gave thanks with generous hearts, and were in good favor with all people. The Lord saved many more.

The people of the first church were connected in authentic relationships by a common purpose. The result was they grew in their love for the Lord and their devotion to one other, and the gospel continued to be heard and received by more people. This first church was not just an anomaly. As the gospel spread into different regions, a local church was established in each of those regions.

Hebrews 10:24-25 confirms that the regular meeting together with a local community of believers is to be a central part of each Christian's life until Christ returns. "And let us consider how to stir up one another to love and good works, not neglecting to meet together, as is the habit of some, but encouraging one another, and all the more as you see the Day drawing near" (Hebrews 10:24-25).

What is the common purpose of the church and why is it necessary in the context of authentic relationships?

_____

_____

_____

_____

_____

_____

COMMON PURPOSE

Randy Frazee in his book *The Connecting Church* describes the first church as, "having a common purpose... all believers were one heart and mind." They had "the common belief and purpose built on the teachings of Jesus." [1]

WHAT COMMON PURPOSE(S) DO YOU SEE IN THE FOLLOWING SCRIPTURES?

Read the following Scriptures and record your response.

I CORINTHIANS 15:1-4

Now I would remind you, brothers, of the gospel I preached to you, which you received, in which you stand, and by which you are being saved, if you hold fast to the word I preached to you—unless you believed in vain. For I delivered to you as of first importance what I also received: that Christ died for our sins in accordance with the Scriptures, that he was buried, that he was raised on the third day in accordance with the Scriptures.

Our first, primary, common purpose is embracing the gospel.

EPHESIANS 4:4-6

There is one body and one Spirit—just as you were called to the one hope that belongs to your call—one Lord, one faith, one baptism, one God and Father of all, who is over all and through all and in all.

We are unified as a body in our belief, commitment, and eternal hope that comes from the Father, Son, and Spirit.

MATTHEW 28:18b-20

"All authority in heaven and on earth has been given to me. Go therefore and make disciples of all nations, baptizing them in the name of the Father and of the Son and of the Holy Spirit, teaching them to observe all that I have commanded you. And behold, I am with you always, to the end of the age."

We are all called with the same calling to go and make disciples, teaching them to observe Christ's teachings.

As a follower of Christ...

- You are united with all other followers of Christ because of your core belief in the gospel (Philippians 1:27).
- You have a common calling, identity, and purpose (1 Peter 2:9; Philippians 2:14-16a).

AUTHENTIC RELATIONSHIPS

—

What makes a relationship authentic?

According to the model of the first church, you are to live out your Christian beliefs in the context of authentic relationships in the church community. In 1 Corinthians 12:12 Paul describes the church as one body with many members and each member having a unique function. The members are all interconnected and interdependent. The things you are called to do as part of the church cannot effectively be done in any way other than through honest relationships in a close-knit community of believers.

How can you stir up (motivate and stimulate) and encourage others "to love and good works" (Hebrews 10:24-25) if you do not know others well enough to know their gifts, joys, struggles, etc? How can others do that for you if you do not allow them to know you in the same way?

WHAT ARE THE BENEFITS OF BEING INVOLVED IN A LOCAL COMMUNITY OF BELIEVERS?
Read the following Scriptures and record your response.

HEBREWS 3:12-13
Take care, brothers, lest there be in any of you an evil, unbelieving heart, leading you to fall away from the living God. But exhort one another every day, as long as it is called "today," that none of you may be hardened by the deceitfulness of sin.

We live in close relationship with each other so we know when someone is struggling and can come along beside her and exhort, encourage, and admonish her so that her heart is not hardened; others can do that for me also.

FDQ: The importance of exhortation (Hebrews 3:12-13): The word "exhort" means to come alongside in a close connection (as with your arm around the person). To stimulate, remind, speak what needs to be spoken every day. There is a sense of immediacy, cannot "get to it later." Must be done daily, can be done in a corporate setting but most significantly one-to-one in a deep, trusting relationship.

HEBREWS 13:17a
Obey your leaders and submit to them, for they are keeping watch over your souls, as those who will have to give an account.

Godly leadership in the local church provides protection, godly counsel, and accountability for me.

1 THESSALONIANS 5:14-15
[A]nd we urge you, brothers, admonish the idle, encourage the fainthearted, help the weak, be patient with them all. See to it that no one repays anyone evil for evil, but always seek to do good to one another and to everyone.

I am able to admonish, encourage, help, and be patient with all, and all are to do the same for me.

How have you benefitted from being involved in your church community?

Take time to pray and ask God who He wants you to encourage.

FDQ: This may be a good time to pass out blank cards to your group to write someone a note of encouragement.

WE ARE FAMILY

—

Because you are in Christ, you are a child of God, and that makes you part of the family of God with all His other children. Neil Anderson, in his book, *Who I am in Christ*[2], talks about the insecurity a person faces when a significant relationship is threatened by desertion, danger, or destruction. Being involved in a close-knit community of believers is one of the best ways to tangibly experience God's unconditional love and security as expressed in Romans 8: "nothing can separate us from the love of God." When the church responds like the family of God, a hurting person can be nurtured and loved in a way that brings healing and promotes spiritual maturity. It is to be the training ground that gives opportunity to grow in God's grace toward one another. As God develops His character in you, you will grow in caring for others.

WHAT ARE THE DIRECTIVES GIVEN TO YOU?

Read the following passages and circle the directives.

ROMANS 12:10

Love one another with brotherly affection. Outdo one another in showing honor.

ROMANS 15:1

We who are strong have an obligation to bear with the failings of the weak, and not to please ourselves.

ROMANS 15:5-6

May the God of endurance and encouragement grant you to live in such harmony with one another, in accord with Christ Jesus, that together you may with one voice glorify the God and Father of our Lord Jesus Christ.

GALATIANS 6:2

Bear one another's burdens, and so fulfill the law of Christ.

FDQ: What do you think it means to "bear one another's burdens"? (Galatians 6:2)
"To bear" means to come alongside someone in support but not to take the person's load. (See Galatians 6:5)

EPHESIANS 4:32

Be kind to one another, tenderhearted, forgiving one another, as God in Christ forgave you.

JAMES 2:1

My brothers, show no partiality as you hold the faith in our Lord Jesus Christ, the Lord of glory.

COLOSSIANS 3:12-14

Put on then, as God's chosen ones, holy and beloved, compassionate hearts, kindness, humility, meekness, and patience, bearing with one another and, if one has a complaint against another, forgiving each other; as the Lord has forgiven you, so you also must forgive. And above all these put on love, which binds everything together in perfect harmony.

Which of these family characteristics seem to come easily to you? Which ones are difficult? Why?

_____

_____

_____

_____

_____

_____

FDQ:
- How have you experienced these characteristics lived out in your church family? How have these experiences impacted your relationship with God?
- Have you experienced these characteristics NOT lived out in your church family? How did/has that impacted you?
- Why might someone resist being involved in a church community?

Jesus established a high standard for how the family of God is to love one another.

JOHN 13:34-35

"A new commandment I give to you, that you love one another: just as I loved you, you also are to love one another. By this all people will know that you are my disciples, if you have love for one another."

Based on how Jesus loved, how are you to love?

Sacrificially, thinking of others' best over my comfort.

What is accomplished when the family of God loves each other as Jesus loved/loves us?

When we love one another well, we show Jesus to the world.

CONFLICT AND SIN IN THE FAMILY

——

The Father's Guidelines for Resolution and Restoration

When you live in close relationship with others, even in the family of God, you will have conflict; however, Scripture provides clarity and direction for resolving conflict in a biblical way. First, be sure you have forgiven the person for how you think she may have sinned against you as well as confessed your own sins in the situation/relationship (see Part 6 Lesson 1 - My Forgiving & Confessing Heart). Make sure you have taken the steps to reconcile (see Part 6 Lesson 2 - My Reconciling Heart).

"

All sin is serious and dishonors God. But to help you think through whether an offense is too serious to be overlooked, ask yourself if the sin is:

- Publically dishonoring God
- Damaging your relationship
- Hurting other people
- Hurting the offender[3]

TARA BARTHEL

DO NOT JUDGE INDISCRIMINATELY.

MATTHEW 7:1-5
"Judge not, that you be not judged. For with the judgment you pronounce you will be judged, and with the measure you use it will be measured to you. Why do you see the speck that is in your brother's eye, but do not notice the log that is in your own eye? Or how can you say to your brother, 'Let me take the speck out of your eye,' when there is the log in your own eye? You hypocrite, first take the log out of your own eye, and then you will see clearly to take the speck out of your brother's eye."

This passage is not saying do not judge, but do not judge indiscriminately with the wrong motive. Be sure you have evaluated your own heart before you speak truth into another person's life.

LET THIS BE YOUR ATTITUDE.

PHILIPPIANS 2:3-4

Do nothing from selfish ambition or conceit, but in humility count others more significant than yourselves. Let each of you look not only to his own interests, but also to the interests of others.

EPHESIANS 4:29

Let no corrupting talk come out of your mouths, but only such as is good for building up, as fits the occasion, that it may give grace to those who hear.

Conflict Resolution

MATTHEW 18:15-17

"If your brother sins against you, go and tell him his fault, between you and him alone. If he listens to you, you have gained your brother. But if he does not listen, take one or two others along with you, that every charge may be established by the evidence of two or three witnesses. If he refuses to listen to them, tell it to the church. And if he refuses to listen even to the church, let him be to you as a Gentile and a tax collector."

The passage is clear that you are to first speak to the offender privately. If the offender is not receptive to your admonishment, you are to take one or two witnesses along to establish evidence. This is not to browbeat or to condemn the person, but to encourage repentance and reconciliation. The ultimate goal is the unity of the body of Christ to glorify God and show Christ to the world. If this step is ineffective, you are to take the matter to the church. This is by no means permission to gossip to the whole church about the situation. You are to take this to the shepherd(s) of your church, and let them determine the next step. Some churches have an elder board, and the men serving on that board provide spiritual leadership as the shepherds of that church community.

It is your responsibility to do what God directs in calling a person to repentance. It is not your responsibility to convince the other person to see her sin. It is not your responsibility to change the other person's heart. Only the Holy Spirit can do that. If the other person is not willing to repent, continue praying for her heart.

The Scripture "let him be to you as a Gentile and a tax collector" (Matthew 18:17) means to treat the person as one who is not a true follower of Christ. Treat the person as Jesus treated the tax collector and Gentile—with concern, respect, and with the desire that they come to know the Father.

See also, 1 Corinthians 5.

WHEN YOU THINK SOMEONE HAS SINNED AGAINST YOU OR WHEN YOU THINK THERE IS A NEED TO ADMONISH, FIRST CONSIDER THE FOLLOWING:

PROVERBS 19:11

Good sense makes one slow to anger, and it is his glory to overlook an offense.

In Humility

COUNT OTHERS

more significant

THAN YOURSELVES.

PHILLIPIANS 2:3b

Admonishment

You are called to admonish. To admonish means "to warn." Admonishing is a ministry of restoration. It is a picture of someone being caught in a snare (trap) and you are called to help.

LUKE 17:3-4

"Pay attention to yourselves! If your brother sins, rebuke him, and if he repents, forgive him, and if he sins against you seven times in the day, and turns to you seven times, saying, 'I repent,' you must forgive him."

JAMES 5:19-20

My brothers, if anyone among you wanders from the truth and someone brings him back, let him know that whoever brings back a sinner from his wandering will save his soul from death and will cover a multitude of sins.

GALATIANS 6:1

Brothers, if anyone is caught in any transgression, you who are spiritual should restore him in a spirit of gentleness. Keep watch on yourself, lest you too be tempted.

What does it mean to be "spiritual"?

A Christ-follower; one filled with the Holy Spirit.

What does it mean to "restore"?

To correct. It is used especially as a surgical term of setting a bone out of joint; or in other contexts of the strengthening or sustaining of a worn down people (Lightfoot) Linguistic and Exegetical Key to GNT (Greek New Testament), Accordance Software (2018).

What attitude should you have when you admonish an offender?

SERVING THE FAMILY

PERSONALIZE HOW YOU CAN SERVE GOD'S FAMILY AS EACH SCRIPTURE INSTRUCTS.

Read the following Scriptures and record your response.

1 CORINTHIANS 12:4-7

Now there are varieties of gifts, but the same Spirit; and there are varieties of service, but the same Lord; and there are varieties of activities, but it is the same God who empowers them all in everyone. To each is given the manifestation of the Spirit for the common good.

Spiritual gifts are given to serve the body.

There are four lists of spiritual gifts: 1 Corinthians 12, Romans 12, Ephesians 4, and 1 Peter 4. Each person is given a unique blend of spiritual gifts to live out the varied grace of God (manifold – multi-faceted) (1 Peter 4:10).

ROMANS 12:13

Contribute to the needs of the saints and seek to show hospitality.

I can invite people into my home for meals. I can contribute financially for a particular need.

GALATIANS 6:6

Let the one who is taught the word share all good things with the one who teaches.

I can give tithes and offering to my local church to support the pastors and general financial needs of the church.

What other ways of serving one another come to your mind?

How do you think God has gifted you? For what do you have passion?

How are you using your gift(s) to serve others in the family of God in this season of life?

Take time to write a note to someone in your community who has encouraged or blessed you.

CONTRIBUTE

TO THE

needs of the saints

AND

SEEK TO SHOW

hospitality.

ROMANS 12:13

Nothing Replaces the Family of God

In today's Internet world, Christians have access to biblical teaching, sermons, devotionals, Bible studies, and even on-line interaction with other believers. For that reason many people may not see the need to be involved in a local community of believers; however, in this lesson you have learned the biblical mandate, the directives, and the blessings of being involved in a local church.

PRAYING FOR THE FAMILY

——

Paul's prayers for the saints give you a beautiful example of how to pray for one another. Look up the following prayers. Choose one to pray out loud.

EPHESIANS 1:15-20

EPHESIANS 3:14-21

COLOSSIANS 1:9-14

END YOUR STUDY...

Summarize what you learned from this lesson

"COMMUNITY"

——

A personal testimony

In 1997 we moved to a new area, which meant new schools for our kids, new neighbors to meet, and a new church to connect with. Did I mention that we were also new believers? We had come to Christ at a church in Southern California, and two months later, we were in Northern California. The word "community" was not the buzzword then, but we knew we needed to be with other believers.

Upon recommendation from our church in So Cal, we set off to the Bay Area with a single name and phone number. After driving up north on a Sunday, we reached out to Joe that night. Joe warmly welcomed us with an invitation to his small group that met on Tuesday nights. We went.

At first we thought we were in the wrong group. We were in our late 20's and the average age of the other attendees was about 60. However, as the weeks passed, we realized this was the very best group for us. These empty nesters had life experience, wisdom, and time. Having time was a key component to building relationships. They had time to help us move into a house; they had time to watch our kids in a pinch; they had time to invest in us spiritually.

Although we were really connected to our small group, we didn't feel connected with the teaching at the church. As new believers, it was difficult to understand the sermons and make life applications that would spur us on. But thankfully we had Tuesday nights to help us with understanding.

At one point we decided to look for another Sunday morning option. Looking for something more like our Southern California church, we set out church shopping for a couple of months. Sunday after Sunday we tried out different churches, all the while still attending our small group each Tuesday night. Graciously each week our small group would ask about our latest church experience. With no judgment and no expectation, our small group family continued to invest in us.

After a few of months of trying out different churches, we decided that really our small group family was the community we needed and loved. We made a commitment to attend the small group church. The Sunday morning sermons became more meaningful as time went on. Our community stretched into other ministries as we served. But our roots run deep with this small group of people that changed our lives. We will be forever grateful.

Reflection

Thank the Lord for your church family. Record your prayer.

ALL WHO BELIEVED

were together

AND HAD ALL THINGS

in common.

ACTS 2:44

LESSON 4

Abiding in Suffering

Just as you are to abide in the Father through His Word, prayer, and community, so you are to abide in Him through suffering. In this lesson you will examine the certainty and purpose of suffering.

FDQ:
1) Review — What does it mean to abide?
2) Why would we choose to include a lesson on suffering in Part 7 — My Abiding Heart?
3) What are some of the truths you have learned in *My Heart Unveiled* that can help you understand the doctrine of suffering?

THE CERTAINTY OF SUFFERING

——

Suffering shows no favoritism. The fall of man (Genesis 2:17; Genesis 3:16-19) assured that all people will suffer. Sin resulted in all creation being vulnerable to death, decay, disease, destruction, and despicable acts. Our loving Father never delights in wickedness (Psalm 5:4; Isaiah 5:20), and He grieves over the suffering world. Yet, He remains sovereign over and determines suffering for His purposes.

"

Modern Western culture sees no value in suffering and it does its best to minimize it. In older cultures suffering has always been viewed "as an expected part of a coherent life story, a crucial way to live life well and to grow as a person and a soul." But the meaning of life in Western society is individual freedom.... [If] the meaning of life is individual freedom and happiness, then suffering is of no possible "use." In this worldview, the only thing to do with suffering is to avoid it at all costs, or if it is unavoidable, manage and minimize the emotions of pain and discomfort as much as possible. [1]

TIMOTHY KELLER

FDQ: How have you seen the secular view of suffering played out?

Biblical worldview stands in stark contrast to popular secular worldview. No one lives in individual freedom. All people are enslaved to either sin or righteousness (Romans 6:17-18). The highest quality of life is lived as one yielded to Christ. Humble submission to Christ is the essence of true freedom.

THE OPPORTUNITY IN SUFFERING

——

The Bible teaches that one of the privileges of being in Christ is that you will have the opportunity to suffer for the sake of Christ. "For it has been granted to you that for the sake of Christ you should not only believe in him but also suffer for his sake" (Philippians 1:29). God has appointed specific sufferings for you that will be for your best good (Romans 8:28-29) and for His glory. "Yet if anyone suffers as a Christian, let him not be ashamed but let him glorify God in that name" (1 Peter 4:16).

FDQ: "granted" χαρίσθη aor. ind. pass. χαρίζομαι (G5919) to give graciously. "God has granted you the high privilege of suffering for Christ; this is the surest sign that He looks upon you w. favor" (Lightfoot). As noted in Linguistic and Exegetical Key to GNT (Greek New Testament), Accordance Software (2018).

THE PRIVILEGE OF SUFFERING

———

Paul was acquainted with suffering. After saving Paul on the Road to Damascus, the Lord told Ananias, the prophet whom He sent to open Paul's eyes, that He would "show [Paul] how much he must suffer for the sake of my name" (Acts 9:16). Paul endured unimaginable trials over his lifetime.

CONSIDER HOW PAUL RESPONDED TO HIS CIRCUMSTANCES. WHAT DID HE CHOOSE?

Look up the following Scriptures and **record** your response.

2 CORINTHIANS 4:8-10

2 CORINTHIANS 11:23-38

Paul chose to trust God in the midst of his circumstances, and he remained steadfast in the hope of Christ. He chose to not be driven to despair.

In your suffering you will be faced with a crossroad of choice, either to trust God or to trust your own ways of handling the suffering and the fear that it entails. If you do not trust God, you will rely on your control responses: fighting, fleeing, or feeling paralyzed. Consequently, you will not be able to access the presence and the power of Christ.

The greatest gifts
I HAVE RECEIVED IN LIFE
HAVE ENTAILED
the greatest suffering.

ELISABETH ELLIOT

A HIGH HOPE
——

Paul experienced first-hand the inspired words he recorded in Romans 8. As children of God we are "fellow heirs with Christ, provided we suffer with him in order that we may also be glorified with him. For I consider that the sufferings of this present time are not worth comparing with the glory that is to be revealed to us" (Romans 8:17-18; see also Luke 24:25-26; 2 Corinthians 4:17; 1 Peter 4:13; 5:1, 10).

In light of the glory that will be "revealed to [you]" and the "living hope" that you have in Christ, you are to "rejoice, though now for a little while, if necessary, you have been grieved by various trials, so that the tested genuineness of your faith—more precious than gold that perishes though it is tested by fire—may be found to result in praise and glory and honor at the revelation of Jesus Christ" (1 Peter 1:6-7).

"Suffering" Defined

What qualifies as suffering in this present time? Suffering includes "all the daily anxieties, tensions, and persecutions you face." (see Romans 8:17; Luke 9:23; 2 Timothy 3:12; Hebrews 12:6-7.) It is the futility of the present age—all calamity, disease, and death. Suffering has a broad scope and includes "any suffering you meet on the road to heaven and endure by trusting in Jesus." [2]

Elisabeth Elliot (wife to Jim Elliot and missionary to the Auca Indians, today known as the Waidani Tribe) defined suffering as "having what you don't want, or wanting what you don't have." Suffering covers the gamut and is not quantified nor qualified. Every act of obedience to God is a choice to die to self, which is a form of suffering (see Matthew 16:24-26.) You are never to minimize or trivialize your personal suffering nor someone else's. But suffering is "not for nothing." Whether you are suffering persecution directly for Christ's sake or you are suffering from any other life circumstance, you have the potential to glorify God in your suffering. Elisabeth Elliot claimed, "The greatest gifts I have received in life have entailed the greatest suffering."

"Glorified" Defined

What does it mean to be glorified? You will share in God's glory by being conformed to the image of Christ (Romans 8:29) so that you will enjoy all that Christ enjoys—God and all His gifts. This inheritance is so great that every trouble you may encounter is small by comparison.

Praise be to God that eternal glory will far outweigh your worst suffering. "Present sufferings must be seen in light of the promise of eternal happiness in God. The scales can't be balanced in this life alone." [3] (See 2 Corinthians 4:17-18.)

Peter also teaches that suffering is the path to glory. In 1 Peter he writes, "But rejoice insofar as you share Christ's sufferings, that you may also rejoice and be glad when his glory is revealed" (1 Peter 4:13).

The Path to Glory

Scripture places "strong emphasis on the principle that suffering is the path to glory."[4] (See Romans 8:16-18.) This was the Messiah's path (Isaiah 53:3; Luke 24:26; Mark 8:31). Jesus learned obedience through what He suffered (Hebrews 5:8-9; see also Hebrews 2:10). "Jesus moved from untested obedience into suffering and then through suffering into tested and proven obedience."[5] Jesus was tested and tempted in every way yet without sin. His tested perfection makes Jesus the Perfect Savior. He bore the wrath of all sin and as a result He experienced suffering representative of every kind of human suffering. So Jesus not only paid your debt and secured for you an eternal life, but He also intimately understands and meets you in your pain and suffering. Jesus suffered not so you would never suffer, but so you could endure suffering as He walks with you through it.

WHAT DO THE FOLLOWING VERSES TEACH REGARDING YOUR FUTURE GLORY?

Read the following Scriptures and record your response.

COLOSSIANS 3:4

When Christ who is your life appears, then you also will appear with him in glory.

I will be with Him.

1 JOHN 3:2

Beloved, we are God's children now, and what we will be has not yet appeared; but we know that when he appears we shall be like him, because we shall see him as he is.

I will be like Him.

REJOICE IN SUFFERING

Paul tells his readers in Romans 5 to rejoice in suffering not only because of the guarantee of future glory but also because suffering presently produces endurance, character, and hope (Romans 5:2-5). As you suffer you can be assured that you are becoming more spiritually fit (endurance). As your faith is tested, you are being approved and you are becoming more Christ-like (character). As a result, your hope will increase and expand and you will be certain that God is faithful to keep His promises to make all things right. (See also Matthew 5:4, 10-12; Acts 14:22; 2 Corinthians 12:9-10.)

Peter and James share the same message as Paul.

WHAT DO YOU THINK IT MEANS TO REJOICE IN SUFFERING?

It does not mean that you are happy but that you are sustained and comforted in your suffering because your future is not attached to your circumstances. You have a future beyond your suffering.

When you reflect on the fact God sent His only Son to redeem you, you realize how blessed and privileged you are. Christ is not only in you but also going through your suffering with you. Because You are called to be a living sacrifice (Romans 12:1), you are able to offer your suffering to Christ as a sacrifice of praise (Hebrews 13:15).

REWRITE THE FOLLOWING VERSES AS A PERSONAL PRAYER. HOW DO THESE TRUTHS BRING YOU COMFORT?

1 PETER 1:6-7

In this you rejoice, though now for a little while, if necessary, you have been grieved by various trials, so that the tested genuineness of your faith—more precious than gold that perishes though it is tested by fire—may be found to result in praise and glory and honor at the revelation of Jesus Christ.

Thank you Father that suffering will not last forever and thank you that the trials in my life are refining my faith and will bring me to glory. Through suffering, you are becoming more and more precious to me, O God.

FDQ: What does it mean to be tested or refined by fire? "Like fire working on gold, suffering destroys some things within us and can purify and strengthen other things" (Timothy Keller, *Walking with God through Pain and Suffering*, 228.)

JAMES 1:2-4

Count it all joy, my brothers, when you meet trials of various kinds, for you know that the testing of your faith produces steadfastness. And let steadfastness have its full effect, that you may be perfect and complete, lacking in nothing.

Father, please help me to receive with joy and cooperate with you when various trials come into my life, trusting that you are growing my faith through each one.

"

If suffering was the means by which the sinless Christ became mature, we in our sinfulness need it that much more. Significantly, James uses the same language of "perfection" or "maturity" in relation to Christians. Just as suffering led to maturity through obedience for Christ, so it leads to maturity through perseverance for us.[6]

JOHN STOTT

GOD USES SUFFERING TO MATURE YOU

———

There are many benefits that come through suffering, including the following:

Suffering humbles you and helps you realize your desperate need for God. It uncovers your vulnerability and the areas in which you are relying on someone or something other than Him.

2 CORINTHIANS 1:8-10

For we do not want you to be unaware, brothers, of the affliction we experienced in Asia. For we were so utterly burdened beyond our strength that we despaired of life itself. Indeed, we felt that we had received the sentence of death. But that was to make us rely not on ourselves but on God who raises the dead. He delivered us from such a deadly peril, and he will deliver us. On him we have set our hope that he will deliver us again.

2 CORINTHIANS 12:7-10

So to keep me from becoming conceited because of the surpassing greatness of the revelations, a thorn was given me in the flesh, a messenger of Satan to harass me, to keep me from becoming conceited. Three times I pleaded with the Lord about this, that it should leave me. But he said to me, "My grace is sufficient for you, for my power is made perfect in weakness." Therefore I will boast all the more gladly of my weaknesses, so that the power of Christ may rest upon me. For the sake of Christ, then, I am content with weaknesses, insults, hardships, persecutions, and calamities. For when I am weak, then I am strong.

Suffering provides an opportunity for you to go deeper in your relationship with Christ.

1 PETER 4:19

Therefore let those who suffer according to God's will entrust their souls to a faithful Creator while doing good.

In the midst of suffering, you are to be confident in God's sovereignty, trust God completely, and live faithfully while doing good.

PHILIPPIANS 3:7-11

But whatever gain I had, I counted as loss for the sake of Christ. Indeed, I count everything as loss because of the surpassing worth of knowing Christ Jesus my Lord. For his sake I have suffered the loss of all things and count them as rubbish, in order that I may gain Christ and be found in him, not having a righteousness of my own that comes from the law, but that which comes through faith in Christ, the righteousness from God that depends on faith—that I may know him and the power of his resurrection, and may share his sufferings, becoming like him in his death, that by any means possible I may attain the resurrection from the dead.

God always wants us to go deeper than our emotions, what we are feeling. Our faith must be based on objective truth. Outside of God's faithfulness, you cannot be faithful to Him. Ask God to help you always live faithfully to Him.

Suffering increases your capacity to care well for others.

There is no way to truly empathize and sympathize with others unless you have personally endured suffering. As you endure the pain of suffering and experience God's comfort, you will be able to comfort others.

2 CORINTHIANS 1:3-5
Blessed be the God and Father of our Lord Jesus Christ, the Father of mercies and God of all comfort, who comforts us in all our affliction, so that we may be able to comfort those who are in any affliction, with the comfort with which we ourselves are comforted by God. For as we share abundantly in Christ's sufferings, so through Christ we share abundantly in comfort too.

Suffering reveals your attachments (idols)—the things that compete with your knowing and trusting God.

It gives opportunity to evaluate who/what is truly important to you.

FDQ: If you do not abide in Christ through suffering you will be prone to try to escape/control your suffering. What things are you apt to do to escape suffering?
In what ways are you trying to guard or keep others from having to walk through suffering? Are you using control-responses? What are your fears?
If someone is struggling with the above, it may be beneficial for her to work through the My Heart Unveiled chart.

What are some benefits you have received through your suffering?

What are some specific ways that suffering has matured you?

"5 THINGS I LEARNED THROUGH SUFFERING"

―――

A personal testimony

A few years ago I went through a near-death medical emergency. I spent several weeks in the hospital and my recovery was very difficult. As I passed through my suffering, the Lord was kind and faithful to teach me several things. Five key things I learned were the following:

1. Greater certainty of my faith (John 5:24; 11:25).

2. Greater humility before God and a greater understanding that I have no control over my life. God is the one who gives life and breath (Acts 17:25; Colossians 1:17).

3. Greater optimism for life and desire for fruitful labor (Philippians 1:21-25).

4. Greater skill in dealing with stress, tension, and anxiety. I learned in a new way how to repeatedly give to Jesus with all my strength the things that were eating me up. And each time I did, I said to myself, "Your peace is more powerful than my pain and I cast my troubles on you because I am certain you care for me" (see 1 Peter 5:6-7).

5. Greater appreciation for my family and my church.

A HIGH VIEW OF GOD

Having a high view of God is essential to suffer well. Set your gaze on Him rather than on the seemingly hopeless situation or circumstance. By setting your gaze on Him— remembering His glory, sovereignty, power, and tender mercy--you will be able to rest in Him who is your Hope. Reflect on these truths.

God alone is worthy of all praise.

REVELATION 4:11

"Worthy are you, our Lord and God, to receive glory and honor and power, for you created all things, and by your will they existed and were created."

God is sovereign. He is in ultimate control of the world—all things great and small.

ISAIAH 46:9b-10

"I am God, and there is no other.... My counsel shall stand, and I will accomplish all my purpose."

God is supreme.

ROMANS 11:33-36

Oh, the depth of the riches and wisdom and knowledge of God! How unsearchable are his judgments and how inscrutable his ways! "For who has known the mind of the Lord, or who has been his counselor?" "Or who has given a gift to him that he might be repaid?" For from him and through him and to him are all things. To him be glory forever. Amen.

God is immutable.

JOB 23:13-14

"But he is unchangeable, and who can turn him back? What he desires, that he does. For he will complete what he appoints for me, and many such things are in his mind."

God is eager to show mercy and kindness to those who trust in Him.

EXODUS 34:6b

"The LORD, the LORD, a God merciful and gracious, slow to anger, and abounding in steadfast love and faithfulness...."

Why is having a high view of God essential to suffer well?

YOU ARE NOT ALONE

——

God promises to walk with you in your suffering. Pain, sadness, fear, doubt, envy, even horror and anger are all (natural, instinctual) responses to suffering that remind you to bring your suffering—all that you are experiencing and feeling—before the Father with honest pleas for mercy and to trust that you are not alone. In 2 Timothy 4:16-17, Paul spoke this wonderful truth, "At my first defense no one came to stand by me, but all deserted me. May it not be charged against them. But the Lord stood by me and strengthened me, so that through me the message might be fully proclaimed and all the Gentiles might hear it. So I was rescued from the lion's mouth." The Lord Jesus was with Paul, and the Lord Jesus is with you.

Not only is God always present with you, He also always hears you. "I love the LORD, because he has heard my voice and my pleas for mercy. Because he inclined his ear to me, therefore I will call on him as long as I live" (Psalm 116:1-2). The word "inclined" represents a beautiful picture of how God bends down to listen to you. Like a mother who bends down to look into the face of her child with her full attention, so Your Father attends to you. Thanks be to God that He is always with you and always hears you.

WRITE OUT THE FOLLOWING SCRIPTURES THAT PROMISE HIS PRESENCE AND PROVISION IN SUFFERING.

PSALM 23:4a

Even though I walk through the valley of the shadow of death, I will fear no evil, for you are with me....

PSALM 57:1-3a

Be merciful to me, O God, be merciful to me, for in you my soul takes refuge; in the shadow of your wings I will take refuge, till the storms of destruction pass by. I cry out to God Most High, to God who fulfills his purpose for me. He will send from heaven and save me....

ISAIAH 43:2-3a

"When you pass through the waters, I will be with you; and through the rivers, they shall not overwhelm you; when you walk through fire you shall not be burned, and the flame shall not consume you. For I am the Lord your God, the Holy One of Israel, your Savior...."

IN THE MIDST OF SUFFERING, WHAT CAN YOU DO TO SURVIVE?

——

1. Spend time with the Lord every day.

Take time to quiet yourself before the Lord. Ask Him what He wants to speak to you about and take time to listen.

When you read the Word, ask the Lord to give you an encouraging Scripture (a statement, a promise, a command) that you can keep in your mind. Write it down on a notecard and read and reflect on it throughout the day. Save these cards and re-read them often. These will serve as a lifeline to truth.

2. Confide in one or two trusted friends.

Be willing to honestly share your struggle and heartache. Ask them to faithfully pray for you and give them permission to speak truth into your life.

3. Cry out to Lord.

As the Psalmists did in the Psalms of Lament (e.g. Psalms 22, 86, 142), cast your cares on Him and recall Who He is. Pray through the Psalms.

4. Acknowledge your pain.

It is natural to resist pain, but choose to feel your pain in order to grieve your hurt or your loss and to receive what the Lord has for you through your suffering.

5. Remember that God's mercies are new every morning (Lamentations 3:22-23).

6. Do not be anxious about tomorrow (Matthew 6:34).

Trust the Lord will give you what you need for each day.

7. Journal.

Take time to record what is on your mind and troubling your heart. This is a great way to process.

8. Record your thanksgivings.

Every day make yourself write down at least one thing for which you are thankful. Ask the Lord to bring these things to mind and keep a running list.

9. Keep a list of answered prayers.

Recall, remember what the Lord has done.

10. Stay involved in community.

You may be tempted to withdraw from others, but being with others will provide needed support and help you not be self-focused.

11. Serve someone else.

This will encourage you.

12. Listen to worship music.

13. Get outside for some exercise. Enjoy nature.

14. Be sure to get proper rest and nutrition.

15. Pray and Listen.

Pray that the suffering you are experiencing will increase your faith, your love for the Lord and others, and your ability to endure affliction. (See 2 Thessalonians 1:4.)

When you are suffering, what practical things help you?

How have others helped you through suffering?

WHAT TO DO AND NOT DO

———

Here are some things for you to consider when God calls you to walk alongside someone who is suffering:

Listen. Listening is the most important thing you can do besides praying for the person. Giving the sufferer the time and space to share her thoughts, how and when they come up, is a gracious gift. Listen without interrupting and without giving advice. Allow her to share her doubts, fears, and frustrations.

Do not compare her situation to yours (or something you have gone through in the past). Each person's suffering is unique to them. When you say you understand or share your story, you minimize her pain.

Allow her to share her pain. You cannot relieve her pain or fix her pain. Come alongside her and comfort her in her pain. Sit with her quietly as she cries and cry with her. Your tears let her know you are suffering with her and that she is not alone.

Physical touch is important. A hand on her knee, an arm around her shoulder, or a long hug tenderly communicate your care.

Say, "I'm glad to see you" rather than "How are you doing?" This lets her know you want to be around her; she is not a burden to you, and you are not expecting her to be "okay."

Leave her a text message. She may not want to talk on the phone, but she will be glad to see a text message from you. It does not need to be long, just enough to let her know you are thinking of her and praying for her.

Be slow to redirect to truth. A time will come for you to speak truth and share Scripture, but wait for the appropriate time. Trust the Holy Spirit to direct you.

Send a note or card.

A personal testimony

After my son passed away, these were a few things that were and were not helpful:

Do:

- Be available.
- Listen without offering advice.
- Let her talk about the loved one and share memories. (It was important to me that my son was remembered by others.)
- Call and let her know you are praying for her. Do this daily at first.

Don't:

- Ask how she is feeling or coping.
- Ask what she needs; she probably doesn't know.
- Ask what verse she is leaning on.
- Be reluctant to bring up her loss; she will be glad you remember.

So rejoice, for suffering is not for nothing. Your great hope is that one day you will see and savor the glory of God Himself (Romans 5:11) in your redeemed and glorified body, fully able to enjoy the new heavens and new earth free from sin and its corruption (Romans 8:22-23). (See Part 7 Lesson 5)

"THE PRIVILEGE OF SUFFERING"

———

Within minutes of receiving Christ, Helen Roseveare was told by Bible teacher Graham Scroggie that he hoped one day she would have the privilege of suffering for her Savior (Philippians 3:10). She prayed after her conversion for the privilege of being a missionary.

Dr. Helen Roseveare was a famous English missionary to the Congo. At age 28 she arrived in the Congo (Zaire), where she founded a training school for nurses who would serve as nurse-evangelists. In 1964, Helen was one of ten missionaries taken by some men by brutal force. In the moments of that horrific night, her tortured heart cried,

> " "My God, my God, why have You forgotten me, forsaken me?"... Suddenly Christ had been there. No vision, no voice, but His very real presence. A phrase came into my mind, "led as a lamb to the slaughter", and I saw as it were the events in the garden of Gethsemane, the trial scene, the scourging of Christ, the long march out to Calvary bearing the cross, to the crucifixion....For my sake, He went as a willing sacrifice.[1]

Helen along with the other missionaries were held in harsh captivity for five months, not knowing when the brutal captors would kill them or rape them. On one horrific night, she was beaten, bruised, and raped. She was terrified and felt utterly alone. She felt that God had failed her. She thought He could have stepped in. She reached what seemed to her ultimate point of despair. Yet, even as her heart cried out against God for His "failure," He met her in that despairing moment with His presence and spoke what she needed to hear. He gave her courage to trust Him and to endure.

Referring to this offense, Helen spoke these words in her Urbana '76 Conference address:

> " One word became unbelievably clear, and that word was "privilege." He didn't take away pain or cruelty or humiliation. No! It was all there, but now it was altogether different. It was with Him, for Him, in Him. He was actually offering me the inestimable privilege of sharing in some little way the edge of the fellowship of his suffering.
>
> In the weeks of imprisonment that followed and in the subsequent years of continued service, looking back, one has tried to "count the cost," but I find it all swallowed up in privilege. The cost suddenly seems very small and transient in the greatness and permanence of the privilege.[2]

The missionaries were finally rescued. The rebels had destroyed the hospital and killed many of the people they had served. Helen returned to the UK on furlough. After a year at home, the African brethren asked her to return to help rebuild what was destroyed. For a year they had carried on alone, so she committed to go back. "During the sea-voyage, I became conscious of the old fears again. Why on earth am I going back?"[3] God, however, continued to show His faithfulness to her throughout the years of rebuilding.

She returned to the UK in 1973, where she remained until she went home to be with the Lord at age 91 (1925-2016).

The theme "privilege" underlined everything in Helen's Christian life. In her later years she shared:

> If we love the Lord Jesus, He himself said, "If you are going to follow me, take up your cross and follow me." Where was He going? He was going to Calvary.
>
> The death to the self-life is the death to my ambitions, my rights to be who or what or where I wish. The giving of that over to Jesus and letting Him really live His life in and through us under any circumstance, will involve suffering. It is a privilege to suffer for the Lord Jesus.[4]

"The Privilege of Suffering" Works Cited:

1 • Roseveare, Helen. He Gave Us a Valley. Christian Focus Publications, Scotland, UK, 2013, p. 35.
2 • Taylor, Justin. "A Woman of Whom the World Was Not Worthy—Helen Roseveare (1925 – 2016)." The Gospel Coalition 7 December 2016, https://blogs.thegospelcoalition.org/justintaylor/2016/12/07a-woman-of-whom-the-world-was-not-worthy-helen-roseveare-1925-2016/. Accessed 9 May 2017.
3 • Roseveare, Helen. He Gave Us a Valley. pg. 50.
4 • Taylor, Justin. "A Woman of Whom the World Was Not Worthy—Helen Roseveare (1925 – 2016)." The Gospel Coalition 7 December 2016, https://blogs.thegospelcoalition.org/justintaylor/2016/12/07a-woman-of-whom-the-world-was-not-worthy-helen-roseveare-1925-2016/. Accessed 9 May 2017.

"ABIDING IN SUFFERING"

———

A personal testimony

But as for me, the nearness of God is my good; I have made the Lord GOD my refuge,
that I may tell of all Your works.

PSALM 73:28 (NASB)

Worry has been my companion for years but it has never been my friend. As the Lord has refined my heart, I've recognized my own sin tendency to mistrust His goodness towards me and His sovereignty over all. It was no surprise to me in the latter part of my pregnancy with my second child that I began to entertain all kinds of dreadful scenarios about what kind of suffering was just around the corner. There was never reason to be expecting any sort of trial, yet for whatever reason I was just uncomfortable with so many unknowns. I presented my fears to the Lord daily and found myself weary from taking every thought captive. Yet, I was continuously comforted as I tried...desperately tried...to rest in the character of the One who I was learning was providential and omnipotent. My mentor reminded me and steadied my soul with the following: "You're imagining the story ahead of you without imagining the God who will go there with you in it."

So, after my completely uncomplicated pregnancy finally culminated in a beautiful labor and delivery at 41.5 weeks, my son was born. His heart rate dropped twice after delivery and so he was sent to the NICU just to be certain that his respiratory and heart status was stable. He was fine at 20 minutes of monitoring, but they decided to keep him in the NICU overnight. I thought I had faced, and escaped, the reality of something going wrong as I had feared. Then, one of the NICU physicians asked if we would be okay if she ran an ultrasound on his head because of his abnormally large circumference and increased fontanelle gap. We agreed. One thing led to another and twenty-four hours later we sat in front of the pediatric neurologist as she explained multiple daunting brain abnormalities in our son's head.

That should have been tragic news, but at that precise moment God began to give us grace sufficient for the time. Sure, we wept, grieved, and questioned what all of it would mean: would he ever be able to see, hear, walk, talk, relate, etc.? The questions began to swirl in my mind, but, almost immediately, God quieted my heart, mind, and soul with His sweet presence and gentle reminder that He, in fact, created my son just as he should be and that his story was already ordained as I had prayed all along according to Psalm 139. I could share detail after detail about how God providentially led us to discover his diagnoses at such an early age when many people don't find out for years. Instead, I want to testify to the way that the Lord has ordained, sustained, and even worked good in our trials over the last four months of my son's life.

Morning after morning following the diagnoses, I woke up at 5am to grab my Bible, my blank journal, and a playlist of songs filled with worship music that honestly expressed raw emotions and a steady trust in God during suffering. I engaged my closest friends to help me fight the uncertainties ahead for our family. I started memorizing more Scripture and continued memorizing my Catechisms. And in these last four months I have learned:

1. The nearness of God is truly my good. Like the psalmist, I made him my refuge. God has worked miracles already in my son's life, and I've seen wonders as he's developed in ways that he simply shouldn't be able to do with a missing part of his brain. Yet, Jesus has also led us through some scary days of his head swelling and fevers threatening to initiate seizures. He has been my refuge in both scenarios. I will testify about the Lord's work in my son's life—whether it's healing in the earthly realm or the anticipation of wholeness and healing in the heavenly one someday.

2. If I knew then what I know now, I wouldn't have dreaded and avoided the trial I am now living out. My reality now with this trial is concurrent with a greater measure of God's grace and nearness—and I wouldn't trade this for a life without it. It's hard to describe to people, but this trial is God's kindness towards me. He has wounded me and is humbling my pride, but He is so gracious to me in doing so. He does not promise to never bring suffering; in fact, He prepares us for just the opposite. Yet, and it's a resounding yet in my world right now, He grants His presence, His word, His people to both comfort and sustain us in it. One scene in C.S. Lewis's The Chronicles of Narnia's *The Lion, the Witch, and the Wardrobe* portrays this perfectly. Mrs. Beaver describes Aslan, the Lion Ruler of Narnia, to little Lucy. Lucy then asks Mr. Beaver, "Is he quite safe?" Mr. Beaver replies, "'Course he isn't safe. But he's good."

The Lord is sovereign over all and this means He gets to choose how He will bring Himself the most glory. We can rest in the tension that His glory getting comes with great comfort giving to us. We are not cursed in our sufferings and trials. Rather, we are blessed to endure with Him.

"FINANCIAL SUFFERING"

A personal testimony

After working many years in the corporate world in San Francisco, my husband and I left our respective firms to start our own rental property business. We had a very comfortable life—we owned and managed over 100 rental units (spread out in San Francisco, San Jose, Pleasanton, and the Central Valley); we were partnering up with a family member on a promising new business venture; we were homeschooling our five children (all under 12 years old at the time); and we lived in our comfortable Pleasanton home on seven acres of rolling hills. Everything was going well until 2008, when the real estate market crashed and our business ventures, along with our significant investments, dissipated.

One by one, all of our rental properties and eventually our beloved home were swept up into our bankruptcy. We lost everything—my worst nightmare.

For several years, we were utterly broken financially. It was incredibly humbling to live day-by-day, not knowing how we would get enough money for the next month's rent (and many months we had to ask our family and friends to help out). Some days I suffered well, leaning into the Lord and trusting in Him. Many more days I did not suffer well: I felt shame, anger, fear, and resentment.

The ugliness of my heart was exposed in my suffering, but God faithfully carried me through that time.

PSALM 66:10-12

For you, O God, have tested us; you have tried us as silver is tried. You brought us into the net; you laid a crushing burden on our backs; you let men ride over our heads; we went through fire and through water; yet you have brought us out to a place of abundance.

I believe that the "place of abundance" the Psalmist refers to in this Psalm is not limited to physical blessings. Though the Lord can, of course, bless us physically (as He did Job after Job suffered), He gives us something far more precious in our suffering—a sweeter and deeper communion with Him.

Michael Goff, when writing about the grief and suffering he endured when his first-born was diagnosed with a rare disease, said, "[I]n God's gracious leading, he made my suffering an easel which held up the canvas of my heart. In that suffering, God painted a fresh vision of himself for me and in me." Goff, "Trust God Through Your Tears," desiringgod.org (April 1, 2017).

In the midst of, and through, suffering, God breaks us and then changes and molds us more into Christ's image. "This is God's universal purpose for all Christian suffering: more contentment in God and less satisfaction in self and the world." John Piper, "The Seminary of Suffering," desiringgod.org (October 31, 2012).

I may have lost my earthly treasure, but I gained something far more valuable in return—"the tested genuineness of [my] faith—more precious than gold that perishes" (1 Peter 1:7a).

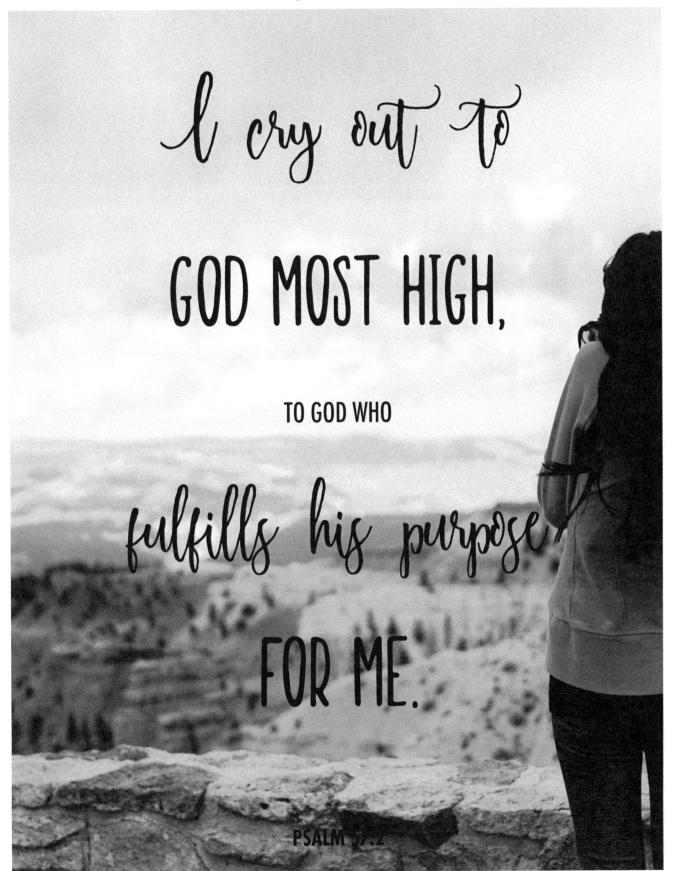

I cry out to GOD MOST HIGH, TO GOD WHO fulfills his purpose FOR ME.

PSALM 57:2

"A REFUGE IN TIMES OF TROUBLE"

———

A personal testimony

Before my husband's first surgery for cancer, I bought him a print of a ship being tossed by waves in a storm at sea. A quote by Charles Spurgeon was written at the bottom which read, "I have learned to kiss the waves that throw me up against the Rock of Ages."

We don't like hardship; naturally, we want life to be easier, less complicated.

I want comfort and to feel like I know what each day has in store; and yet, I'm so thankful I have a Heavenly Father who will allow hardship in my life, my husband's life, my children's lives—if it means we will draw closer to Him.

These circumstances have made me love Him more deeply. They've brought my husband and me closer and allowed me to love him in sickness as well as good health. They've humbled him and stripped away pride in physical abilities. My children have been able to see their dad place his hope in Christ and not a desired outcome.

The Lord is kind. He truly is a place of refuge and strength.

END YOUR STUDY...

Summarize what you learned from this lesson

Reflection

Choose a Scripture from this lesson to meditate on. Thank God that He is with you in your suffering, remembering it is a privilege to suffer for the Lord Jesus.

LESSON 5

Abiding in the Hope of Heaven

As you saw in Lesson 4, no follower of Christ is exempt from suffering. Jesus said, "In the world you will have tribulation" (John 16:33a.) In the book of Revelation Jesus also warned, "Do not fear what you are about to suffer…. Be faithful unto death, and I will give you the crown of life" (Revelation 2:10).

FDQ: "Tribulation" in Greek is "thlipsis," which means "pressure, pressing together, affliction, distress or oppression." This word is also translated in the Bible as "trouble, anguish, persecution or burden."

Your ultimate hope will be realized only after you die (unless the Lord Jesus returns before your death). The Apostle Paul said, "If in Christ we have hope in this life only, we are of all people most to be pitied" (1 Corinthians 15:19). But praise God that your hope goes so much deeper and beyond this life! In this final lesson you will be encouraged to abide in the reality of heaven.

"

It is the hope of eternal life in heaven. Our resurrection is not to another period of earth life. It is a resurrection to eternal life with God in heaven [and the new earth].... It is resurrection to abide forever in the presence of the Lord (Rev. 21:3) where "God shall wipe away all tears from their eyes; and there shall be no more death, neither sorrow, nor crying, neither shall there be any more pain" (Rev. 21:4). It is a resurrection to "rest from their labors" (Rev. 14:13). It is a resurrection to drink the water of life (Rev. 21:6) and to eat of the tree of life (Rev. 22:2).[1]

MIKE WILLIS

YOUR LIFE IS A VAPOR

FDQ: Do you think about your life as a vapor?

Your life is "a vapor that appears for a little while and then vanishes away" (James 4:14b, NASB). Review the following verses that affirm the brevity of life:

1 PETER 1:24
"All flesh is like grass and all its glory like the flower of grass. The grass withers, and the flower falls...."

PSALM 144:4
Man is like a breath; his days are like a passing shadow.

PSALM 102:11
My days are like an evening shadow; I wither away like grass.

PSALM 39:4-5
"O LORD, make me know my end and what is the measure of my days; let me know how fleeting I am! Behold, you have made my days a few handbreadths, and my lifetime is as nothing before you. Surely all mankind stands as a mere breath!"

Moses understood this and he asked the Lord, "So teach us to number our days that we may get a heart of wisdom" (Psalm 90:12). Understanding the brevity of life is an essential element of wisdom.

FDQ: Why is understanding the brevity of life an essential element of wisdom?
What things do we seek to have now that we may not receive until heaven?

YOUR LIFE WILL NEVER FULLY SATISFY YOU

———

Not only is your life short, but very little in your life will turn out the way you hope it will. And even if it does, your heart will not be fully satisfied. The most wonderful moments of your life are but echoes of what your heart ultimately longs for.

"

The enjoyment of God is the only happiness with which our souls can be satisfied. To go to heaven, fully to enjoy God, is infinitely better than the most pleasant accommodations here.... [These] are but shadows; but God is the substance. These are but scattered beams; but God is the sun. These are but streams; but God is the ocean.[2]

JONATHAN EDWARDS

All people desire to "live happily ever after." Everyone is searching for that someone or something that will fulfill their deepest longings. As a follower of Christ, however, you have "found him whom...[your] soul loves" (Song of Solomon 3:4a). This is not wishful thinking or a fairy tale. It is "your life...hidden with Christ in God" (Colossians 3:3b). And your truest and happiest life has yet to begin!

FDQ: Do you live daily as one who is loved by God and desires to love Him in return?

READ THE FOLLOWING VERSES ABOUT THE JOYS OF HEAVEN AND UNDERLINE THE WORDS THAT INDICATE THAT FACT.

2 CORINTHIANS 5:8
Yes, we are of good courage, and we would rather be away from the body and at home with the Lord.

PHILIPPIANS 1:21, 23
For to me to live is Christ, and to die is gain.... My desire is to depart and be with Christ, for that is far better.

ISAIAH 65:17-18
For behold, I create new heavens and a new earth, and the former things shall not be remembered or come into mind. But be glad and rejoice forever in that which I create; for behold, I create Jerusalem to be a joy, and her people to be a gladness.

"

[C]onsider that we all desire to be happy. We all have the same goal—Joy. We search for it in different places and in different ways. But in the end, there is only one source of ultimate pleasure: "In your presence is fullness of joy, at your right hand are pleasures forevermore." Psalm 16:11[3]

RANDY ALCORN

HEAVEN — OUR ULTIMATE HOPE AND HOME

———

God has set before you the hope of heaven—to encourage you and strengthen you in this life (Hebrews 6:18; Colossians 1:5). The writer of Hebrews states that this is "a sure and steadfast anchor of the soul, a hope that enters into the inner place behind the curtain" (Hebrews 6:19). As a follower of Christ, you are a citizen of heaven now; your true citizenship is in the New Jerusalem.

EPHESIANS 2:6
[God] raised us up with him [Christ] and seated us with him in the heavenly places in Christ Jesus....

PHILIPPIANS 3:20-21
But our citizenship is in heaven, and from it we await a Savior, the Lord Jesus Christ....

How might it change the way you live if you daily viewed heaven as your true and ultimate home?

Scriptures command you to "set your hope fully on the grace that will be brought to you at the revelation of Jesus Christ" (1 Peter 1:13b), and to "seek the things that are above, where Christ is, seated at the right hand of God." You are to "[s]et your minds on things that are above, not on things that are on earth" (Colossians 3:1-2). Likewise, 2 Corinthians 4:18 reminds believers to "look not to the things that are seen but to the things that are unseen. For the things that are seen are transient, but the things that are unseen are eternal."

In Hebrew 11's "Hall of Faith," we see that the Old Testament saints "acknowledged that they were strangers and exiles on the earth. For... they desire[d] a better country, that is, a heavenly one" (Hebrews 11:13b,16). Focusing on the hope of heaven is how these Old Testament saints were able to both suffer and endure temptations well:

> By faith Moses, when he was grown up, refused to be called the son of Pharaoh's daughter, choosing rather to be mistreated with the people of God than to enjoy the fleeting pleasures of sin. He considered the reproach of Christ greater wealth than the treasures of Egypt, for he was looking to the reward.... [They] conquered kingdoms, enforced justice,... stopped the mouths of lions,... escaped the edge of the sword, were made strong out of weakness, became mighty in war, put foreign armies to flight,... [were] tortured, refusing to accept release, so that they might rise again to a better life.... Others suffered mocking and flogging, and even chains and imprisonment. They were stoned, they were sawn in two, they were killed with the sword. They went about in skins of sheep and goats, destitute, afflicted, mistreated[,]... wandering about in deserts and mountains, and in dens and caves of the earth (Hebrews 11:24-26; 33-38).

The discipline of focusing on heaven and on the fact that you will see the Lord face-to-face when your faith becomes sight (2 Corinthians 5:7) will steady you during the many ups and downs of this life and inspire you to "renounce ungodliness and worldly passions, and to live self-controlled, upright, and godly lives... waiting for [your] blessed hope (see Titus 2:12-13). Abiding in the hope of heaven not only helps you to suffer well but also helps you to resist temptations to sin, for suffering and temptations can be "two sides of the same coin."

"

The effect of this kind of focus is to make our present pain seem small in comparison to what is coming: "I consider that the sufferings of this present time are not worth comparing with the glory that is to be revealed to us" (Romans 8:18; see also 2 Corinthians 4:16–18).[3]

JOHN PIPER

You need to constantly remind yourself that your hope, which goes behind the curtain into the Holy of Holies (Hebrews 6:19), is not a hope for this life only but ultimately in what Christ's death and resurrection accomplished for you. This is the hope of eternal life with Him, which will ultimately and definitely come when Christ returns in His glory.

WHAT DO YOU LEARN ABOUT YOUR HOPE?

Read the following Scriptures and record your response.

1 PETER 1:3-6a

Blessed be the God and Father of our Lord Jesus Christ! According to his great mercy, he has caused us to be born again to a living hope through the resurrection of Jesus Christ from the dead, to an inheritance that is imperishable, undefiled, and unfading, kept in heaven for you, who by God's power are being guarded through faith for a salvation ready to be revealed in the last time. In this you rejoice....

Our hope is precious and never changes. Our salvation is being guarded, so that our standing before God is secure and certain.

1 JOHN 3:2b

[W]hat we will be has not yet appeared; but we know that when he appears we shall be like him, because we shall see him as he is.

The amazing and overwhelming promise is that we will be like Him and this will be the completion of our sanctification.

ROMANS 8:23b-24a

[W]e ourselves, who have the firstfruits of the Spirit, groan inwardly as we wait eagerly for adoption as sons, the redemption of our bodies. For in this hope we were saved.

Our bodies will be redeemed and our adoption will be complete.

JOHN 14:2-3

"In my Father's house are many rooms. If it were not so, would I have told you that I go to prepare a place for you? And if I go and prepare a place for you, I will come again and will take you to myself, that where I am you may be also...."

Jesus is preparing for us a home so that we can be with him forever.

1 THESSALONIANS 4:16-17

For the Lord himself will descend from heaven with a cry of command, with the voice of an archangel, and with the sound of the trumpet of God. And the dead in Christ will rise first. Then we who are alive, who are left, will be caught up together with them in the clouds to meet the Lord in the air, and so we will always be with the Lord.

We will always be with the Lord!

"

We will constantly be more amazed with God, more in love with God, and thus ever more relishing his presence and our relationship with him. Our experience of God will never reach its consummation.... It will deepen and develop, intensify and amplify, unfold and increase, broaden and balloon.[5]

SAM STORMS

WHAT HAPPENS WHEN I DIE (BEFORE CHRIST'S SECOND COMING)?

———

"

Although we don't have as many details as we might want, the Bible clearly teaches that at our death we go from earth to Paradise, and then come back to the renewed earth in our new resurrected bodies as citizens of the New Jerusalem (Revelation 21). It's then that heaven and earth will be joined together and we'll be residents of one really grand city.[6]

ELYSE FITZPATRICK

When a believer dies and she is away from the body, she will be "at home with the Lord" (2 Corinthians 5:8b). When the dying thief on the cross asked Jesus to remember him, the Lord told him, "Truly, I say to you, today you will be with me in paradise." (Luke 23:43).

However, only after Christ returns for His Second Coming will the deceased believer receive her glorified body, receive her full reward, and enjoy the fullness of the renewed heaven and earth (see Philippians 3:20-21; Luke 14:14; Revelation 21).

WHAT HAPPENS WHEN CHRIST RETURNS?

The exact order of events when Christ returns is not revealed in Scripture. However, the Bible teaches that when Jesus returns in all His glory, several things will happen.

WHAT DO YOU LEARN CONCERNING WHAT HAPPENS WHEN CHRIST RETURNS?

Read the following Scriptures and list your response.

MATTHEW 25:31-34

" When the Son of Man comes in his glory, and all the angels with him, then he will sit on his glorious throne. Before him will be gathered all the nations, and he will separate people one from another as a shepherd separates the sheep from the goats. And he will place the sheep on his right, but the goats on the left. Then the King will say to those on his right, 'Come, you who are blessed by my Father, inherit the kingdom prepared for you from the foundation of the world.'"

There will be judgment of all people and the believers will inherit the kingdom.

PHILIPPIANS 2:10-11 (NASB)

[A]t the name of Jesus every knee will bow, of those who are in heaven and on earth and under the earth, and...every tongue will confess that Jesus Christ is Lord, to the glory of God the Father.

Everyone will bow to and confess Christ's name, whether they want to or not.

2 TIMOTHY 4:7-8

I have fought the good fight, I have finished the race, I have kept the faith. Henceforth there is laid up for me the crown of righteousness, which the Lord, the righteous judge, will award to me on that day, and not only to me but also to all who have loved his appearing.

We will be rewarded with the crown of righteousness.

PHILIPPIANS 3:20-21

But our citizenship is in heaven, and from it we await a Savior, the Lord Jesus Christ, who will transform our lowly body to be like his glorious body, by the power that enables him even to subject all things to himself.

He will change our bodies to be like His glorious body. He will subject all things to Himself.

ISAIAH 25:6-9

On this mountain the LORD of hosts will make for all peoples a feast of rich food, a feast of well-aged wine, of rich food full of marrow, of aged wine well refined. And he will swallow up on this mountain the covering that is cast over all peoples, the veil that is spread over all nations. He will swallow up death forever; and the LORD God will wipe away tears from all faces, and the reproach of his people he will take away from all the earth, for the LORD has spoken. It will be said on that day, "Behold, this is our God; we have waited for him, that he might save us. This is the LORD; we have waited for him; let us be glad and rejoice in his salvation."

The Lord will prepare an amazing wedding feast for us. We will be completely satisfied and will rejoice greatly in His salvation.

OUR CITIZENSHIP

IS IN

heaven.

PHILLIPIANS 3:20a

THE JUDGMENT SEAT OF GOD AND THE GREAT WHITE THRONE JUDGMENT

———

Again, although all of the details of the final judgment are not revealed in Scripture, there appears to be two judgments when Christ returns: the Judgment Seat of God (see Romans 14:10b; 2 Corinthians 5:10) and the Great White Throne Judgment (see Revelation 20:11-15).

ROMANS 14:10b

[W]e will all stand before the judgment seat of God....

REVELATION 20:11-15

Then I saw a great white throne and him who was seated on it.... And I saw the dead, great and small, standing before the throne, and books were opened. Then another book was opened, which is the book of life. And the dead were judged by what was written in the books, according to what they had done.... And if anyone's name was not found written in the book of life, he was thrown into the lake of fire.

REVELATION 3:5

The one who conquers...I will never blot his name out of the book of life. I will confess his name before my Father and before his angels.

As a follower of Christ, you need not fear the Great White Throne judgment where Christ will separate the sheep from the goats (see Matthew 25:31-46) because you can be assured that you are His sheep and that your name is written in "the book of life" (see Revelation 20:15). No condemnation awaits you because you have been saved by Christ's atoning work on the cross (see Romans 8:1-2).

However, even as a follower of Christ you will have to give an account of your life to Christ before the Judgment Seat of God (see 2 Corinthians 5:10). Read the following verses about this judgment:

ROMANS 14:12

So then each of us will give an account of himself to God.

1 CORINTHIANS 3:12-15

Now if anyone builds on the foundation with gold, silver, precious stones, wood, hay, straw—each one's work will become manifest, for the Day will disclose it, because it will be revealed by fire, and the fire will test what sort of work each one has done. If the work that anyone has built on the foundation survives, he will receive a reward. If anyone's work is burned up, he will suffer loss, though he himself will be saved, but only as through fire.

EPHESIANS 6:8b

[W]hatever good anyone does, this he will receive back from the Lord....

REVELATION 22:12 (NIV)

"Look, I am coming soon! My reward is with me, and I will give to each person according to what they have done."

2 CORINTHIANS 5:10

For we must all appear before the judgment seat of Christ, so that each one may receive what is due for what he has done in the body, whether good or evil.

FDQ: "Evil" in this verse can mean "of a bad nature."

The word "appear" in 2 Corinthians 5:10 means, "to make manifest," "to make clear," "to make visible," or "to reveal."

"

To be made manifest means not just to appear, but to be laid bare, stripped of every outward façade of respectability, and openly revealed in the full and true reality of one's character.[7]

PHILIP E. HUGHES

This is the "bema" (translated "court" or "tribunal") judgment where everything you have done in your life, including all of your motives and desires, will be disclosed and made bare to you before Christ. The purpose of this judgment is not to condemn you but to reward you for the good works you did for God's glory—rewards for all of the work that is not burned up in the fire of God's judgment. (See 1 Corinthians 3:12-15.)

"

The failures and shortcomings of … believers … will enter into the picture on the Day of Judgment. But — and this is the important point — the sins and shortcomings of believers will be revealed in the judgment as forgiven sins, whose guilt has been totally covered by the blood of Jesus Christ.[8]

ANTHONY HOEKEMA

The most beautiful aspect of this bema judgment is that when you stand before Christ you will more fully realize the depth of your sin and the depth of Christ's atonement (see 2 Corinthians 5:21). Although you are presently grateful for His work on the cross, when all of your life is laid bare before Him and you, your gratitude will be increased ten thousand-fold so that forever and ever you will be propelled to worship Christ. You will sing and shout with all of the heavenly hosts, which will number "myriads of myriads and thousands of thousands," this verse: "Worthy is the Lamb who was slain, to receive power and wealth and wisdom and might and honor and glory and blessing!" (Revelation 5:11-12).

You may never fully grasp the greatness and depth of God's love for you—the love He had for you when He wrote your name in the book of life even before He created the world (see Revelation 13:8) and the love He displayed when He formed His plan of redemption to unite you to Him through Christ. (See Ephesians 1.) When Christ returns and your adoption is consummated and you receive your new body (see Romans 8:23), all of history from the Garden of Eden (see Genesis 2) to the final defeat of Satan (see Revelation 20) will have come full circle, and you will revel in God's majesty and His intimacy forever! (See Revelation 22:1-5.)

COLOSSIANS 3:1-2

If then you have been raised with Christ, seek the things that are above, where Christ is, seated at the right hand of God. Set your minds on things that are above, not on things that are on earth.

Be heavenly minded:

- When you see something beautiful in nature (e.g., a full moon or a sunset), think "these are but scattered beams, but God is the sun"! How beautiful God will be to you when you see Him face-to-face!

- Every day, purpose to think that you are one day closer to seeing Him and being in His presence. Embrace the brevity of life!

- When you are enjoying a wonderful and pleasurable moment, whether alone or with others, imagine what these moments will be like in the New Jerusalem, without any sin—no more tears, death, mourning, crying, nor pain, "for the former things have passed away" (Revelation 21:4).

- When you are going through various suffering, remind yourself that these temporary pains are not worth comparing with the glories of heaven that you will experience one day very soon.

- When temptations are luring you, recall to mind the fact that you will stand before the Lord at the bema judgment, where you will give an account of your life to God. (See Romans 14:12.)

Let us be women who "long for His appearing" (2 Timothy 4:8 (NIV)) because "He who testifies to these things says, 'Surely I am coming soon.' Amen. Come, Lord Jesus!" (Revelation 22:20).

END YOUR STUDY...
Summarize what you learned from this lesson

Reflection

Meditate on this verse, reflecting on the importance of abiding in Christ.

And now, little children, abide in him, so that when he appears we may have confidence and not shrink from him in shame at his coming.

1 JOHN 2:28

"

Do not let yourselves be so absorbed by anticipations of what you are going to do and where you are going to be tomorrow that you have no leisure to think of what you are going to do and where you are going to be through the eternities.... Live in the continual contemplation of that blessed future, and Him who makes it...; fasten [your heart and your hope] to the anchor of your souls which hath entered within the veil.[9]

ALEXANDER MACLAREN

PART 7 WORKS CITED

Lesson 1: Abiding in God's Word

1 • Whitney, Donald. Spiritual Disciplines for the Christian Life. NavPress, Colorado Springs, Colorado, 2014, pg. 46.
2 • Pope, Janet. His Word in My Heart. Moody, Chicago, Illinois, 2013, pgs. 30-31.
3 • Swindoll, Chuck. Growing Strong in the Seasons of Life. Zondervan, Grand Rapids, Michigan, 1994, pg. 61.

Lesson 2: Abiding in Prayer

1 • As defined by Wycliffe Bible Translators. See https://www.wycliffe.org/prayer/why-we-pray.
2 • Miller, Paul. A Praying Life. NavPress, Colorado Springs, Colorado, 2009, pgs. 25, 32-39, 117, 201-203.
3 • Carson, D.A., A Call to Spiritual Reformation: Priorities from Paul and His Prayers. Baker Academic, 1992, pg. 33.

Lesson 3: Abiding in Community

1 • Frazee, Randy. The Connecting Church. Zondervan, 2001.
2 • Anderson, Neil. Who I am in Christ. Bethany House Publishers, 2001.
3 • Barthel, Tara. Living the Gospel in Relationships. Peacemaker Ministries, Billings, Montana, 2007, pg. 60.

Lesson 4: Abiding in Suffering

1 • Keller, Timothy. Walking with God through Pain and Suffering. Dutton, New York, New York, 2013, pg. 23.
2 • Piper, John. "Children, Heirs, and Fellow Sufferers." Desiring God, 21 April 2002, http://www.desiringgod.org/messages/children-heirs-and-fellow-sufferers. Accessed 9 May 2017.
3 • Alcorn, Randy. "C.S. Lewis on Heaven and the New Earth: God's Eternal Remedy to the Problem of Evil and Suffering." Desiring God, 28 Sept. 2013, http://www.desiringgod.org/messages/c-s-lewis-on-heaven-and-the-new-earth-god-s-eternal-remedy-to-the-problem-of-evil-and-suffering. Accessed 9 May 2017.
4 • Stott, John. The Message of Romans. InterVarsity Press, Downers Grove, Illinois, 1994, pg. 235.
5 • Piper, John. "How Did Jesus Learn Obedience and Become Perfect?" Desiring God, 30 June 2016, http://www.desiringgod.org/interviews/how-did-jesus-learn-obedience-and-become-perfect. Accessed 9 May 2017.
6 • Stott, John. The Cross of Christ. InterVarsity, Downers Grove, Illinois, pg. 308.

Lesson 5: Abiding in the Hope of Heaven

1 • Willis, Mike. "Hope: The Anchor of the Soul." Truth Magazine, 19 Oct. 1989, http://www.truthmagazine.com/archives/volume33/GOT033268.html. Accessed 9 May 2017.
2 • Edwards, Jonathan. Sermons and Discourses, 1730-1733 (The Works of Jonathan Edwards Series, Volume 17.) Yale University Press, 1999, from sermon delivered in 1733 entitled "The True Christian's Life, A Journey Towards Heaven."
3 • Alcorn, Randy. "Longing for God and Joy, from Augustine." Eternal Perspectives Ministries, 11 Feb. 2008, http://www.epm.org/blog/2008/Feb/11/longing-for-god-and-joy-from-augustine. Accessed 9 May 2017.
4 • Piper, John. "Rejoicing in Pain." Desiring God, Nov 2 Devotional, http://www.desiringgod.org/articles/rejoicing-in-pain. Accessed 9 May 2017.
5 • Storms, Sam, as quoted by Alcorn, Randy, "Heaven Would be Hell without God," 24, April 2018, https://www.desiringgod.org/articles/heaven-would-be-hell-without-god. Accessed 5 May 2018.
6 • Fitzpatrick, Elyse. Home, How Heaven and the New Earth Satisfy Our Deepest Longings. Bethany House, Minneapolis, Minnesota, 2016, pg. 91.
7 • Hughes, Philip E. The Second Epistle to the Corinthians; The New International Commentary on the New Testament. Eerdmans, Grand Rapids, Michigan, 1992, pg. 180.
8 • Venema, Cornelius. The Promise of the Future. Banner of Truth, Edinburgh. 2000, pg. 402.
9 • MacLaren, Alexander. MacLaren's Commentary — Expositions of Holy Scripture. Delmarva Publications, 2014.

APPENDIX A

Two-Minute Testimony Guidelines

The story of our personal journey to salvation through Jesus Christ is one of, if not the most important tool we have in communicating the gospel to others. Because it's our own unique story, it conveys a message that's relevant and real to people, much in the same way parables were to Jesus' audiences, and to us.

Many of us have different testimonies about what God has done and is doing in our lives. We also may have various versions of our conversion testimony—the account of our salvation story from lost sinners to redeemed sons and daughters of God. Some versions may be quite lengthy, which may be appropriate in some situations. But we should all have a summarized version of our conversion testimony, as well. Many times, we only have a limited amount of time with people, or they may not be interested in listening to all the details of our lives. Take Paul, for example. His testimony is perhaps the most well-known and influential testimony in history. However, set up a timer and read the summarized version of his testimony (Acts 22:3-16). How long did it take? Under two minutes! If Paul can share his story in less than two minutes, all of us should be able to do the same.

Prayerfully prepare your story. Spend sufficient time asking God to reveal to you what to share and how to share it. Praise him again for saving you and giving you abundant life!

Consider your audience. Assess the age, familiarity with God, the Bible, and Christ, and other factors that may influence how you share and what you share with those who will be listening to you.

Avoid clichés or terminology unfamiliar to the unsaved or unchurched. We often use unclear, overused, or even inaccurate terms when sharing a testimony. Examples often include: 'I prayed the prayer'; or 'My walk with God has gotten strong'; or 'I asked Jesus into my heart'. Every statement you make should be as clearly understandable to your audience as possible. If you're speaking to a group of people who are primarily unsaved and aren't familiar with the Bible or language we use in the church or commonly with other believers, then be careful not to use those words or terms.

Speak the truth accurately. For example, according to the Bible, it is not true to say, "I've been a Christian all of my life." No one is born a Christian. You may not remember the day or events that led you to place your faith in Christ, but there was still a point in time when you went from a state of unredeemed sinner to redeemed child of God (Romans 10:9-10). It's therefore important, to include important details such as how you came to understand your sin, repentance, forgiveness, grace, salvation, eternal life, etc. A good model to use is to explain the following:

1. An illustration to introduce yourself (you can even weave this throughout your story)
2. Your life before Christ
3. How you came to realize your need for Christ & how you surrendered your life to him
4. How your life is different now that you live for Christ

Enjoy the opportunity and privilege of sharing how God has revealed his amazing love and truth through your own story!

APPENDIX B

A Cry for Help - Fighting Fear and Anxiety

PSALM 18:1-6

I love you, O Lord, my strength. The Lord is my rock and my fortress and my deliverer, my God, my rock, in whom I take refuge, my shield, and the horn of my salvation, my stronghold. I call upon the Lord, who is worthy to be praised, and I am saved from my enemies. The cords of death encompassed me; the torrents of destruction assailed me; the cords of Sheol entangled me; the snares of death confronted me. In my distress I called upon the Lord; to my God I cried for help. From his temple he heard my voice, and my cry to him reached his ears.

PSALM 18:27-36

For you save a humble people, but the haughty eyes you bring down. For it is you who light my lamp; the Lord my God lightens my darkness. For by you I can run against a troop, and by my God I can leap over a wall. This God—his way is perfect; the word of the Lord proves true; he is a shield for all those who take refuge in him. For who is God, but the Lord? And who is a rock, except our God?—the God who equipped me with strength and made my way blameless. He made my feet like the feet of a deer and set me secure on the heights. He trains my hands for war, so that my arms can bend a bow of bronze. You have given me the shield of your salvation, and your right hand supported me, and your gentleness made me great. You gave a wide place for my steps under me, and my feet did not slip.

PSALM 28:7

The LORD is my strength and my shield; in him my heart trusts, and I am helped; my heart exults, and with my song I give thanks to him.

PSALM 31:1-8

In you, O Lord, do I take refuge; let me never be put to shame; in your righteousness deliver me! Incline your ear to me; rescue me speedily! Be a rock of refuge for me, a strong fortress to save me! For you are my rock and my fortress; and for your name's sake you lead me and guide me; you take me out of the net they have hidden for me, for you are my refuge. Into your hand I commit my spirit; you have redeemed me, O Lord, faithful God. I hate those who pay regard to worthless idols, but I trust in the Lord. I will rejoice and be glad in your steadfast love, because you have seen my affliction; you have known the distress of my soul, and you have not delivered me into the hand of the enemy; you have set my feet in a broad place.

PSALM 34:4; 18

I sought the Lord, and he answered me and delivered me from all my fears.... The Lord is near to the brokenhearted and saves the crushed in spirit.

PSALM 55:22

Cast your burden on the LORD, and he will sustain you; he will never permit the righteous to be moved.

PSALM 56:3-4

When I am afraid, I put my trust in you. In God, whose word I praise, in God I trust; I shall not be afraid. What can flesh do to me?

PSALM 57:1-3

Be merciful to me, O God, be merciful to me, for in you my soul takes refuge; in the shadow of your wings I will take refuge, till the storms of destruction pass by. I cry out to God Most High, to God who fulfills his purpose for me. He will send from heaven and save me; he will put to shame him who tramples on me. God will send out his steadfast love and his faithfulness!

PSALM 73:23-26

Nevertheless, I am continually with you; you hold my right hand. You guide me with your counsel, and afterward you will receive me to glory. Whom have I in heaven but you? And there is nothing on earth that I desire besides you. My flesh and my heart my fail, but God is the strength of my heart and my portion forever.

PSALM 116:1-7

I love the LORD, because he has heard my voice and my pleas for mercy. Because he inclined his ear to me, therefore I will call on him as long as I live. The snares of death encompassed me; the pangs of Sheol laid hold on me; I suffered distress and anguish. Then I called on the name of the LORD; "O LORD, I pray, deliver my soul!" Gracious is the LORD, and righteous; our God is merciful. The LORD preserves the simple; when I was brought low, he saved me. Return, O my soul, to your rest: for the LORD has dealt bountifully with me.

PSALM 121:1-2

I lift up my eyes to the hills. From where does my help come? My help comes from the Lord, who made heaven and earth.

PROVERBS 3:5-6

Trust in the LORD with all your heart, and do not lean on your own understanding. In all your ways acknowledge him, and he will make straight your paths.

ISAIAH 26:3

You keep him in perfect peace whose mind is stayed on you, because he trusts in you.

ISAIAH 41:10

[F]ear not, for I am with you; be not dismayed, for I am your God; I will strengthen you, I will help you, I will uphold you with my righteous right hand.

ISAIAH 55:8-11

"For my thoughts are not your thoughts, neither are your ways my ways, declares the Lord. For as the heavens are higher than the earth, so are my ways higher than your ways and my thoughts than your thoughts. For as the rain and the snow come down from heaven and do not return there but water the earth, making it bring forth and sprout, giving seed to the sower and bread to the eater, so shall my word be that goes out from my mouth; it shall not return to me empty, but it shall accomplish that which I purpose, and shall succeed in the thing for which I sent it."

MATTHEW 11:28-30

"Come to me, all who labor and are heavy laden, and I will give you rest. Take my yoke upon you, and learn from me, for I am gentle and lowly in heart, and you will find rest for your souls. For my yoke is easy, and my burden is light."

JOHN 14:27

"Peace I leave with you; my peace I give to you. Not as the world gives do I give to you. Let not your hearts be troubled, neither let them be afraid."

PHILIPPIANS 4:4-8

Rejoice in the Lord always; again I will say, rejoice. Let your reasonableness be known to everyone. The Lord is at hand; do not be anxious about anything, but in everything by prayer and supplication with thanksgiving let your requests be made known to God. And the peace of God, which surpasses all understanding, will guard your heats and your minds in Christ Jesus.

Finally, brothers, whatever is true, whatever is honorable, whatever is just, whatever is pure, whatever is lovely, whatever is commendable, if there is any excellence, if there is anything worthy of praise, think about these things.

HEBREWS 4:14-16

Since then we have a great high priest who has passed through the heavens, Jesus, the Son of God, let us hold fast our confession. For we do not have a high priest who is unable to sympathize with our weaknesses, but one who in every respect has been tempted as we are, yet without sin. Let us then with confidence draw near to the throne of grace, that we may receive mercy and find grace to help in time of need.

HEBREWS 13:6

So we can confidently say, "The Lord is my helper; I will not fear; what can man do to me?"

1 PETER 5:6-7

Humble yourselves, therefore, under the mighty hand of God so that at the proper time he may exalt you, casting all your anxieties on him, because he cares for you.

APPENDIX C

Do The Next Thing

From an old English parsonage,
Down by the sea,
There came in the twilight,
A message to me;
Its quaint Saxon legend,
Deeply engraven,
Hath, as it seems to me,
Teaching from Heaven.
And on through the hours
The quiet words ring
Like a low inspiration-
DO THE NEXT THING.

Many a questioning, many a fear,
Many a doubt, hath its quieting here.
Moment by moment,
Let down from Heaven,
Time, opportunity,
Guidance, are given.
Fear not tomorrow,
Child of the King,
Trust them with Jesus,
DO THE NEXT THING.

Do it immediately;
Do it with prayer;
Do it reliantly, casting all care;
Do it with reverence,
Tracing His Hand,
Who placed it before thee with
With earnest command.
Stayed on Omnipotence,
Safe 'neath His wing,
Leave all resultings,
DO THE NEXT THING.

Looking to Jesus, ever serener,
(Working or suffering)
Be thy demeanor,
In His dear presence,
The rest of His calm,
The light of His countenance
Be thy psalm,
Strong in His faithfulness,
Praise and sing,
Then, as He beckons thee,
DO THE NEXT THING.

Author Unknown

APPENDIX D

My Heart Unveiled Chart

COMMON CONTROL-RESPONSES & FEARS

————

CONTROL-RESPONSES:

Flight

Withdrawing
Hiding
People-pleasing
Minimizing sin
Escaping
Denying
Acting as a martyr/victim
Avoiding conflict
Fantasizing
Focusing on another's sin
Blaming others
Lying/deceiving
Numbing

Fight

Arguing
Aggressive
Manipulating
Intimidating
Convincing
Anger
Escaping
Acting as a martyr/victim
Being negative or critical
Condemning
Focusing on another's sin
Blaming others
Lying/deceiving
Being passive-agressive

UNDERLYING BELIEFS/FEARS:

- Fear of the unknown
- Fear of the future
- Fear of failure
- Fear of missing out
- Fear of rejection

- Fear of consequences
- Fear of exposure
- Fear of pain and suffering
- Fear of loss (health, financial, relationship, security, reputation)

My Heart Unveiled

My situation

My response

| FEELING | THINKING | CHOOSING |

Why am I responding this way?

| PERCEIVED NEED/DESIRE | CONTROL-RESPONSES | UNDERLYING BELIEF/FEARS |

Steps to walk in obedience

| GOD'S TRUTH | ACTION STEPS |

(Refer to My Heart Unveiled Instructions on p. 118)

Made in the USA
Monee, IL
19 August 2022

11986060R00250